EARLY WRITINGS

Lippmann in his office at *The New Republic* in 1915

WALTER LIPPMANN

EARLY WRITINGS

INTRODUCTION AND

ANNOTATIONS BY

ARTHUR SCHLESINGER, JR.

LIVERIGHT / NEW YORK

The articles in this collection were first published in
The New Republic in the years 1914–1920 and are reprinted
by permission of the publisher.

Standard Book Number: 87140-503-2
Library of Congress Catalog Card Number: 70-114385

Designed by Marshall Henrichs

Manufactured in the United States of America

CONTENTS

v

CONTENTS

UNREST

ARTS AND OTHER MATTERS

FOREWORD

Walter Lippmann was twenty-four when, in 1913, he was invited by Herbert Croly, whom he had not met but whose *Promise of American Life* he had read, to help found *The New Republic. A Preface to Politics* had just been published and was soon to be followed by *Drift and Mastery*; Lippmann was already a recognized intellectual leader of his generation. Lincoln Steffens had picked him as the young man with "the ablest mind that could express itself in writing." Lippmann "caught on right away," Steffens later wrote; "keen, quiet, industrious, he understood the meaning of all that he learned."

It was on Steffens's recommendation that Lippmann in 1912 went to Schenectady to work for the newly elected Socialist mayor, the Reverend George R. Lund, former pastor of a fashionable Presbyterian church. The episode was brief. From the start, Mr. Lippmann was a student of politics, rather than a practitioner.

The first issue of *The New Republic* (price: ten cents) came out on Saturday, November 7, 1914, and carried a lengthy comment by Lippmann on "Force and Ideas." With time out during World War I as a captain in military intelligence, then as an aide to Colonel House before and after the Armistice negotiations, Mr. Lippmann was to remain on *The New Republic* staff until the fall of 1921. There were few weeks in which he did not write either notes or signed articles. Croly was "first among equals," the acknowledged but untitled chairman of the editorial board; but Lippmann, along with the other editors—Francis Hackett, Walter Weyl,

Philip Littell and Alvin Johnson—was free to develop his own themes and views.

The assembling of the writings in this book presented a problem other than the hardship of leaving out so much of merit. All the early *New Republic* files had mysteriously disappeared. Fortunately, Mr. Lippmann had kept most of his original manuscripts and deposited them at Yale University. By matching manuscripts against copies of *The New Republic,* the authorship of many unidentified notes was fixed. All of them were written for the week; that they are so little dated is the more remarkable. They appeared in a journal whose purpose, Mr. Lippmann said, "was not partisan, factional, personal or ideological; it was educational"; its editors wanted it to be "informed, disinterested, compassionate and brave."

Since some of the personages and controversies described here have faded from memory, Arthur Schlesinger, Jr. in his annotations recreates the stage on which they moved.

GILBERT A. HARRISON
Editor-in-Chief
The New Republic

INTRODUCTION

ARTHUR SCHLESINGER, JR.

"We are living and shall live all our lives now," Walter Lippmann wrote in *The New Republic* in 1917, "in a revolutionary world." This proposition, which might be taken either as highly banal or highly incendiary, was in Lippmann's case a vivid and sustained perception of the radically unstable character of the time in which he was growing up.

Born in the Victorian tranquilities of 1889, he was stirred by the ferment of the Progressive era and became a socialist before he left Harvard in 1910. His socialism soon evaporated in any dogmatic form; but it left behind a residue in the shape of a belief in the necessity for rational planning and purpose to master the incipient chaos of modern society. He was one of the first Americans to read Freud, and this doubtless contributed to his sense that he was living in an age of the transvaluation of values.

It was a decade of the rise and collapse of great hopes. It began with the euphoria of Roosevelt's 1912 campaign, the first campaign in American history to be based on a truly modern analysis of industrial society. When TR succumbed to jingoism, the young men transferred their dreams to Wilson; and for a season Wilson seemed to them a leader not only for America but for all mankind. Then Wilson, in their view, capitulated to the old order at Versailles, and the decade concluded in disillusion over the peace and in the shame of the Red Scare.

Whether optimistic or pessimistic about the chances of a

policy of mastery prevailing over a policy of drift, Lippmann throughout these years had an intense conviction that the "acids of modernity" (his phrase a decade later in *A Preface to Morals*) were eating away at all the inherited certitudes. The revolution, he wrote in 1917, "goes deeper than any man had dared to guess. . . . Western civilization is approaching not the end of its potential resources, but the end of its resources as they are now organized." Reconstruction was the vital need of the age. "A planless, drifting uncontrolled society," he said in 1914, "is no longer fit to survive in the modern world. . . . The underlying notion of modern radicalism has been to substitute a conscious social control for accident and confusion, to unify the nation's resources so that they can be used for a purpose." In urging the task of reconstruction, however, Lippmann was animated more by commitment to reason than by faith in reason—or at least by faith in the capacity of reason to conquer the irrational in man. This tension between his passion for reason and his acknowledgment of irrationality accounts, I think, for the poignancy of much of his writing. "We, too, can blunder into horror."

He had many doubts about the organization of the American government. "Only the most revolutionary changes in the congressional system," he wrote in 1917, "can save representative government in America." As for the Presidency:

> The concentration of all vitality in the Presidency has become something like a disease in which there is feverish activity at the center, a cold inertia in all the parts.
> We expect of one man that he shall speak for the nation, formulate its needs, translate them into a program. We expect that man to instill these purposes and this program into a parasitic party system, drive his own party to enact them, and create an untainted administrative hierarchy through which to realize his plans. We expect him to

oversee the routine, dominate group interests, prepare for the future, and take stock of possible emergencies. No man can do it. . . . As the thing works today, if the President is absorbed in a foreign complication everything else comes to a dead stop. . . . The President is burdened with the task of a benevolent despot and then denied the authority and resources to make even a despotism effective. In the system of checks and balances, it is the checks alone which seem to have much vitality.

His writings on foreign affairs still have acute meaning half a century later. He warned eloquently against the "frame of mind where the scale of courage is measured by what the wildest jingo proposes as the correct method of licking creation. . . . There is in America today the beginning of that very military arrogance which we are told this war is being fought to abolish." He warned too against the tendency to base foreign policy on abstractions. "We are an inveterately legalistic people, and have veiled our real intentions behind a mass of technicalities. . . . Our fundamental interest in this crisis is not a complicated system of rights but a definite and practical and tangible end"—the defense of the Atlantic world. This point underlay his repressed differences with Wilson. Much of his *New Republic* writing on foreign affairs reads as if it were addressed to an audience of one and explains his ultimate rejection of Wilsonianism. The democrats of Europe had hailed Wilson, he wrote in 1919,

> because they saw, more accurately than anyone who directed American policy, that the substantial realization of Mr. Wilson's program was a vital American interest. . . . They assumed that he understood this. . . . But in the test, the American program was treated like so many other ideals, as something distant, unrelated, and of no material consequence.

Nor should one overlook Lippmann's startling prescience about what we now call the underdeveloped world. "The relation between government and the financing of backward countries," he wrote in 1916,

> is the central problem of modern diplomacy. . . . We
> cannot turn our backs on the weak countries. We must
> act in order to make them strong. The central motive
> of a democratic foreign policy must be the modernization
> of the feeble and distracted nations.

His range, as these pages make clear, was exceedingly wide; and a new generation which (like all new generations) supposes its own problems uniquely gratuitous and awful may be interested to discover the extent to which other young men have struggled with similar problems in other times. It has been our nation's good fortune that Walter Lippmann did not stop his struggle in 1920. We have benefited from his wisdom for half a century since; and, with luck, we will continue to learn from him for a long time to come.

WAR AND PEACE

FORCE AND IDEAS

Every sane person knows that it is a greater thing to build a city than to bombard it, to plough a field than to trample it, to serve mankind than to conquer it. And yet once the armies get loose, the terrific noise and shock of war make all that was valuable seem pale and dull and sentimental. Trenches and shrapnel, howitzers and forts, marching and charging and seizing—these seem real, these seem to be men's work. But subtle calculations in a laboratory, or the careful planning of streets and sanitation and schools, things which constitute the great peaceful adventure of democracy, seem to sink to so much whimpering futility.

Who cares to paint a picture now, or to write any poetry but war poetry, or to search the meaning of language, or speculate about the constitution of matter? It seems like fiddling when Rome burns. Or to edit a magazine—to cover paper with ink, to care about hopes that have gone stale, to launch phrases that are lost in the uproar? What is the good now of thinking? What is a critic compared to a battalion of infantry? This, men say, is a time for action, any kind of action. So, without a murmur, the laboratories of Europe are commandeered as hospitals, a thousand half-finished experiments abandoned. There was more for the future of the world in those experiments than we dare to calculate. They are tossed aside. The best scholarship has turned press agent to the General Staff. The hope of labor is absorbed, the great plans built on the surplus of wealth are dropped, for the

3

armies have to be financed. Merely to exist has become a problem, to live finely seems to many a derelict hope.

Yet the fact remains that the final argument against cannon is ideas. The thoughts of men which seem so feeble are the only weapons they have against overwhelming force. It was a brain that conceived the gun, it was brains that organized the armies, it was the triumph of physics and chemistry that made possible the dreadnought. Men organized this superb destruction; they created this force, thought it, dreamed it, planned it. It has got beyond their control. It has got into the service of hidden forces they do not understand. Men can master it only by clarifying their own will to end it, and making a civilization so thoroughly under their control that no machine can turn traitor to it. For while it takes as much skill to make a sword as a ploughshare, it takes a critical understanding of human values to prefer the ploughshare.

That is why civilization seems dull and war romantic to unimaginative people. It requires a trained intelligence to realize that the building of the Panama Canal by the American Army is perhaps the greatest victory an army ever won. Yet the victories of peace are less renowned than those of war. For every hundred people who can feel the horrors of the battlefield, how many are there who feel the horror of the slum? For every hundred people who admire the organization of war, how many are there who recognize the wasteful helter-skelter of peace?

It is no wonder, then, that war, once started, sweeps everything before it, that it seizes all loyalties and subjugates all intelligence. War is the one activity that men really plan for passionately on a national scale, the only organization which is thoroughly conceived. Men prepare themselves for campaigns they may never wage, but for peace, even when they meet the most acute social crisis, they will not prepare themselves. They set their armies on a hair-trigger of preparation. They leave their diplomacy archaic. They have their

4

troops ready to put down labor disputes; they will not think out the problems of labor. They turn men into military automata, stamp upon every personal feeling for what they call the national defence; they are too timid to discipline business. They spend years learning to make war; they do not learn to govern themselves. They ask men to die for their country; they think it a stupid strain to give time to living for it.

Knowing this, we cannot abandon the labor of thought. However crude and weak it may be, it is the only force that can pierce the agglomerated passion and wrong-headedness of this disaster. We have learnt a lesson. We know how insecurely we have been living, how grudging, poor, mean, careless has been what we call civilization. We have not known how to forestall the great calamity. We have not known enough, we have not been trained enough, ready enough, nor radical enough to make our will effective. We have taken the ideas that were thrust upon us, we have believed what we were told to believe. We have got into habits of thought when unnecessary things seemed inevitable, in panic and haste we stumbled into what we did not want.

We shall not do better in the future by more stumbling and more panic. If our thought has been ineffective we shall not save ourselves by not thinking at all, for there is only one way to break the vicious circle of action, and that is by subjecting it endlessly to the most ruthless criticism of which we are capable. It is not enough to hate war and waste, to launch one unanalyzed passion against another, to make the world a vast debating ground in which tremendous accusations are directed against the Kaiser and the financiers, the diplomatists and the gun manufacturers. The guilt is wider and deeper than that. It comes home finally to all those who live carelessly, too lazy to think, too preoccupied to care, afraid to move, afraid to change, eager for a false peace, unwilling to pay the daily costs of sanity.

We in America are not immune to what some people

5

imagine to be the diseases of Europe. Nothing would be easier for us than to drift into an impossible situation, our life racked and torn within and without. We, too, have our place in the world. We have our obligations, our aggressions, our social chasms, our internal diseases. We are unready to deal with them. We are committed to responsibilities we do not understand, we are the victims of interests and deceptive ideas, and nothing but our own clarified effort can protect us from the consequences. We, too, can blunder into horror.

November 7, 1914

DEFINING TERMS

We live these days in an atmosphere of large words. Militarism, aggression, freedom, peace, national survival, destiny, race, we speak of them glibly as if we knew just what they meant. But where, for example, in the gradation from Tolstoi to Bernhardi does a man become a militarist? What constitutes aggression? Was it aggressive for Germany to send the gunboat Panther to Agadir, or for France to seize Morocco? Was England aggressive or defensive in South Africa, in Persia? Is it aggressive to try to monopolize the trade of backward countries? Are protective tariffs aggressive? Was Austria aggressive when it set up a tariff against Serbia's commerce in pigs? Would it be aggressive for Italy to "redeem" Trieste? Were we aggressive when we took the Philippines? Is the Monroe Doctrine aggressive? And what is a war for freedom? Would the crushing of the Hohenzollerns by the Allies be a liberation of the German people? Was our refusal to recognize Huerta an act to further self-government in Mexico? What is peace? Are tariff wars, concession wars, labor wars, diplomatic wars, armaments races, all aspects of peace? What is national survival? Do nations die? Can nations be destroyed by the enemy? Is national destiny written in the stars or in the newspapers? When national destiny tells Greece, Serbia and Bulgaria in turn that its destiny is to control the Balkan peninsula to the exclusion of the others, what about the destinies that can't be satisfied? Above all, what about race? Who are the chosen people? When German Emperors have

7

English mothers and Russian cousins, how do they know which race they belong to? When Englishmen sweat Englishmen in nasty slums, who are the chosen people then?

November 21, 1914

VERA CRUZ

In April 1914 Wilson had ordered United States marines to occupy Vera Cruz. Though the idea behind this intervention was to help the Mexican Revolutionists against the counter-revolutionary Huerta regime, a number of Mexicans were killed in the fighting, and Huerta was enabled to whip up nationalist emotions against the United States. Wilson's purpose throughout was to avoid American intervention against the Mexican Revolution, but his methods were not always helpful. [*A.S., jr.*]

Now that the American troops are to evacuate Vera Cruz, it is fair to ask why they were sent there and what they have accomplished. If we remember correctly, it was said at the time that the flag had been insulted by a Huertista, and American dignity required an act of reprisal. We presume that this comic-opera reason was not the one which actually inspired the President. For it was clear that the Administration favored the Constitutionalists, and that after the fall of Torreon the darling idea of destroying Huerta seemed about to be realized. There was a chance, however, that a new shipment of arms would help the Federals. By seizing Vera Cruz we could prevent the "Ypiranga" from landing her cargo, and so deprive Huerta of the weapons he needed. We seized Vera Cruz, but the arms were landed at Puerta Mexico. Nevertheless Huerta fell, and the President's policy was called a success. There was just one rift in the lute. When Huerta

9

fell, no one else arose. And at this moment conditions in Mexico are said to be worse than at any time within the memory of man. Constitutional government is as far off as it ever was. The needed land reforms are not in the least likely to be carried out, foreigners are not safe in Mexico, and the country is prostrate. What have we accomplished? For what purpose did American and Mexican soldiers die at Vera Cruz? To what end did we intervene?

The President is a silent and secretive man, and he has the air of profound intentions. His hand has been free because the news was constantly suppressed, because Europe was unable to interfere, and because this country shared his dislike of Huerta and his genuine desire for peace. Moreover, there never was any question that Mr. Wilson was eager to serve the Mexican people, and to prevent any aggression by the United States. Because Americans admired his idealism, they resolved to trust his methods. It seemed inconceivable that he should be without definite policy, that the action at Vera Cruz was merely feeble and impulsive reprisal, and that behind the brooding and the watching and the waiting and the impressive silence there was not some large and well-defined idea. Yet when the troops leave Vera Cruz on Monday they will leave the Mexican problem completely unsolved. A good intention does not constitute a good policy. The President is, if anything, further from a solution than he was when Mr. Taft so genially bequeathed the difficulty to him. Mr. Wilson has no Mexican policy, yet Mr. Wilson has interfered in Mexico. Mr. Wilson wished to establish self-government in Mexico; he leaves it in chaos. Mr. Wilson wishes peace and deplores aggression; Mr. Wilson seized a paltry excuse for aggression, and then shrank feebly from the consequences. He has blown hot and cold, has favored different factions, has put embargoes on arms and allowed arms to go in.

We find it hard to understand why we should evacuate Vera Cruz when more trouble is just about to begin. Perhaps

Mr. Wilson has given up all hope of doing more than to allow Mexico to work out her own agony. For whatever influence he may have had will be lessened by this empty rattling of the sword and hasty retreat. From Vera Cruz he had at least a tangible leverage on Mexico. It might have been possible to justify the taking of Vera Cruz if Mr. Wilson had used it as a base from which to exert pressure in the direction of some definite policy. Vera Cruz in American hands was a big, impressive physical fact. Vera Cruz evacuated now is an object lesson to Mexico that our attitude is capricious and without underlying plan. The latest dispatches say that while we are withdrawing the army, we shall not restore the customs money until order is restored. In other words we are to weaken our hold, but we are not to let go. We are still intervening. But it is a serious business to interfere in another country, and only the most genuine reasons can ever justify it. By withdrawing now we show that our intervention was unjustified, for we leave with nothing essential accomplished. Mr. Wilson is abandoning the instrument through which his opinions could be given some weight in Mexico. From Washington his words will beat the air. And if foreigners are killed or plundered now, what will he do? Will he be ready to admit that he has failed, that he can do nothing about Mexico, that our intervention has achieved nothing? Or will he, with great determination, seize Vera Cruz again?

November 21, 1914

TIMID NEUTRALITY

> The attitude of our own government
> during the last three months shows
> how worthless the present treaties,
> unbacked by force, are, and how
> utterly ineffective mere passive neu-
> trality is to secure even the smallest
> advance in world morality. *Theo-*
> *dore Roosevelt in The New York*
> *Times, November 8, 1914.*

Whenever a man like Theodore Roosevelt suggests that the
disarmament of peaceful nations will not produce peace on
earth, a cry goes up that he is spoiling for a fight. It is
assumed at once that if only he had had the chance, we
should by this time have overrun Mexico, gotten ourselves
embroiled with Japan, and have sent an army to the battlefield of Flanders. And so we say: "Thank God for Bryan, for
the peace treaties, for a small navy and a small army."

Well, you may be thankful for them if you like. You may
be glad that you have managed to avoid the risks of living on
this planet; but don't talk about the need for world cooperation, the sanctity of treaties, an international court and an
international police. Don't assume that the world will heed
you, don't mistake your private good-will for the universal
morality of nations. For if you do you make yourself the
victim of your naivete, and your dreams will turn to despair.

12

Though the world may love you as it loves St. Francis, the world will ignore you as it ignores him.

We were all surprised at the war, stunned at the idea that such things could happen. And then we took to reading Bernhardi, Cramb, Bülow, Fullerton, and we discovered that this war had been a long time in the minds of the men who know Europe. Their speculations seem to us unbelievably cynical and cold-blooded. We learn with astonishment that the strategists of Europe had military plans drawn, that every well-informed person in England, France, Germany, and Belgium knew that Germany would probably strike through Belgium, that the Germans had built railways from Aix-la-Chapelle, that England knew where she would land her expeditionary force. We discovered, in short, that our surprise was due to our ignorance and to our miscalculation of motives. And yet, in the face of this, it is assumed that security and peace in the future can be guaranteed by more ignorance and more miscalculation. It is assumed that by not doing anything, by pretending that peace is the reward of the peace-loving, neutrality will be assured and treaties made invincible.

Chiefly because Colonel Roosevelt is free from that delusion, we believe that of all Americans commenting on the war his judgment is the ripest. We reject as the idlest superstition the idea that he enjoys war and despises peace. We honor him and respect him for his courage in shouldering the inevitable risk of misunderstanding which is the portion of anyone who faces a brutal situation with intellectual integrity.

The situation which Colonel Roosevelt has faced is this: How is it possible to create the beginnings of international order out of the nations of this world? Not out of a world of pacifists, not out of a world of Quakers, but out of this world, which contains only a small minority of pacifists and Quakers. For it is peace on earth that men need, not peace in heaven, and unless you build from the brutalities of earth, you step out into empty space.

The first question that arises is the maintenance of treaties. We have seen them violated not only in Belgium but in Manchuria and China. We have seen the Hague conventions, to which our signature is attached, torn up and thrown to the winds. Undefended towns have been bombarded, exorbitant levies made, hostages taken. We have not even protested. We have watched the paper structure of good-will collapse. And yet when a man like Roosevelt insists that we must create no more valueless paper, he is denounced as an American Bernhardi and the twin of the Kaiser. On this same score *The New Republic* will no doubt be accused as a militarist organ, hostile to the good faith of the world.

If we range ourselves with Roosevelt on this question, it is because we believe that treaties will never acquire sanctity until nations are ready to seal them with their blood. England may not have been too scrupulous about treaties in the past, but to-day she stands irrevocably committed. If she makes treaties now they may mean something, and that is an incalculable advance for the human race. So with us. It is our business to make no treaties which we are not ready to maintain with all our resources, for every scrap of paper is like a forged check, an assault on our credit in the world. We must not permit ourselves to fall into the plight of Germany, where our word is distrusted by the nations. For there can be no morality of nations so long as promises are idly given and idly broken. So long as that condition prevails, distrust and suspicion will rack the world, and behind a facade of delusive promises the nations will continue to arm.

So when Colonel Roosevelt says that our neutrality does not carry with it the obligation to be silent when our own Hague conventions are destroyed, he is taking an active step towards ultimate peace. Had we protested against the assault on international morality when Belgium was invaded, our faith in public law would have been made somewhat real. For unless someone some time is ready to take some chance for the sake of internationalism, it will remain what it is to-day, an object of derision to aggressive nations. Had the United States, as the courted neutral, stood out for the neutrality of Belgium and the rules of the Hague, ruthlessness would have received the severest jolt it ever imagined. We do not think the United States should have gone to war. We alone cannot undertake to police the world. But we might alone, or with the help of the other neutral nations, have used the pressure of our diplomacy, and so laid the foundations of effective world opinion against international cynicism. A precedent would have been established which could react on all the future. The beginnings of world organization would have been tested in fire, and the hope of peace would have taken on at least the shadow of reality.

Against all this it may be said that because we acted so as to preserve the good-will of Europe, we shall be able to exercise a guiding influence in the settlement of the war. It is an idea which gratifies not only our desire to keep out of trouble, but our vanity and our hope that we shall do great things with small difficulty. The nation is doomed to disappointment. For while the settlement may be made by a peace congress held under the presidency of the United States, the decisions will be determined by the balance of power in which the war results. The nations of Europe will have sacrificed so much that they will settle the issues in accordance with their own strength and position. And when we enter the congress with nothing but a record of comfortable neutrality, an acquiescence in the violated Hague conventions, and an array of vague treaties for a half-conceived future, our voice may well be disregarded. We shall be treated as we deserve to be treated, as a nation of well-meaning people who run no risks, and build their faith upon their simple and uncritical desires.

November 21, 1914

LIFE IS CHEAP

When a military expert wishes to be very technical and professional he refers to the killed, wounded, and missing as the wastage of an army. To those who do not share his preoccupation with the problems of grand strategy, the word connotes a cold and calculated horror based on a fatal disregard of human cost. It is natural, then, to fall back upon the old platitude that in war life is cheap; cheaper than guns, cheaper than dreadnoughts, cheaper even than intelligent diplomacy.

If we go behind this simple idea, however, we find curious distinctions reflected in ordinary feelings about the war. There was General Joffre's statement that the French would not waste men in furious assaults. In England this was received with approval, mixed with the feeling that the British were standing the worst of the racket. Most curious, however, was the English attitude towards the Russians. The Russians were conceived as an inexhaustible horde which could be poured endlessly against German guns. The value of individual Russians was ridiculously low as compared with individual Englishmen. In America the loss of two thousand Austrians would seem as nothing beside the loss of two thousand Englishmen. If the Canadians were to suffer heavily, we should feel it still more, no doubt.

When the *Titanic* sank, it was very noticeable that the anguish of the first-cabin passengers meant more to the newspapers than did that of the crew or steerage; and of the first-cabin passengers, it was the well-known people in whom was dramatized the full terror of the disaster. When a man is run over, the amount of space given to a report of the accident

16

seems to depend very closely either on his social importance in the community, or on whether he is injured under circumstances which might apply to highly regarded elements of the population. The injuries of foreign-born laborers on construction work are hardly reported. It is estimated that one man is killed for every floor added to a skyscraper, but the fact does not rise to the level of popular interest. The value of a life seems to increase only as it emerges from a mass and becomes individualized. So long as great populations remain politically inert, so long as they can be treated in lumps, so long as they can be manipulated from above, they will be lightly used or easily disregarded.

It is in time of peace that the value of life is fixed. The test of war reveals it. That is why democracies tend to be peaceful. In them the importance of each person has been enlarged, and the greater the equality, the less able are small groups to use their fellows as brute instruments. Democracies are compelled to look toward peaceful adjustments because the cost of war is too tremendous for them. The mere fact that at a certain level of comfort and self-respect the birth-rate declines makes the conservation of life imperative. It is in democracies based on fairly well distributed economic opportunity and a modicum of education that birth ceases to be a wholesale accident and becomes a considered purpose. France is such a democracy, and France does not spend life easily. The large measure of equality which she has achieved by a prudent birth-rate, a tolerable level of well-being, and a tradition of human rights, has made dreams of lavish conquest forever impossible to her. She will defend what she has with superb courage, but she cannot dominate the world.

There, perhaps, is the most important relation between social reform and the problem of peace. The aggressors of the future are likely to be the nations in which life is cheap, and the hope of international order rests with those countries in whom personality has become too valuable to be squandered. This is why the whole world waits the democratization of Germany, Russia and Japan.

But even the so-called democracies are far from a decent sense of the value of life. Here in America life is extraordinarily cheap. There is almost no task so dull, so degrading or so useless but you can find plenty of human beings to do it. You can hire a man to walk up and down the avenue carrying a sign which advertises a quack dentist. You can hire rows of men for the back line of the chorus, just standing them there to fill up space. You can hire a man to sit next to the chauffeur; he is called a footman and his purpose is to make the owner of the car a bit more comfortable and a great deal more magnificent. There are women known as lady's maids whose business it is to dress up other women. There are flunkeys whose mission it is to powder their hair, put on white stockings and gold-trimmed knee-breeches and flank the threshold of great houses. It is possible to hire any number of caretakers for empty houses, bellhops to fetch for you, even mourners to mourn for you.

Every city is full of women whose lives are gray with emptiness, who sit for hours looking out of the window, who rock their chairs and gossip, and long for the excitement that never comes. Unloved and unloving, and tragically unused, the world seems to have passed them by. Our cities are full of those caricatured homes, the close, curtained boarding houses to which people come from the day's drudgery to the evening's depression, the thousands of hall bedrooms in which hope dies and lives the ghost of itself in baseball scores and in movies, in the funny page and in Beatrice Fairfax, in purchased romance and in stunted reflections of the music-hall.

It is not strange that in war we spend life so easily, or that our anxiety to lower the death-rate of babies, to keep the sick alive, to help the criminal and save the feeble-minded, seems to many a trifling humanitarianism. The notion that every person is sacred, that no one is a means to some one else's end, this sentiment which is the heart of democracy, has taken only slight hold upon the modern world. It is still hardly questioned that men should die to protect concessions, to collect debts, to hold markets, to glorify their king, to avenge imaginary insults. In the industrial world men are used as "hands," kept waiting in idle crowds to fill casual jobs, put at work that exhausts and pays almost nothing, blocked in occupations from which they cannot learn, from which they become forever unfitted to escape. Women are used as drudges, as recreation, as things to jest about or to appropriate, because all through our civilization there runs an appalling insensitiveness and disregard. We have not yet made life dignified and valuable in itself, we have not yet made it a sufficient treasury of good things, have not infused it with the riches which men will not wantonly waste.

Human life will become valuable as we invest in it. The child that is worth bearing, nursing, tending and rearing, worth educating, worth making happy, worth building good schools and laying out playgrounds for, worth all the subtle effort of modern educational science, is becoming too valuable for drudgery, too valuable for the food of cannon. It is because for some years we have been putting positive values into life that this war appalls us more than it would have appalled our ancestors. And just so far as we can induce the state to sink money and attention in human beings, by just so much do we insure ourselves against idle destruction.

This is the best internal defense against those amongst us who may be dreaming of aggression. Every dollar and every moment of care devoted to increasing the individual importance of people, all skill and training, all fine organization to humanize work, every increase of political expression, is a protection against idle use of our military power, against any attempt to convert legitimate and necessary preparation for defense into an instrument of conquest. It may be said with justice that the man is dangerous who talks loudly about military preparation and is uninterested in social reform. It is the people engaged in adding to the values of civilization who have earned the right to talk about its defense.

December 19, 1914

A LITTLE CHILD

SHALL LEAD THEM

Henry Ford's celebrated "peace ship" had set sail
in a quixotic effort to bring World War I to an end.
[*A.S., jr.*]

Mr. Henry Ford's peace trip has aroused violent resentment
in America since the day it was announced. Men laugh at it
with helpless anger. They regard it as humiliating. They want
to break something at the thought of it. Yet there is hardly
one of Mr. Ford's opponents who doesn't long for peace,
and hope secretly that America may help to bring it about.
Something in the protests seems a little too loud. May it not
be that we are shouting at Mr. Ford because he has done us
the inconvenience of revealing some of the American character a little too baldly? Is our indignation like that of the
man making faces at himself in a mirror?

The first fact about Mr. Ford is that he is a very rich man.
Whatever he says is therefore sure of a hearing in America.
We have always acted instinctively on the theory that golden
thoughts flow in a continuous stream from the minds of mil-
lionaires. Their ideas about religion, education, morality, and
international politics carry weight out of all proportion to
their intrinsic importance; and though we have not admitted
that riches make wisdom, we have always assumed that they
deserve publicity.

This automatic obeisance to wealth is complicated by our

notions of success. We Americans have little faith in special knowledge, and only with the greatest difficulty is the idea being forced upon us that not every man is capable of doing every job. But Mr. Ford belongs to the tradition of self-made men, to that primitive Americanism which has held the theory that a successful manufacturer could turn his hand with equal success to every other occupation. It is this tendency in America which instals untrained rich men in difficult diplomatic posts, which puts business men at the head of technical bureaus of the government, and permits business men to dominate the educational policy of so many universities. Mr. Ford is neither a crank nor a freak; he is merely the logical exponent of American prejudices about wealth and success.

But Mr. Ford reveals more of us than this. He reflects our touching belief that the world is like ourselves. His attitude to the "boys in the trenches" is of a piece with his attitude to the boys in the Ford plant, kindly, fatherly, and certain that Mr. Ford knows what is best. His restless energy and success appear as a jolly meddlesomeness. He gives his boys good wages and holds them to good morals. He is prepared to do likewise for the boys in Flanders and around Monastir. Why shouldn't success in Detroit assure success in front of Bagdad? If Mr. Ford is unable to remember that all men are not made in his own image, it is not strange. Have Americans ever remembered it? Has our attitude towards the old world ever assumed that Europe was anything but a laborious effort to imitate us?

Mr. Ford serves as a reminder of another amiable trait in our character, our belief in the absolute validity of moral judgments. We have never taken much stock in the theory of Socrates that the good man to be really good must really be wise.

> "Ez fer war, I call it murder,—
> There you hev it plain an' flat;
> I don't want to go no furder

21

Than my Testyment fer that;
God hez said so plump an' fairly,
It's ez long ez it is broad,
An' you've gut to git up airly
Ef you want to take in God."
                The Biglow Papers

These verses were written by an American about the Mexican War of 1845, but they express Mr. Ford and Mr. Bryan of to-day. They go no further than their Testament, and what they will not see is that you have to go further than your Testament if you are ever to realize the principles which it embodies.

In common with most Americans Mr. Ford believes that evil can be eradicated by the spontaneous recognition of it. "The two notes that will be sounded," says Mr. Ford's secretary, "are faith and moral suasion." Oh, America! home of Christian Science, of blue laws, of the Sherman act, of letter-writing diplomacy, of moral indignation, of "prosperity" and "sunshine," of prohibition and Billy Sunday, and the new freedom and the promises of the Republican party. We are too good for this wicked world.

                                    December 4, 1915

ARE WE PRO-GERMAN?

Ralph Barton Perry was a professor of philosophy at Harvard; his book of 1912, *The New Realism,* had established him as among the most promising of the younger American philosophers. He was also the brother-in-law of Lippmann's close friend Bernard Berenson. He is remembered today particularly for his splendid biography *The Thought and Character of William James* (1935). In both world wars Perry was an eloquent proponent of an advanced American role. [*A.S., jr.*]

Mr. Ralph Barton Perry, who addresses us in another column, is a professional philosopher, and to our certain knowledge a good one. It is part of his daily business to use words accurately. Will he then be kind enough to say what the epithet "pro-German" conveys to his mind? The term has become incomprehensible to us. We advocate closer political union with the British Empire. We argue against the propaganda of those who wish to build a navy larger than England's, and urge a navy larger than Germany's. We say that the measure of German ambition in this hemisphere is one of the criteria of American preparedness. We point out that the real argument against an embargo on munitions is the sympathy of America for the Allies. We support the Anglo-French loan, saying that this country is fortunate in being able to help the cause most of us sympathize with. We were one of the very first journals to follow Colonel Roosevelt in

23

his plea that America should have protested against the violation of Belgium (see "Timid Neutrality," p. 12). And yet, according to Professor Perry, *The New Republic* is pro-German.

What seems to trouble Professor Perry is that after sixteen months of devastating war we prefer to waste as little energy as possible in hating the Germans. So he poses the question: "Is there, or is there not, a moral issue involved in the present war?" There is no need to hesitate over an answer. There is a moral issue, a supreme moral issue. It turns on the question of whether this awful slaughter and waste is to help towards a just and lasting peace. The moral issue is whether we can make the war count for or against a civilized union of the nations. All other questions are trivial or subsidiary compared to that. The guilt of German diplomacy, the ruthlessness of German arms are secondary. The question now is not who started the war, but to what end the fighting is to lead.

The accusation that we are evading the moral issue and becoming "pro-German" has but one excuse. Our accuser is emphasizing the origin of the war, whereas we are emphasizing its purposes and results. This difference of emphasis is what he calls "pro-German," and the only basis for his suspicion is that we have at various times criticized certain statements made by infuriated spokesmen of the Allies. When Frenchmen talk of making the Rhine their frontier; when the Japanese move aggressively against China; when the Italians play a part extremely dubious and selfish; when careless people talk glibly of "carving up" Austria-Hungary or "crushing" Germany, anyone interested in the future of the world has to speak out. For the point to remember is that while a nation may enter the war with clean hands, there is no guarantee that it will emerge with clean hands. We may believe that in July, 1914, the cause of France and England was the cause of humanity. The question now is what will their cause be in July, 1916?

This moral issue is so desperately important, the task of

24

reconstructing the world is so infinitely difficult, that consuming hatred seems to us a luxury. It is the refuge of those who are too angry to think. It is the solace of those who have nothing more helpful to do. There seem to be two groups of people who avoid this impotence of hate. They are the soldiers who have met the enemy, and the non-combatants whose minds are concentrated on the future. The issues are too real for these people to sit at ease and brood on blame and punishment.

"Easy tolerance" . . . "willingness to forget" . . . "intellectualism" . . . It is a world steeped in agony, and those who can bring it nothing but their indignation have little cause to be proud. This is especially true of those members of neutral nations whose life-work it is to use their minds. Never did the world need its coolest thought so much as now. Never did it come with poorer grace that a professional thinker should deride the effort to employ human reason.

December 18, 1915

TRADE AND THE FLAG

Commissioner of Immigration Frederic C. Howe formulates three principles which he believes ought to be worked into any program of preparedness. The first is that the cost of armament should be paid for out of direct taxation graded to throw the chief burden on the well-to-do and very rich. Differences of detail aside, this has been the contention of *The New Republic* since an increase of military forces became a practical political issue. Commissioner Howe's second postulate is that "there should be no profit from war." This is an impossible ideal, short of complete communism; but if Commissioner Howe means that the chief munitions should be made in government plants, that prices of other munitions should be regulated, and that special war profits should be reached by drastic taxation, then we can heartily agree.

The third point is by far the most interesting because there has been so little discussion of it. It is that the greatest source of diplomatic friction in the modern world centers about finance in backward countries. Commissioner Howe argues against the acceptance by the United States of the doctrine that the flag follows the investment of the citizen, that armed force should ever be used either to secure concessions, to protect them, or to collect debts. As we understand him, he wishes the government to wash its hands of responsibility for American investors and traders in backward countries.

To see what this means consider the case of Mexico. There are large American investments in that country. During the revolution they have depreciated, much money has been lost, a number of Americans have been murdered. There has been a demand for intervention, resisted by President Wilson. Finally a government has been set up in Mexico under General Carranza. The United States has "kept its hands off"; the doctrine that the flag covers the investment has not been enforced. In other words, we have had a demonstration of the principle which Commissioner Howe advocates. A few days ago there was a circumstantial report in the New York *Times* that General Carranza will be refused loans in Wall Street. It was pointed out that the Mexican government is already in arrears of $64,000,000, and that no obligations of any kind have been met since the end of 1914. Mexican credit has been ruined "almost beyond repair." The article states that it is only a question of weeks or months before the Carranza government falls, and that the bankers are unwilling to lose money in Mexico. Finally it suggests that Carranza might secure loans if he permitted an American commission to take charge of the collection and disbursement of government revenues until the defaulted obligations are redeemed.

Commissioner Howe will have no difficulty in understanding the meaning of this. Through the control of credit the financiers are in a position to pass sentence of death on a foreign government and to put an effective veto on the clear intention of our own government. For without credit what can Carranza do? If he tries to raise funds by taxation he will evoke a revolution among his own people. If he tries to borrow outside of recognized banking circles he must deal with speculators and usurers, and yield concessions which would be ruinous to Mexico. Without funds he cannot police or administer his country. Yet the bankers can hardly be blamed if they insist on some security for the money they are asked to lend. Mexico must borrow. Our government can hardly say to the investor, "We will not protect you, but you must lend money." If we withdraw protection from the investor we have no case against him if he takes us at our word and refuses to invest. Yet his refusal to invest destroys the Carranza government and upsets the Wilson policy towards Mexico.

This is the sort of consideration Commissioner Howe has neglected to deal with. International laissez-faire is no solution of the real danger to which he points. What he wishes to avoid is war to protect investments. But the facts of a given case may require investment in order to preserve the peace. In our judgment he is right in believing that the relation between government and the financing of backward countries is the central problem of modern diplomacy. We differ only when he insists that the problem can be solved by divorcing government from finance.

In casting about for a better solution, a somewhat closer analysis is necessary. It is clear that British investments in the United States or French investments in England are not a diplomatic problem. The flag need not cover the investor. And the reason is that these investments are made in countries which have comparatively strong and modern governments. The problem arises only in the weak nations, like Mexico or China or Haiti. But even in these nations there are differences. Some groups of investors desire only security and equal opportunity. Others have more sinister ambitions. They intrigue to control the weak government in order to secure monopolies or to force their own government to establish a protectorate. In both cases the problem is how to establish a strong modern government in the backward country. Once that is done, the flag ceases to follow the investment.

Commissioner Howe's policy of hands off will not establish strong government in weak countries. As in the case of Mexico, it may actually keep the weak governments weak. And so long as they are weak, disorder will reign, nationals will be murdered, and peoples will be embroiled. We need a much more positive policy. We cannot turn our backs on the weak countries. We must act in order to make them strong. The central motive of a democratic foreign policy must be the modernization of the feeble and distracted nations. That is

28

the only way to end the worst cause of diplomatic fraction. That is the only program of peace which really deals with the trouble.

How to translate this intention into a concrete policy to vary with the circumstances of each case. In some countries, China, for example, where weakness has produced bitter international rivalry, the only solution is probably joint action by the less aggressive Powers against the more aggressive. Some kind of international protectorate may have to be devised as a shield behind which China can gather its own strength. In certain Latin-American countries stability may be attained best by a Pan-American protectorate. In others, as in Cuba, a single Power may act to establish satisfactory government. Whatever the method, one thing is clear: if we are to avoid the dangers that Commissioner Howe has in mind, we must be prepared to take affirmative action on the causes from which these dangers arise. It is the old story of draining the swamp rather than of dodging the mosquitoes.

There is another point to be borne in mind. When companies are formed for investment and trade in backward countries, the policy of those companies is a matter of great public concern. What they do in Latin-America or in China is not a matter of business alone, it affects profoundly the foreign relations of the United States. At the worst these companies may wreck a weak government, or they may by aggressive and monopolistic enterprise bring on dangerous friction with a great Power. They may produce trouble in which American lives are lost. It is not enough to say to them, as Commissioner Howe suggests, we shall not back you up by force of arms. It is necessary to regulate them and keep them under public control. What is needed is a clear understanding about the kind of investment, the sort of trade policy, which the American people are ready to support.

No such understanding exists to-day, and we are in the perilous position of being open to unlimited liability for the action of Americans in the undeveloped nations. One administration may refuse to protect them at all, another may back them up at all times. The result is a foreign policy which has no consistency, in which it is impossible to count the costs and know what the responsibilities are. One of the very greatest services that any statesman could do for America to-day would be to work out a body of principles defining and regulating the relation between American diplomacy and American trade in the weak nations. Anyone who can contribute to that service will be dealing with the realities that underlie the problem of war and peace.

February 26, 1916

AN APPEAL

TO THE PRESIDENT

Sir: A week ago Thursday night you spoke to members of your party, but you appealed to the whole nation. You stood in the shadow of what the public believed was a break with Germany. You used words then which no man in your position would have used unless they were meant to indicate what was in your mind about the crisis which is upon us. You asked us whether we were ready to go in only when the interests of America are coincident with the interests of mankind. Those are brave words, and if we judge the American people correctly they are ready to go in on these terms. But they will want to know what those words mean. They will want you to enunciate not only a great aspiration but a great policy. It is to help what little we can towards formulating such a policy that we venture to address you.

To do that it is necessary to analyze America's policy since the war began. We have been officially neutral. We have claimed the protection which international law promises to neutral life and trade. We have claimed the right to export munitions to any belligerent who was physically able to fetch them. We have seen the protection of international law broken down by both groups of fighting powers, murderously on the part of Germany, quietly and effectively on the part of Great Britain. We have seen the law of nations grossly violated in the case of Belgium, in lesser ways by the Allies. We have seen the smaller neutrals like Holland, Sweden, Norway, Denmark, and Greece helpless in the great conflict. The neutrals have proved their impotence to protect their rights in the midst of war.

At last one form of outrage upon us has become intolerable. Germany's conduct of submarine warfare overshadows everything else, and you have led us to the breaking point. We are threatening to suspend diplomatic relations. But you must realize better than any one else that this in itself would be an empty gesture unless there were behind it the distinct understanding that another outrage meant action of a kind which would damage Germany. Therefore, with the rupture of relations we are brought to the verge of war. Let us remember what this means. It means that we are abandoning neutrality in order to preserve the recognized rights of a neutral. What possibility is there, Mr. President, that we can by fighting attain the object for which we go to war? To declare war now in the old fashioned way is to join the Allies. This means first of all that we accept the British Orders in Council as the basis of sea law. We yield at once a very large portion of the neutral rights for which we have been contending.

But there is a deeper consideration. Can we by going to war with Germany obtain the kind of guaranty which we desire? Suppose that in conjunction with the Allies we beat Germany to the ground and are in a position to dictate the terms of peace. What guaranty can we extract from Germany which will prevent for the future such crimes as the sinking of the Lusitania? We can obtain a promise from Germany. Nothing more. But promises we have already had, and the reason we are now in a crisis with Germany is not that she will not promise but that she will not fulfill her promise.

Moreover, if you break with Germany now, if you declare war upon her, on what terms will you resume relations, on what terms will you make peace? How will you know when you have won what you are contending for? When Germany sues for peace, offers apologies and reparation, and makes promises for the future? You have had all these things from Germany, and the fearful fact is that when military necessity is great enough, the promises are worthless. Then, too, if you go into the war, on what basis will you go in? Will you sign the pact of the Allies not to make a separate peace? You could not do that. You would not dare to pledge the future of this country in a compact the purposes of which have never been defined. You can not pledge us to Russia and Italy and Japan. You would not entangle us in the ambitions of Italy for the control of Trieste and the Dalmatian coast, in the ambitions of Russia to obtain Constantinople.

Yet if we declare war, join the Allies, sign their pact, we shall have begun for the purpose of vindicating our right to travel at sea, but we shall end by fighting to change the political control of the Near East. And when it is all over we shall not have the slightest idea whether we have attained the object for which we fought.

This, Mr. President, is a situation which requires a different kind of action, a situation which offers you an unparalleled opportunity for constructive leadership. With all respect we submit the following suggestions:

Neutrality in the old meaning of the term has ceased to be possible. It has no way of defending itself except by abandoning its neutrality. The reason why neutrality is so helpless is that each neutral has tried to protect its specific rights under the law of nations, whereas the true principle is to uphold the law whether your rights are violated or not. Only when all nations are ready to act in behalf of the general rule will that rule come to have any binding force. A common defense of rights is the only way individual rights can be maintained.

What does this mean? It means that we must abolish the old doctrine of neutrality. It means that we no longer intend to be neutral between the violator and his victim. We have learned from this war that one attack on law is followed by another, and that if lawbreaking is permitted at one point the

33

anarchy infects every one. Therefore, we must say that from now on the United States is not neutral. It intends to use its moral power, its economic resources, and in some cases its military force against the aggressor.

How does it define the aggressor? The aggressor is the nation that will not submit its quarrel to international inquiry, that will not suspend action until the world has had a chance to pass judgment upon it, or that pursues its quarrel after the world has decided against it. With such a nation the United States will have no intercourse, against it will be employed the resources of America.

How can this principle be applied in the present crisis? By announcing to Germany that we shall not only break off negotiations but aid her enemies until she agrees to abandon submarine warfare against commerce, until she agrees to evacuate Belgium, France, and Serbia, to indemnify Belgium, and to accept the principle that in the future all nations shall use their resources against the Power which refuses to submit its quarrel to international inquiry. If Germany accepts this program, we shall agree to resume intercourse, and not to furnish special aid to her enemies; we shall agree to become one of the guarantors of Belgium's integrity, and to assist in maintaining the inviolability of buffer states which may be created after the war by refusing to furnish their invaders with supplies of any kind. Futhermore, we shall accord to Germans equal rights with Americans in all American protectorates, and we shall refuse to furnish any kind of aid to any Power which does not apply the open door in its protectorates and non-self-governing territories.

If you adopt some such policy as that, Mr. President, you will have turned this crisis to the service of mankind. You will have done more than any one else has ever done to put a sanction behind the law of nations. You will have transformed what may be a meaningless rupture into a significant event. You will have a thousand times better chance of stopping specific submarine outrages, and at the same time you will have done a very great deal towards organizing the world against the lawbreaker.

The worst that can happen to this plan, Mr. President, is that it can fail. But you will have set mankind thinking, and you will be in a position to use the older and cruder methods of plunging into war without definition of purpose or sight of the goal. But what if it is a success? You will have established the precedent that an injury to one is an injury to all, you will have put the power of the United States behind nations like Belgium which are the wards of mankind, and can exist only in a world where international law is respected. You will have pledged this country to the principle that only in a world where Belgium is safe can the United States be safe. You may lead Germany back into the family of nations, ready to acknowledge that there is a greater law than the law of her interests.

A Germany which has accepted the program suggested would be a chastened Germany, a Germany with whom liberal Europe could begin to negotiate. It has been your ideal, and the ideal of the American people, that we might make some contribution to the healing of this disaster. Until now there has been no opportunity. To have intervened would have been to meddle. But here our rights are involved. We have some standing in the conflict. We have injuries to redress, we have great power to exert. The opportunity has come. For when you break with Germany you are in a position to state what the break shall mean, and on what terms you will resume intercourse. Make those terms coincide with an international program. Make this crisis count. Here is a way by which you can translate into action the aspiration of your speech on Jefferson Day. There is a way of making the interests of America coincident with the interests of mankind. Here is a program which meets your splendid challenge:

Are you ready for the test? Have you the courage to go in? Have you the courage to come out according

35

as the balance is disturbed or readjusted for the interests of humanity?

You stand, Mr. President, before a choice such as comes to few men. You are at the crest of opportunity.

April 22, 1916

MR. WILSON'S

GREAT UTTERANCE

The address before the League to Enforce Peace actually was delivered on May 27, not May 22. In this speech Wilson declared, "We are participants, whether we would or not, in the life of the world. The interests of all nations are our own also. We are partners with the rest." After setting forth basic principles of the peace, he added, "I am sure that I speak the mind and wish of the people of America when I say that the United States is willing to become a partner in any feasible association of nations formed in order to realize these objects and make them secure against violation." [*A.S., jr.*]

President Wilson's declaration on May 22nd at the dinner of the League to Enforce Peace may well mark a decisive point in the history of the modern world. No utterance since the war began compares with it in overwhelming significance to the future of mankind. For us in America it literally marks the opening of a new period of history and the ending of our deepest tradition. For this speech and the policy it foreshadows, it will be said of Mr. Wilson that he lived in a time of supreme opportunity, that he had the vision to grasp it and the courage to declare it, that on the central issue of modern life he chose the noble part .

These are big claims, but they are easily upheld. The

United States is the richest and potentially, so far as the near future is concerned, the most powerful nation on earth. We have become converted to a program of armament and industrial preparedness which will make our power count. The question they are asking in Japan, in Latin-America, and in Europe is: What does America intend to do with this power? In a world prostrated by war, in a world bled white with death and destruction, what is the meaning of this arming and preparing on the other side of the Atlantic? Let us not fool ourselves as to their answer. The fact that we think we are arming for defense will not convince Europe or Asia. They are worldly wise and know that all nations, no matter how aggressive, always call preparedness national defense. And virtuous as we may believe ourselves to be, let us not forget that no one else takes us at our own valuation. The rise of a great military and naval Power in the New World is certain to frighten all mankind, unless the intention of that Power is clearly defined and openly guaranteed.

The most damnable thing we could do with our strength would be to use it for purely national purposes. As surely as the earth turns on its axis, a new balance of power would be set up to offset us, and a new race of armaments incited. To be heavily armed, to "go it alone," to seek security in isolation, would in every human probability bring into existence alliances against us. The final tragic absurdity of preparedness for national defense alone is that, after all the cost and trouble, a nation is not one bit better defended. What would it profit us to build a "supreme navy" as some madmen urge, if the result were to align the navies of Japan and England against us?

Mr. Wilson's speech means that he has done some real thinking on the problem of national defense. His conclusion is that of a growing body of people in all the important countries of the world. It is that security cannot be had by any one nation alone, no matter how well armed it is. Security cannot be had by force divided among "sovereign" nations.

It can be had only by force which is unified under the control of nations that cooperate. Armament cannot defend one section of mankind. To be of any use it must defend an organization of mankind. Because the readiness to kill and be killed is certain to be the decisive factor in human government for a long time to come, the path of progress is not the abolition of force but the improvement of the purposes for which force is used. The proposal made by the League to Enforce Peace, and supported by the President, is that in the future force shall be used to defend the community of nations.

Mr. Wilson deserves the gratitude of all decent men for having announced that America is ready to use its force for this civilized end. The whole preparedness agitation, which has been running wild of late by piling jingoism on hysteria, is given a new turn. It becomes our contribution to the world's peace, the only kind of peace in which we can find our own safety. Mr. Wilson has broken with the tradition of American isolation in the only way which offers any hope to men. Not only has he broken with isolation, he has ended the pernicious doctrine of neutrality, and has declared that in the future we cannot be neutral between the aggressor and the victim. That is one of the greatest advances ever made in the development of international morality. His speech means that America is ready to act on the belief that war is no longer a matter between two "sovereign" states, but a common world-problem of law and order in which every nation is immediately concerned. There is something intensely inspiring to Americans in the thought that when they surrender their isolation they do it not to engage in diplomatic intrigue but to internationalize world politics. They will surrender it for that, though they would have resisted bitterly a mere entanglement in the manoeuvers which prepare new wars.

Mr. Wilson has chosen a good moment to make his historic statement—and it may justly be regarded as the first practical step towards peace. When America is talked of as peace-maker, Europeans have naturally asked what we have to contribute for that work. While we clung to isolation we had nothing to offer, but now we have committed ourselves to upholding the peace of Europe. We have said to the nations: "You may count on us to employ our power to curb any nation which attempts to destroy the peace you organize." Mr. Wilson has introduced a new factor, and a decisive one, into the calculations of European governments. Think what it means. To England it means our aid as against an aggressor and an end to the fear that the British commonwealth can be challenged and destroyed. To France it means that in a war of defense she would be guaranteed by the joint power of Britain and America. To Belgium it means that she becomes the ward not only of these competing nations, but also of a Power which cannot be accused of any selfish designs upon her. The future violator of Belgium would face at once the united arms of western civilization. To Germany it means security in return for the abandonment of aggression. It offers her the choice between arming again to meet all Europe and finding real safety in a league of the Western World. Let that alternative once be offered to the German people, and if radical and social democratic Germany does not make the decent choice, it is because Germany is incapable of learning anything. For our part we have no question that a people as educated as the Germans will make the right choice once the opportunity is offered with convincing sincerity. You can fool and frighten a people into aggression once, but when the price is as terrible as the price has been, you cannot do it again if there is a plain alternative in sight.

Our offer to join in a guaranty of the world's peace opens up the possibility of a quick and moderate peace. It gives to the liberals of Europe a practical thing to work with. They are now in a position to confront the extremists and say to them: "You tell us we must fight till the enemy is crushed, or there is no safety for our children. But to crush the enemy is to come near to crushing ourselves. You offer us the phantom peace of total exhaustion, followed by insurrection and riot and degeneracy. But here is a chance to organize security before we are shattered, and to guarantee that security with the untouched vigor of the richest people on earth. That is a better defense than anything you promise us. It is time to stop talking highflown martial nonsense, and begin to adjust concrete problems."

Let no one suppose that Mr. Wilson made his offer without realizing its significance. It is a fact that there are definite assurances from the Foreign offices, both of France and England, that such a league is desired. There is excellent reason for believing that Berlin is favorable to the idea. It may be said at last without any exaggeration that the first move towards peace has been made.

June 3, 1916

AMERICA TO EUROPE,

AUGUST, 1916

The "Dublin executions" referred to the hanging of
fifteen Irish republican leaders after the Easter Rising
in Dublin. See Yeats's poem "Easter 1916." [*A.S., jr.*]

As the war goes into a third year the minds of Europe are
beginning to turn towards the settlement. In Germany the desire for peace is no longer concealed. It is possible to predict
with confidence that among the Allies the submerged longing
for an end of the agony will burst forth as soon as the present
offensive on all fronts has come to some kind of conclusion.
Whether the result is success or failure or indecision, a new
impulse to negotiate will almost certainly appear.

Just now the most useful service of American opinion
would be to give people in Europe a working knowledge of
what to expect of the United States. Hotheads in all the warring countries have insisted that America will not count,
either because it has stood aloof or because it has been unneutral. But the more sensible men know that America is
bound to count merely because of its immense bulk and latent power. They know that the schism of Europe is too deep
for any lasting adjustment by the Peace Congress unless the
semi-detached influence of America is brought in to guarantee stability. Europe will remain on a predatory basis if it is
divided into two well matched alliances. Only the intervention

42

of the neutral world can give power to the liberals in all countries and make a just peace possible and durable.

If the settlement is made by the belligerents alone, instead of by a council of nations, a disastrous peace is almost sure to be constructed. Assuming, for example, that Grey represents liberal England and von Bethmann-Hollweg moderate Germany, if these men meet they will feel behind them constantly the dangerous pressure of the von Reventlows and the Northcliffes, the Pan-Germans and the "ginger" groups, the forces of jingoism and wrath. The extremists on both sides have a tremendous appeal to their people when they say that no faith can be put in the enemy. But if the neutrals under the leadership of the United States will guarantee by force the terms of the settlement some hope exists of an arrangement in the interests of peace rather than as a measure of relative power. The attitude of the United States may prove to be crucial, and it is of the utmost importance that Europe should form accurate expectations about the United States.

America's action is contingent upon European policy. That is to say, the amount of responsibility America can be made to assume will depend on America's judgment of the good faith, the liberalism and the ambitions of the major belligerents. It is a tremendous task to arouse the United States from its isolation, and it will not be achieved unless the American people can be convinced that they are exchanging their historic policy for a policy of greater promise.

Were Germany triumphant, able to annex new territory and to terrorize Europe, the United States would remain aloof, and would merely arm heavily. But at present no such result seems possible. To dominant American opinion the exhaustion of Germany is a matter of time and the price the Allies are willing to pay. The really important consideration to-day is this: How will the Allies use their victory? On that depends America's attitude towards Europe.

To Englishmen especially we feel that we have a right to speak frankly, and to tell them what we fear. They must not

43

be deceived by the attitude of Americans living in England, or by upper-class feeling in the big cities of the United States. There is a school of American opinion which is more pro-Ally than the Allies, as full of futile hate against Germany as the *Morning Post* or the *National Review*. There are Americans who have always looked upon the British Tory as the apex of the social pyramid. But though noisy and prominent they are utterly unrepresentative, and their political power in a matter like this is very small. Two other factions in our population need to be considered, the organized Irish and Germans. The Dublin executions have done more to drive America back to isolation than any other event since the war began. It will be a long time before official America will be able to come to open agreement with any alliance of which Britain is the dominant partner. As for the Americans of German descent, their pro-Germanism has been a good deal exaggerated because of the action of leaders whom they have not repudiated. In our judgment they would not prove an insuperable obstacle to American participation in European affairs, provided that the status quo America was called upon to guarantee were not vindictive to Germany.

The great mass of American opinion can be won only by proof that Europe is dominated by liberals. An arrangement with Tories and chauvinists and imperialists is unthinkable, and Americans are watching with some misgiving the internal politics of Britain and Germany. They would take no responsibility for the peace of Europe if policy is to be dictated by men like Carson, Northcliffe and Curzon. The news which has come to us in the last few months has been a serious setback to the propaganda for an abandonment of isolation. Among the most important items of such news are these:

The proposal for a war after the war by means of tariffs, boycotts, and what not. If this is attempted, it will drive us into isolation. If successful, it will ultimately push us into the arms of Germany.

The muddle of Ireland, which has made America question

44

the liberalism of Britain and the sincerity of her talk about small nationalities or the good faith of her interest in Poles, Danes, and Alsatians.

The activity of Japan and Russia in China.

The publication of a blacklist. This is regarded by most Americans as a disruption of the world's commerce, not as a military measure against Germany. With Germany and all the adjoining neutrals blockaded, America sees no sense in the measure, and regards it as an attempt to destroy Germany, not as an effort to conquer her military power. It is regarded by Americans as insulting and as an invasion of their rights.

We do not believe that these measures represent the will of liberal England. They represent the reaction of wartime. But they have done and are doing infinite harm to any effort which might induce America to guarantee the settlement. We had got along pretty far in our willingness to join. President Wilson has made a speech which in its significance outweighs any statement of foreign policy made since the Monroe Doctrine was proclaimed. But the realization of this promise hangs on the victory of liberalism in Europe and especially in England. In its bearing upon the future the war of parties within the nations may be more significant now than the war of the nations.

July 29, 1916

PERISHABLE BOOKS

Maximilian Harden, editor of *Die Zukunft,* and the Social Democratic leaders Wilhelm Liebknecht and Eduard Bernstein were German critics of the war, as Shaw, Dickinson, Russell, Angell and Bryce were, in varying degree, skeptical observers of the war in Great Britain. Houston Stewart Chamberlain, an early racist, married Wagner's daughter and became a German citizen in 1916. Ernst Lissauer, a German poet and playwright, is remembered for the notable line in his *Hassgesang gegen England*: "Gott strafe England." Friedrich von Bernhardi was the German general, militarist and nationalist. Gilbert Murray had written in defense of British war aims. [*A.S., jr.*]

Much that has been written and said during the war by eminent men will not be pleasant reading to them in the years to come. The famous ninety-three German professors will never point with pride to their manifesto. They will never be glad that they signed their names to it. Lissauer will not be proud of his Hymn of Hate, and the biographer of Admiral von Tirpitz will have to do some tall explaining before his hero shines in splendor. The Kaiser's speeches will sound even more incredibly silly, and Mr. Houston Stewart Chamberlain will be a literary joke for a long time to come.

There will be a whole library of books written in all countries which will supply the social psychologist with a mountain of evidence on the instability of the human mind. It is interesting to speculate how the books will be classified. There will be one section devoted to races. It will include all those disquisitions on the intrinsic qualities of the Teutonic, the Latin, the Slav, and the Anglo-Saxon genius, books which are merely elaborate ways of repeating the old barbaric vanity of a Chosen People. In the years to come when Englishmen and Germans meet and gossip they will think it very funny that their learned men invented a race mythology to justify the clash of empires. They will scoff at those books which treat this war as bred in the soul of two "races" from the beginning of time. They will remember that in the 'eighties the most fashionable adjective for an Englishman was Teutonic and the bogey words were Latin and Celtic. They will see again what they knew before the war, that race theories follow the flag and that race mythologies reflect the course of diplomacy. Perhaps even Americans will see that our turn from admiration of the Japanese to suspicion is not a product of new learning about race psychology but the result of political and economic friction in California and in China.

Another section of the library will be devoted to annihilation theories, to books based on the old barbaric delusion of omnipotence. Nothing will altogether equal the books and statements which promised to wipe out a whole people. Men will wonder how even in the fury of war any one could have supposed that a nation was like an individual and that you could cut off its head, or that you could destroy a people by killing its soldiers.

Then there will be the books written by fair-minded men whose only fault was an excess of gregariousness, books like Professor Gilbert Murray's, which find for war purposes that the diplomacy of the Entente has ever been inspired by unwavering wisdom and righteousness. Of those books it will probably be said that the authors being moral men had to find a moral explanation for their patriotism, and were afraid to make the candid statement that they wanted to win the war.

There will be utterances of sedentary people who enjoyed the war, who found that it improved their character, gave them purpose in life, zest in existence, and sound sleep at night. The world will not laugh at these books. It will put them on the shelf beside the works of the Marquis de Sade. Nor will it deal more gently with those arguments which showed that Bernhardi was not alone in believing that war is a holy thing, and the only way of curing the vices of peace. Europe counting its dead, its maimed, its shattered, and its bastards, suffering under the poverty of exhaustion, will say that of all the false prophets these are the most damned.

Then there will be a literature produced by American neutrals, books which celebrate a Germany that does not exist on land or sea, and books which are more pro-Allies than the Allies. There will be articles by American professors, one or two of them at Harvard perhaps, which will read like the words of a British Duchess at a garden party for the benefit of Belgian refugees. There will be books, published serially in reputable magazines, read and discussed solemnly at dinner tables, which showed that six months after the end of the war the German army would be put on transports and accompanied by the fleet would sail for New York and steal our gold deposits. Even now those books seem a little dusty and rather worm-eaten.

On the whole the world will prefer to forget these books. What will it care to remember? That to the outer world France was silent and steady and that no hysterical whine was uttered, that the common people of all the nations, not understanding the diplomacy which made the war, struggled for what they believed to be a disinterested cause, that the British soldier fought with humorous contempt and preserved in the trenches a large measure of that kindly humanity and unpretentious gallantry which are the badge of his courage.

And then the world will like to remember the men who, like Lincoln, never said a bitter or foolish thing, the men whose eyes were fixed on the deeper truth that however wrong one belligerent might be, the greatest wrong was the organized anarchy which had permitted it to be. The men who stood out against the herd, who could see through the sins of their own people, will be the moral heroes of the war. Those few men in each nation who spoke for Europe, who had enough iron in their souls to withstand hatred and illusion will grow in the world's estimation. Englishmen today can appreciate Harden and Liebknecht and Bernstein; they will learn to appreciate Shaw and Lowes Dickinson and Bertrand Russell and Norman Angell and Bryce. There is no surer prophecy than that peace will bring a revaluation.

October 14, 1916

BRITISH-AMERICAN

IRRITATION

In August, 1914, Britons and Americans were very close together. Newspapers and public speakers were denouncing
Germany in the same phrases, and so far as outward expression went the English-speaking nations had become one spiritual community. But since 1914 the experience of the two
peoples has diverged. Behind the phrases which inaugurated
the war, behind the simple formulæ which were used to explain its origin, the British have placed their lives, their
wealth, their pride. No wonder then that the slogans of the
war are vivid to Britons as they no longer are to us. For if all
that Americans wrote and said in the first months of the war
was unimpeachable truth, our peace is indeed dishonorable,
and we ought to be fighting alongside the Allies. But events
soon showed that though many of us used much the same
language as the Allies, the words had a totally different pragmatic value. Not only the election, but the campaign conducted by the Republicans, showed that the bulk of the
American people, though they talked like a belligerent, never
intended to be one.

The small minority here who desire American intervention,
and the great mass of the British people who naturally desire
it also, concluded that the stamina of America is decaying
because it did not go to war when it talked like a nation at
war. It was humiliating to look at the gap between American

words and American deeds. Imperceptibly at first, but none the less surely the American people began to close up the gap, but they did it not by squaring their deeds with their words. They began to square their words with their deeds. Having fixed upon non-intervention as a policy, they began to analyze the old phrases, and for over a year we have been witnessing a growing tendency in America to take a less partisan view of the war.

There was plenty of material at hand: the old anti-British tradition implanted in every schoolboy's memory, the blunders at Gallipoli and elsewhere, the Japanese alliance, the indefinite extension of British sea-power, the Irish episode, and a good deal of discourtesy in the British press. More and more Americans began to say that though Germany was the immediate instigator of the war, though the violation of Belgium was the greatest crime since the destruction of Poland, yet the origins of this world-wide conflict were deeper than German militarism, and that the guilt must be distributed, however unevenly. Now it would be a mistake to suppose that America became more neutral because it had weighed the evidence. The truth is that America secured the evidence when it had determined to be neutral.

More and more the war has ceased to look like a clean-cut fight between right and wrong, between democracy and absolutism, between public faith and international lawlessness. Italy, Rumania, Russia with their aggressive programs confuse the situation too much, and the lack of any definition of the Allied objective has filled a growing mass of Americans with the sense that the remedy for this horror is not to be had by a "knockout," but is to be sought in radical reorganization. These obscure and half-formulated reactions have found their expression in the idea of a League to Enforce Peace, an idea which is much closer to effective American opinion to-day than any proposal for downright intervention or an out-and-out alliance with the British Empire. It is a true, though no doubt a pale and unappreciated crystallization, and perhaps even a compensation for the diminishing partisanship of America.

This spiritual change has reverberated in Canada and Great Britain. That America should talk big and not act was bad enough, but that America should soften its tone was worse. If you ask an Englishman to-day what it is that we have done to irritate him so, he will insist that he does not quarrel with us for staying out of the war, he will confess that our neutrality has been ultra-benevolent to the Allies, and sharply discriminating against Germany. Then he will point sadly or angrily to things which have been said, things which are unsympathetic to the reasons which are put out as explaining the Allied cause. He will complain about the alteration in the American temper toward the war. His irritation piques us, of course, and the result is a discouraging cleft in the feeling of the English-speaking peoples.

It is curious and significant that no such division has appeared between France and America. No doubt many Frenchmen are annoyed at us, and feel many contemptuous things. But they have been too discreet to let us hear them, and what is more, they do not talk English. For our part the feeling toward France has reached a pitch of almost ecstatic admiration. It is due to facts that are obvious enough, to the intrinsic lovableness of the French people, to their heroism and clarity and their steadfastness. But these qualities will not in themselves explain the spiritual differences in American feeling for France and Britain. The mere fact that a nation has great qualities will unfortunately not always produce an international friendship, and the situation in America is such that we tend to an unlimited idealization of France and a hypercriticism of Great Britain.

The real explanation surely lies deeper than the spiritual quality of the two peoples. It lies in those portentous historic forces which determine feelings and ideas. Americans have been able to love France as they do, to see the best in

France, because the relationship of the two nations is fundamentally disinterested. But the attitude of Britons and Americans is determined in the last analysis by a dim sense that each means to the other so much of good and evil. Our destinies cross. We are inextricably entangled one with another, we know and the British know that the most terrible consequences are involved in our relationship. The feeling for France is the free friendship men give to those whom they meet only in their leisure. With the British we have to-day the discordant intimacy of business partners and family ties. We know that we cannot live apart, we have not yet learned to live together. We are close up to each other, bound in a common destiny, painfully aware of each other's faults, and a little shrill about announcing them.

The task of sanity is to recognize this and hold it in the front of all discussion. So involved are British-American relations that it is impossible to maintain them as they are. We must go forward to alliance or to enmity. Now and in the years immediately ahead this fearful decision will be made, and on it, more than on any other decision will depend the happiness of the western world. We are living out now the process of that decision, and all the existing irritation is a symptom of it. To find the bases of understanding is the supreme British-American task. We turn for help to the two peoples who will find their security in such understanding, the two peoples most able to mediate, the people of Canada and the people of France.

December 9, 1916

POLTROONS AND PACIFISTS

Of all sneers none is so carelessly thrown as the charge of cowardice. To call a man a coward is almost to obliterate him from discussion. The man who uses the term always implies that he himself, of course, is a brave man. He acquires at once a kind of moral superiority, and puts his opponent on the defensive. Caution and reason thus become positive vices, every honest doubt is made the mark of a timid soul. Those who want twenty dreadnoughts regard as cowards those who want ten; the advocates of forty dreadnoughts look with scorn upon the advocates of twenty. Men who wish to prepare against one possible enemy are cowards in the eyes of those who wish to prepare against two possible enemies. The proposers of a much larger army are tinged with yellow in the eyes of the conscriptionists. In America we are fast getting into the frame of mind where the scale of courage is measured by what the wildest jingo proposes as the correct method of licking creation.

Since all men resent being known as cowards, the jingo has an enormous advantage in any argument. He bullies men into agreeing with him by playing on their fear of appearing to be cowardly. He hammers upon moral cowardice in order to drive people into an attitude of rhetorical bravery. It is an old, old trick, but it works. Take two elderly men both over military age. Let the rumor of war appear. The man who is ready to sacrifice other people's lives at short notice appears as the hero; the moderate person who resists the stampede and braves the denunciation for doing so, is somehow

labelled coward. In the German Reichstag the men who upheld the war party could pose as the gallant pacifists; Liebknecht, who stood up unmoved against the storm, was put
down a coward. But, by any just estimate, where was the
courage and where the timidity? Who had that iron in his
soul of which free men are made? In England there is now
bitter discussion between those who want a sensible peace
and those who will set no limits to their vengeance. Which
position is the easy one, the soft one, the one of the molly-
coddles? Which position requires courage, and which requires
nothing but the willingness to drift with the current?

The courage of the battlefield and the courage of the editorial sanctum are not identical. Courage is not so simple a
virtue. At a dinner table, in a drawing-room, on the stump,
in the Senate, the easy attitude is to follow the loudest decla-
mation, to go with, not against, the violence of the tribe. It
involves usually no risk, and it is almost always a cheap way
to approval. Yet there is no guarantee that the fiber of a
people is sound because no one appears who is willing to
risk the sneers of the angriest. It may be that the people who
are ready to sacrifice popularity, to face ridicule, to stand out
for reason and adjustment, are the people who really have
the bravery that freedom requires. Not to be afraid of being
called a coward has been often recognized as a high order of
courage.

It would be a great gain if our military agitators would use
words like coward and poltroon with more discrimination.
They are not synonymous with a desire for peace, with an
opposition to conscription, with a determination not to in-
vade Mexico because some bandits have committed a crime.
All men less violent than the most violent have not white
hearts and yellow souls. All are not cowards who wish to
weigh carefully the purpose of armaments that mean a break
with the whole tradition of American life. All are not pol-
troons who insist upon analyzing the intention of those who
wish to make us the greatest military nation on earth. All are

not spineless who think that the honor of a democracy is not that of a Spanish grandee.

The cause of preparedness is not helped by floating it upon a stream of jingoism. Many of us think there are powerful reasons for re-defining American policy and preparing armaments to uphold it, but the cause is endangered and made odious by those who treat it as an issue between cowards and heroes. The military propagandists will, if they don't look out, have taken so extreme a position that the American people may regard them as a greater danger than any possible foreign enemy. They are feeding the deep and experienced suspicion of ordinary men that all armament leads to militarism, that any concession provokes the appetite of those who like the virtues of war better than the virtues of peace, who like military equipment for its own sake and propose to rule the nation in its interest.

There is in America to-day the beginning of that very military arrogance which we are told this war is being fought to abolish. It shows itself in contempt for all efforts toward peace, in programs of armament that are the vistas of a nightmare, in denunciation of the virtues that make a free and tolerant people, in a hatred of other points of view, in the attempt to haze and ostracise those who have different opinions, and in the assertion of a brittle, touchy impatience at the thought that anything human can be adjusted without slamming the table and rattling the windows.

The militarists are forcing the issue in such a way as to consolidate the opposition. If the American people have to choose between their virulence and the amiable intentions of the official pacifists they will follow the pacifists. They will risk the Monroe Doctrine and American prestige in the East, they will prefer the defeat of a foreign policy in some future war to any proposal to deliver the country into the hands of those who in the last months have got deeper and deeper into their own violence. The real desire of Americans is to make a civilization in America. They will prepare what is necessary to defend that; they may even be induced to take a share in the policing of the world. But they do not want to be told that war is a gymnasium of the virtues; they know it to be the stinking thing that it is. They want no extra gold lace and no more tom-toms than are necessary. They do not wish to spend their energy in dreaming war games. If they have to fight they will do it sadly, and with as little bombast as possible. Their condemnation of Germany in this war is based on what they believe to be a dangerous military psychology in the rules of Germany, and they are shrewd enough to detect and resent that same psychology when it crops up in America.

January 22, 1916

THE WILL TO BELIEVE

For two and a half years, the war has put upon men's minds a responsibility for which few had any preparation. It is literal truth that so varied a number of people have never before had so tangled and so delicate a situation to deal with. They have had to grope through veils of illusion for judgments which meant life and death to millions. Every man who looks candidly into his own mind knows that it is a haphazard collection of rumors and flashes, of sharp experiences, of jostling memories and hopes, odds and ends of fact, pale little schemes of history. Many people, to be sure, resent any such confession, and insist on walking about in patent-leather certainties. They know, by God, they know, like the fashionable rector in New York City who recently offered to sacrifice ten million European lives for what he called righteousness. They know, oh yes they know that the war must be fought to a finish though they could not define what they mean by a finish if their immortal souls depended upon it. What this kind of assurance comes to really is a moral detachment from the issues of the war. To sit by as a neutral and refuse to consider the awful complications of the struggle is to wash your hands of it, no matter how violently you repeat that you want one side or the other to win. It is to be no less aloof from the actual problems than are those who, seeing only horror, cry peace on any terms.

Yet the effort to find a way through is difficult beyond precedent. We are in the midst of it, and subject to epidemics of all sorts. Journalists especially, hurried and limited as they are, can hardly help feeling that they are stumbling and stuttering most of the time. Unavoidably they say more than they meant or less, they take a tone or an emphasis which is partial and misleading. Like the blind men in the fable they are trying to describe the elephant by touching in casual succession its trunk and its tusks and its tail. And they are compelled to ask the indulgence of their readers if in describing the tusks as hard and bony they appear to be saying that the whole animal is hard and bony.

In *The New Republic,* for example, we have said time and time again that the chief item of American foreign policy must be to find a basis of thorough agreement with the British Empire. We have urged that military preparedness should be adopted to that end, and have hit at those enthusiasts who proclaim their undying love for Britain in one breath and urge America to outbuild her navy in the next. It has been perfectly evident, however, that real understanding could not be reached by fine words and fine sentiments. There are many things in America and Britain that will have to be altered before political alliance is possible. These things have to be talked about with the utmost candor, even though the first effect is to cause irritation rather than allay it. The two peoples will never find a common path by means of after-dinner speeches, Anglo-American snobbery, and a colonialism of spirit. Nor will they find it, as many well-meaning people urge, by suppressions and silences. Whatever the temporary cost, it is only by self-respect which can give and take that the essential understanding will be created. The two nations are not served by flattery, they are merely deceived.

There used to be, for example, continual talk that Germany must be "crushed," and anyone who criticized such talk was regarded as rather "pro-German." Even those who did not indulge in it said that it was useless to protest against it, because as a matter of fact Germany showed no signs of being crushed. What they did not see was that the talk was instantly flashed to Germany, that it played right into the hands of the war party, that it raised false hopes among the Allied peoples, and that it alienated the neutrals. Yet it has been said that to be critical of the extremists among the Allies was to be unfriendly to the Allied cause.

Another source of irritation was the journalistic campaign which asked for specifications as to what the destruction of Prussian militarism meant. The first reaction was to grow angry and say that everybody knew just what it meant. But everybody didn't, and as a result liberals began to fear that the phrase might become a mask for a vindictive policy of territorial aggression. They did not forget that there was a Prussian militarism which had conscripted the body and soul of the German nation, which had played the bully in diplomacy, which had proclaimed a national philosophy intolerable to Europe, which respected no treaty, overran and mutilated Belgium, sank the Lusitania to the widespread applause of the German people, organized sedition and conspiracy on neutral territory, tried to arouse a holy war in the East, stood by while the Armenians were massacred, turned its face against all effort to avert the war, dreamed that it would win supremacy in the world by the most deliberate and ingenious preparation mankind ever knew. Of all people it is the liberal democrat who can say most sincerely that he hates this thing, hates it in Germany, hates an imitation of it at home.

Yet just because the purpose is so real, it is necessary every minute to consider the ways and means of accomplishing it. No one can evade the questions: What are the military objectives which will lead to this result? What must be the condition on the battlefield which is most likely to change the spirit and aims of German policy? Would the change come if peace were made now on the territorial status quo ante, with the present neutral world as added guarantors? Some think it is possible that the memory of this war, the enormous burden of debt, a commercial outlet in Asia Minor, and the existence of guaranties would release the German democracy within the next generation. Others think that even a moderate peace now is undersirable, and that the Allies must secure the prestige of a victory in field before they can dare to enter negotiations. Still others think the Germans are such different clay that peace must rest on victory as absolute as that which the North won in the American Civil War. Our own sympathies lie rather with the second of these groups. That the peace will have to be negotiated, that it cannot be dictated seems to us not only evident but desirable. That it would be better to negotiate after the German army had tasted defeat is probable. But in choosing this probability every one must face the awful gamble on which it rests. No one knows what it would cost to secure a victory on a scale which would compel the German army to retreat say to the Belgian border. To make this choice easily, cocksurely, hastily, without remembering what it means in human agony, without remembering that the result is mere guess-work, is to be rather more extravagant with other people's lives than any half-informed neutral has a right to be.

At no time has *The New Republic* intended to say that now is the moment to end the war. What we have said is that the time is ripe for a discussion of how and when to end the war. As part of that discussion it has been necessary to face as frankly as possible the meaning of a peace negotiated now. It would mean that Middle Europe existed, even though Germany held no foot of conquered territory. It would mean a genuine loss of prestige by the British in the eastern world, and a rather complete destruction of Russian influence in the Balkans and Asia Minor. It is impossible to deny this. But it doesn't follow that Germany dominant in Middle Europe would be able to use it as basis for the domination of all Europe and the world. It is at least arguable that this heterogeneous collection of uneducated and exasperated nationalities would prove ungovernable unless Germany reformed her manners and her methods by a liberalism akin to that of the British in the Dominions. Merely to look at the map and say, this is too much, it's too hideous, is not the final word on the question.

It is well for most of us to be open-minded about Middle Europe, because we may have to be. To be sure, if we happened to be omnipotent, we should not choose Middle Europe as an ideal. We should choose a federalized Austria-Hungary, a Balkan confederation, and a neutralization of the Dardanelles. But if we have to choose between German leadership in the Balkans and its alternative: an everlasting struggle between Germany and Russia in the Balkans, we prefer the German frying pan to the fire itself. After all the accomplished fact is a serious business, and just how Middle Europe is to be unscrambled is difficult to see. The victory we hope for this spring on the western front will take down the Germans as against the French and English, but will it convince Bulgaria and Turkey, and Serbia too, that the Russians are their real protectors?

Neither Middle Europe nor Russia astride the Dardanelles is a permanent or hopeful solution, and it need not be the final one. Middle Europe is likely to exist as a voluntary choice by the chief Balkan nations and Turkey just so long as the only alternative the Allies present is Russian supremacy. But suppose Allied statesmanship could rise high enough to offer these peoples internationalization of the trade routes and of the chief strategic points as the basis of a protected Balkan confederation, then it would not be necessary to take Middle Europe so seriously. A plan of that sort presented to the world by the Allies would probably fulfill their own desires, would awaken liberal enthusiasm, and arouse sentiment in the Near East which would make a German Middle Europe infinitely difficult.

January 13, 1917

AMERICA SPEAKS

On December 18, 1916, Wilson sent a circular note to the belligerent nations suggesting that both sides in the war had reconcilable objectives and proposing that soundings be taken before "injury be done civilization itself which can never be atoned for or repaired," to find out "how near the haven of peace may be for which all mankind longs with an intense and increasing longing." Disappointed by the reaction of Germany and her allies to this note, Wilson delivered an address to the Senate on January 22, 1917, outlining his view of the conditions of peace. "Is the present war," he asked, "a struggle for a just and secure peace, or only for a new balance of power? . . . There must be, not a balance of power, but a community of power; not organized rivalries, but an organized common peace." He called for "a peace without victory . . . a peace between equals. . . . Mankind is looking now for freedom of life, not for equipoises of power." He concluded by saying, "I hope and believe that I am in effect speaking for liberals and friends of humanity in every nation and of every programme of liberty." [*A.S., jr.*]

Everyone who stops to visualize the machinery of the approaching peace congress is appalled at the intricacy of the negotiations which it will require. Nine Allies on one side, four on the other, a score of vitally interested neutrals, life, prosperity, liberty, and security on four continents and the seven seas are involved. For the first time in history the negotiation is to be conducted not by a few men with autocratic powers but by envoys who must consider popular opinion. Obviously such a settlement cannot be made suddenly, without preparation, and without a world-wide background of ideas. The war came, it seemed, without warning; peace cannot come that way. It must come after a gradual lifting of the fog of war, after an uncovering and illumination in which some common understanding is created.

We have all of us to be educated through international discussion for the approaching peace. On December 18th the President, using the prestige of his office, gave great impulse to the discussion. He asked the warring powers to lay down their' formulae of settlement and suggested that the United States would enter a league of nations for the organization of security. After a few days of misunderstanding, because he had used an unclear phrase, the note began to have its effect. The Central Powers answered curtly, and immediately lost whatever psychological advantage they had gained by the Chancellor's offer of peace. Their proposal of a blind negotiation, their dismissal of security as a secondary object, convinced the outer world that the offer was either insincere, or that they wanted merely German peace, or that their own public opinion was in such bad condition that it could not be dealt with openly. The nine Allies by their reply won a great advantage. They specifically put the organization of security first, made territorial claims contingent upon it, and proposed a formula which was ambiguous enough to permit of wide negotiation. Mr. Balfour in his supplementary note reemphasized the point.

Now in accepting the idea of a league, the nine Allies not only made it necessary for Germany to make another move, they made it necessary for the United States to move again. They asked quite rightly what there was behind the President's offer of American aid. To be sure it was a plank in the Democratic platform and the Democrats won at the polls.

The idea had been endorsed by Mr. Hughes, by Mr. Taft, and formerly by Mr. Roosevelt. It had wide non-partisan support. Still the peoples of Europe, faced by the immediate brutal fact of German aggression, knowing the traditional isolation of this country, were entitled to much greater assurance of American support.

It is this support which the President is now arousing. His address to the Senate on Monday is primarily a summons to the American nation to share the responsibilities of the peace. Mr. Wilson is asking his people to prepare themselves for the work which the world has begun to expect of them. It is the beginning of a popular campaign in this country designed to make it certain that when the time comes for a settlement of the war, America will be firm as to its purposes, unified in their support, and conscious of the responsibility. Mr. Wilson knows that he cannot ask the European Powers to clear up the ambiguity of their aims without at the same time clearing up the ambiguity of our own. Not only abroad but here too the fog must be cleared away. He had sent a note to Europe asking for a definition of objects. On Monday he addressed the Senate and began to define ours.

No one supposes that the work of definition is accomplished now or could be accomplished in one note or one address. The fog has lifted only a little; only a few big landmarks are as yet visible. Just as the reply of the Allies was merely a loose statement of principle, so is the President's address. But in essence it comes very close to the prime objects which the Allies have announced. We are as clear as the Allies; we both are clearer and more unanimous than the Germans. Not only has the President recognized Russia's claim to passage of the Dardanelles and Poland's claim to autonomy, he has set America against any attempt to annex occupied territory, and has recognized the justice of liberating peoples held in bondage. It is difficult to see how he could have gone further in accepting as American policy the liberal purposes of the Allied nations.

On one point he seems to us not altogether sound. The passage referring to the freedom of the seas appears to contradict the idea of a league to enforce peace. In an organized world freedom of the seas would certainly not exist for the aggressor. In fact the greatest weapon of the league would be the power to isolate and coerce the law-breaker. It would aim at an absolute blockade of the outlawed power. In time of peace freedom of the seas would of course have to exist, and it may be that the President was thinking of this. He may have meant that maritime discrimination should be prevented. Nevertheless there is a real possibility of confusion in the form of his statement. It does seem to imply a kind of Manchester laissez-faire of the seas, an unworkable and inconsistent idea. What is needed is an organization of the seas which will produce freedom in time of peace and complete blockade and siege against the aggressor in time of war.

The moment is not yet here when it is possible to conclude dogmatically upon all the difficult questions involved in the settlement. The discussion of the next few months will be concerned with them. For the moment the President is bent on creating an atmosphere of negotiation. In this effort he has had to say one thing which was not easy to say. He had to tell the world that America could not share in a settlement which was dictated by the victor to the vanquished. He had to say that only a peace negotiated in a spirit of give and take could be stable enough to justify America in assuming the risks he was proposing. In making that point he used a phrase which will hurt deeply many whose support is required. He said that it must be a peace without victory.

It was an idea that had to be expressed, costly as it may be. So long as the people of the world believe that a lasting peace can be secured by dictation rather than by negotiation, the world will be where it always has been, at the mercy of a teetering balance of power. Peace has never been secured in Europe by that method and never will be, and the Allied spokesmen have generally recognized this. They have told us

that their object was to prevent Germany from winning anything by her aggression. They wanted her to go home with a
sense of futility. They wanted to show that war does not pay,
that nothing can be accomplished by it. The war will not end,
and President Wilson, we take it, would not wish it to end,
till that demonstration is complete. If the Germans think they
are offering peace now because their armies are victorious,
then the war will have to go on till the military situation
changes.

But how long is it to go on after that? Is it to go on till
the Allies can dictate a peace to a prostrate enemy? Are they
to take the position that no peace is possible unless they have
won an absolute decision in the field? Perhaps, but in that
case Europe is likely to be so embittered with its sacrifices
that any larger plan of security must fail. If Europe fights on
in the belief that security can be had only by victory, then
the foundation of a league will be shattered. It is likely to be
the old peace which never lasted because it put all its faith in
military power and ignored international organization.

The President has said that obviously we could not prevent Europeans from following this theory. The matter is in
their hands. But if they did follow it, if they set their hearts
on that rather than on a concert of power, America would
not leave its isolation. A world organized on the creed of
victory is a world in which America must arm to the teeth
and pursue a purely national policy. Americans in the mass
do not want to live in such a world, and they are preparing
to do what they can to make it unnecessary.

Happily they have found a leader who can express that
feeling nobly and eloquently, a man who knows his country-
men well enough to state the tremendous alternative before
them. Organized security or armed isolation—that is the
choice we have to make. The better choice takes courage,
means risks and heavy responsibility. But the man would not
be fit to live who failed to try it after the agony of these
years. This thing must not be repeated if human power can

prevent it. Our vitality, our strength and our potentialities are too great for the mere pursuit of our own interests. All that is valuable in our tradition cries out that we must not sit still in grudging isolation.

The President cannot succeed without the hearty support of the American people. With it he may succeed, and in that success he will have elevated the pride of American citizenship. It will be something to boast of that we have lived in a time when the world called us into partnership, and we went gladly, went remembering what we had always professed, and pledged ourselves to it in a larger theatre. At least it shall not be said that we were too selfish and too timid to attempt it, or that the sources of American idealism have run dry.

January 27, 1917

THE DEFENSE OF

THE ATLANTIC WORLD

In advancing this strategic interpretation of the war, Lippmann and his colleagues on *The New Republic* were seeking to temper a tendency to legalism and moralism in Wilson. This piece was doubtless addressed as much to the President as to the readers of the magazine. [*A.S., jr.*]

We argued last week that it was dangerous and misleading to believe that the United States was taking up arms as the champion of neutral rights under international law. It is no less misleading to believe that we are taking up arms in defense of our own rights alone. If America enters the war on any such flimsy basis as that, it will fight a sterile war, and peace will leave us without the least assurance that we have accomplished anything. The fact is that the Germans have understood America's position in the war far better than we ourselves have understood it, and if we are to deal with them effectively, if we are to fight them well, it is of the first importance that we should understand the business as they feel it. It is a bad general who does not imagine himself in the enemy's place. It is a weak nation that would dribble into war not knowing why, or how, or whither.

All along the Germans have seen two great truths: first, that British command of the sea has become absolute, and has abolished the neutral rights which interfere with it; second, that America's policy has been to protest feebly and without effect against Britain while Germany has been held by threat of war from using the submarine fully to relieve the pressure. The Germans have pointed out quite accurately that the result of this policy has been to close the road to Germany and hold open the road to Britain and France. The German highway we have allowed the Allies to bar, the Allied highway we were ready to keep open at the risk of war. We have not merely been committed theoretically to selling munitions and supplies to any one who can come and fetch them. We have in fact permitted the Allies to cut off Germany, we have been in fact prepared for war to deliver munitions and foodstuffs to the Allies. Stripped of all its technicalities this is the issue, and Germans have not been slow to recognize it.

A number of things have obscured the issue. The first and most spectacular is that no American lives have been lost by the action of the Allies, and consequently their illegalities have never seemed monstrous to most of us. Nevertheless inhumanity is not the real difference. No American lives would have been lost had we acquiesced in Germany's policy as we have in Britain's. American lives would almost certainly have been lost had we refused to agree to Great Britain's "blockade" as we have to Germany's "war-zone" decree. If Britain said we must put into a certain port we have put into it, if Britain said we must not use certain areas of the North Sea we have not used them, if Britain said we could do only a certain amount of trade with Holland, that is all the trade we have done. Nor is there any reason for regarding the submarine war as more deadly than the blockade of Germany. It is well to remember that the German people are suffering anguish as a result of it, that their children's vitality is being sapped, that there is an alarming increase of tuberculosis within the German Empire. The blockade and the submarine are both terrible weapons, and the blockade is the more effective of the two. In choosing between them we are not choosing between legality and illegality, nor even perhaps in the last analysis between cruelty and mercy.

No one can say that this statement of the case does not give Germany her due. It errs if anything in giving her the extreme benefit of every doubt. But when her case has been made with all allowances we are more than ever sure that this nation does right in accepting the blockade and defying the submarine. It does right because the war against Britain, France, and Belgium is a war against the civilization of which we are a part. To be "fair" in such a war would be a betrayal. We would not help Germany to victory. We cannot stand idle as long as there is the least chance of her winning one. If Germany's cause were the better one, this policy would be as outrageous as the Germans believe it is. It is because we cannot permit a German triumph that we have accepted the closure of the seas to Germany and the opening of them to the Allies. That is the true justification of our policy, and the only one which will bear criticism.

It has been obscured for us also by a number of things here at home. We are an inveterately legalistic people, and have veiled our real intentions behind a mass of technicalities. The reason for this legalism just now is to be found in something besides our intellectual habits. We have wanted to assist the Allies and hamper Germany, but we have wanted also to keep out of war. Our government therefore has been driven to stretch technicalities to the breaking point. We have clothed the most unneutral purposes in the language of neutrality. But we have never had any right to expect that we could go on forever without facing the consequences. Having started on the road of assistance to the Allies we have to follow it through. So when we talk about American honor being involved we mean just this: that since we have created an unneutral policy we cannot now abandon it because it is dangerous. Our honor is involved only because in the last

71

thirty months we have made a choice which requires us to keep open the seas that lead to the western Allies. Had our judgment of the issues of the war been favorable to Germany, we would with honor have followed a different policy. Had Britain, for example, been the aggressor, and the violator of Belgium, we could with perfect honor have broken the blockade and acquiesced in the submarine war.

This basic truth has been clouded for us by something more than our legalism. The radical pro-Allies especially along the eastern seaboard have raised the absurd legend that the policy of the administration was either pro-German or at least neutral in effect. Fastening all their attention on the dramatic patience of the President, they often seemed to forget entirely the drastic effects of his inactivity in regard to the blockade. They never seemed able to realize that the decision not to break the encirclement of Germany is one of the great strategic facts of the war. It may indeed be the most decisive victory the Allies have won, and it has earned for us the dangerous hostility of the German people.

Only by a clear grasp of the situation and its gigantic consequences can we steer our course now or in the future. We have chosen to render the Allies definite assistance, negatively by allowing them to close the seas to Germany, positively by insisting that the seas be kept open to them. They must be kept open. This means that to frighten ships away is as much an overt act as to sink them. It means that to sink Norwegian and Dutch ships is as intolerable as to sink American ships. It means that our fundamental interest in this crisis is not a complicated system of rights but a definite and practical and tangible end. The world's highway shall not be closed to the western Allies if America has power to prevent it.

We do not hesitate to say that this should be American policy even though submarines were capable of successful, humane "cruiser warfare." We do not hesitate to say—we have believed it and said it since the beginning of the war— that if the Allied fleet were in danger of destruction, if Ger-

72

many had a chance of securing command of the seas, our navy ought to be joined to the British in order to prevent it. The safety of the Atlantic highway is something for which America should fight.

Why? Because on the two shores of the Atlantic Ocean there has grown up a profound web of interest which joins together the western world. Britain, France, Italy, even Spain, Belgium, Holland, the Scandinavian nations, and Pan-America are in the main one community in their deepest needs and their deepest purposes. They have a common interest in the ocean which unites them. They are to-day more inextricably bound together than most even as yet realize. But if that community were destroyed we should know what we had lost. We should understand then the meaning of the unfortified Canadian frontier, of the common protection given Latin-America by the British and American fleets.

It is the crime of Germany that she is trying to make hideous the highways by which the Atlantic Powers live. That is what has raised us against her in this war. Had she stood on the defensive against France and Britain, had she limited the war to the Balkans and the eastern front where it originated, and clearly thrown in her lot with the western nations, she would have had their neutrality and probably their sympathy. But when she carried the war to the Atlantic by violating Belgium, by invading France, by striking against Britain, and by attempting to disrupt us, neutrality of spirit or action was out of the question. And now that she is seeking to cut the vital highways of our world we can no longer stand by. We cannot betray the Atlantic community by submitting. If not civilization, at least our civilization is at stake.

A victory on the high seas would be a triumph of that class which aims to make Germany the leader of the East against the West, the leader ultimately of a German-Russian-Japanese coalition against the Atlantic world. It would be utter folly not to fight now to make its hopes a failure by showing that in the face of such a threat the western community is a unit.

73

It would be a great mistake to suppose, however, that we are dealing with a single-minded Germany. We wage war on Germany as long as she commits her destiny to those who would separate her from the western world. By rights Germany should be a powerful and loyal member of the Atlantic world, and she will be if this war is effectively fought and wisely ended. Our aim must be not to conquer Germany as Rome conquered Carthage, but to win Germany as Lincoln strove to win the South, to win her for union with our civilization by the discrediting of those classes who alone are our enemies. It is no paradox and no sentimentality to say that we must fight Germany not to destroy her but to force her and lure her back to the civilization in which she belongs. She is a rebel nation as long as she wages offensive war against the western world.

We do not believe that the bulk of the German people or even the better part of her civilian leaders honestly hope to overthrow us. They are gambling we believe on the prospect of an early peace. But if by any chance the submarine should succeed, the party of von Tirpitz would be invincible. We cannot therefore take any chances of allowing the campaign to succeed. It must be made to fail in two ways: by demonstrating that the sea can be kept open, and by enlisting our strength on the side of the Allies. That would be a German failure indeed because it would be clear then that the assault on the West had merely doubled the power of the West.

These, we believe, are the main causes why we are being drawn into the war, the main reasons why we should enter it, and the main objects we should pursue. There could be no greater error than that voiced by Senator Borah when he said, "It ought to be distinctly understood that we are interested alone in protecting our neutral rights as a neutral nation, and that what we have done and all that we may do is for that purpose and no other." A few moments reflection will show that the issue never has been one of neutral rights, that to fight for them alone would be to isolate ourselves

74

from our natural Allies and leave us exposed after the war, and finally that no form of action can be devised which will vindicate all neutral rights, or even those which Germany alone has violated. If we put the matter on the basis of neutral rights we shall never know whether we have vindicated them or not, and our participation in the war would be as futile as a duel of honor.

What we must fight for is the common interest of the western world, for the integrity of the Atlantic Powers. We must recognize that we are in fact one great community and act as a member of it. Our entrance into it would weight it immeasurably in favor of liberalism, and make the organization of a league for peace an immediately practical object of statesmanship. By showing that we are ready now, as well as in the theoretical future, to defend the western world, the cornerstone of federation would be laid. We would not and could not fight to exclude Germany from that league. We would not and could not fight for a bad settlement. The real danger to a decent peace has always been that the western nations would become so dependent on Russia and Japan that they must pay any price for their loyalty. That danger is almost certainly obviated by our participation. For when the peace conference begins some time toward the end of 1917, as it most certainly will, the final arbitrament between liberalism and reaction will be made by the relative power of each. If the liberal forces have the most strength left it is they who will decide the reorganization of the world.

February 17, 1917

THE CONDITIONS

FOR PEACE

There has been much talk of a press cabal to railroad the country into war, or at least of a sudden jingoism and an indecent haste to abandon reason and fight. It is a serious charge, and in so far as it falls upon *The New Republic* we have only this to say: the peace worth having cannot be built on successful terrorism; it cannot be made on the defeat of France and England by a victorious Germany; it cannot be made by the triumph of the dearest weapon of the Pan-German; it cannot be made by the betrayal of the highway on which the Atlantic nations live. There is a time when compromise and submission merely breed violence and tyranny, and in all soberness that time is now. A labor union which submits and submits and submits merely increases the strength of the exploiter. It is only when labor is strong enough to command respect that it can bargain as an equal. So it is with this nation to-day. If we should fail to defy and finally to assist in breaking the German threat, nothing we could ever say about peace would impress itself upon the world. The prospect of a league for peace would be shattered, for no nation in Europe would feel that our participation in it was of any real value. Our pledge to resist aggression in the future would be discounted by our failure to resist it in the obvious present.

February 24, 1917

THE WORLD

IN REVOLUTION

It takes new eyes to see and new words to express what is going on to-day. The world is not only at war but in revolution as well. That revolution goes deeper than any man had dared to guess. The overturn in Russia, the intervention of America, the stirring of China, stupendous as they are, may be merely the prelude to events more drastic still. The whole world faces a famine of food, raw materials, shipping. The productivity of the earth is diminished, the destruction of capital is proceeding at a rate beyond the power of any one nation to repair it. If the worst calamity should happen and the war be prolonged beyond this year the feeding and re-furnishing of the world will tax human ingenuity and science beyond anything of which the ordinary statesman has ever dreamed. Western civilization is approaching not the end of its potential resources, but the end of its resources as they are now organized.

This is the underlying meaning of the present conferences in Washington. The dread which hangs over them is of this shortage which will not end with the end of the war. The hope which inspires them is that the food, the shipping, the credit, and the basic materials of life can be pooled, jointly administered, fairly apportioned, and economically employed. Unless this is done the war cannot be conducted successfully nor a peace made without disaster.

It is almost impossible to estimate the consequences of this

77

revolutionary situation. For one thing it means that a supernational government is being forced into existence—a world authority over the necessities of life. National hoarding, whether of food or ships or materials, is becoming intolerable; economic nationalism, such as Germany practised and the Republican party preached, is being supplanted. We thought we had seen great things when countries like England were swept into national collectivism. We are witnessing greater things to-day in the birth of an international socialism of the commodities on which life depends.

The implications are by no means clear. But certain tentative conclusions it is possible to discern. The organization which we must now create to administer the vital supplies of the Alliance will persist after peace is established. It will control the resources of all the world except Central Europe. It will have become an economic as well as a military league of nations, and membership in it will be an absolute necessity. It is no longer an academic question as to whether Germany will be pleased to enter the League. Germany must enter it in order to be fed and supplied, in order that her industrial life may begin again.

In the last analysis a strong, scientific organization of the sources of material and access to them is the means to the achievement of the only purposes by which this war can be justified. The war started as an exhibition of ruthless nationalism, as an attempt by one nation to pursue its alleged destiny in defiance of the world. It is ending as an amalgamation of the world to defend itself by force, to feed and supply itself on a common basis. That full community has not yet been achieved, but the conference in Washington foreshadows a more statesmanlike continuation of the groping, not altogether enlightened, and somewhat notorious Paris conference.

Only when this supernational economic control is established will the Alliance confront Germany with all its power mobilized. When such a control is established victory will take on a new meaning. It will not imply defeat such as Rome administered to Carthage, but readmission and absorption into the society of nations. In establishing this control we shall be following the evolution of a League of Nations. Economic association will precede political. The statutory machinery of the League will rest on an economic basis. It will crown and formalize an organization already in existence, an organization which draws its strength from the threat of famine and the utter need of security. The nations will approach the peace congress in an advanced state of economic internationalism, and the congress itself will be determined by this fact. That congress cannot finish its work in one session. We may well believe, therefore, that the League of Peace will be a continuation of the Congress of Peace. For, once the whole world is gathered in an assembly, the task of the internationalist will be to keep that assembly from dissolving.

May 5, 1917

THE GREAT DECISION

It is a fearful thing to lead this great,
peaceful people into war, into the
most terrible and disastrous of all
wars, civilization itself seeming to
be in the balance. *Woodrow Wilson*

It has not been an easy decision to make, and it is not made
easily or gaily or restlessly. It has come after as careful
deliberation as human judgment could go through. It is a
conclusion reached by the least jingo and most peaceful of
American Presidents. We have become the enemies of the
German government only after every device of patience and
every ingenuity for peace is exhausted. No government ever
had fuller opportunity to mend its ways, to show to an
anxious world that its crimes were blunders and not the
normal expression of its character. What charity could do
has been done for the German Empire. After outrage upon
outrage, intrigue and assault and cruelty, we have still hoped
and prayed that even among the governing classes there was
a liberal faction which would lead Germany back among the
decent governments. We have endured measureless insult in
the belief that there was a civil group who were ready to act
with liberals everywhere in the pacification of the world.

They have had their chance. Every encouragement has
been extended to them because the American government
was eager to be shown the possibility of peace. In December

80

the President gave them an opportunity to say that they renounced conquest and cared for the organization of a stable international system. They could not accept that offer because they had not renounced conquest. We know now that the official German terms include the subjugation not only of Belgium but of a part of France, that the real intention of that government was to divide the Allies by intrigue and then rob France of her iron mines and Belgium of her freedom. We know those were her terms, and that in order to impose them upon the world she was prepared to destroy the merchant shipping of all nations. That is the revealed plan of Germany's ruling class, be it the party of Bethmann-Hollweg or von Tirpitz.

After that exposure there could be no peace and no mere armed neutrality. In all literalness civilization is hanging in the balance. The success of such a government with such a policy would make the twentieth century a period of profound reaction. It would mean almost certainly the defeat of the Russian Revolution, the absorption of the small nations of Central Europe, the humiliation of France, the monopolization of the road to the East, the disintegration of the British Commonwealth which is to arise out of the Empire, the terrorizing of the Americas, and a fastening upon the whole civilized world of a system of aggressive policies backed by an illiberal collectivism and a thorough conscription of human life. No league of peace could be organized, and for no great nation would fundamental democratic reform be possible. In such a world of terrors only the military virtues could survive.

This is what the President has seen, and this is what has led him to the fearful choice of war. If the European struggle were a war of Tweedledum and Tweedledee he could not have asked for anything more than an attempt to defend American rights as best we could. But after the revolution in Russia the issue is explicit, not merely implicit. There is no longer any doubt that the present German government is the keystone of reaction, that it is the great obstacle to the organization of peace, that it must be resisted and defeated.

The league of peace exists sooner than any of us dared to hope. What was a paper plan and a theoretic vision two years ago is to-day a reality. The liberal peoples of the world are united in a common cause. To be sure they have much to do before their own houses are put in order, and democracy is by no means secure among those who proclaim it. Nevertheless, the nations in which public opinion really counts are all engaged and all on the same side. The cause of the Allies is now unmistakably the cause of liberalism and the hope of an enduring peace. Democracy is infectious—the entrance of the Russian and American democracies is sure to be a stimulus to democrats everywhere, and it is now as certain as anything human can be that the war which started as a clash of empires in the Balkans will dissolve into democratic revolution the world over. A diplomatic tangle over backward territories has unloosed the peoples at home.

For having seen this and said it, for having selected the moment when the issue was so clear, for having done so much through the winter to make the issue clear, our debt and the world's debt to Woodrow Wilson is immeasurable. Any mediocre politician might have gone to war futilely for rights that in themselves cannot be defended by war. Only a statesman who will be called great could have made America's intervention mean so much to the generous forces of the world, could have lifted the inevitable horror of war into a deed so full of meaning. Other men have led nations to war to increase their glory, their wealth, their prestige. No other statesman has ever so clearly identified the glory of his country with the peace and liberty of the world.

Mr. Wilson has created an opportunity which is without parallel. He can mean more to the happiness of mankind than any one who ever addressed the world. Through force of circumstances and through his own genius he has made it a practical possibility that he is to be the first great statesman to begin the better organization of the world. It is a task to which he can give himself without stint or scruple, to which he can subordinate everything else. He can afford to use himself absolutely for this work alone.

The business of mobilizing the nation he can put into expert hands, for it would be a waste if he permitted himself to be swallowed up in the multitude of details which will confront him. In the present temper of the country he need concede nothing to the party machines. He can pick his men without respect to the politicians. He has only to say publicly that the needs of the nation demand the best service available, and public opinion will deal with attempts by Congress or any special interest to clutter up the government and lame it. The President's duty is to free himself from the worries of administrative routine, so that he may be able to devote his entire attention to the great work of shaping the larger outlines of policy.

If that is done there is no need to fear for the future. Mr. Wilson is to-day the most liberal statesman in high office, and before long he is likely to be the most powerful. He represents the best hope in the whole world. He can go ahead exultingly with the blessings of men and women upon him.

April 7, 1917

BEYOND NATIONAL GOVERNMENT

What is being arranged in Washington these days is really a gigantic experiment in internationalism. For the first time in history the food supply, the shipping, the credit, and the man-power of the nations are to be put under something like joint administration. We are witnessing the creation of a supernational control of the world's necessities. The men who are charged with conducting this war are now compelled to think as international statesmen. The old notions of sovereignty no longer govern the facts. Three of the unifying forces of mankind are at work—hunger, danger and a great hope. They are sweeping into the scrap heap the separatist theories that nations should be self-sufficing economically and absolutely independent politically. In order that men should be fed, in order that they may defend themselves, in order that they may make the world safe, they are being forced to create an administration which transcends national government. A new and more powerful machinery of internationalism is being created. It is a true internationalism because it deals not with dynastic and diplomatic alliances but with the cooperative control of those vital supplies on which human life depends. We have entered upon another phase of political unification, a phase greater in its consequences but similar in its methods to the formation of national states in the nineteenth century.

This is the birth of the League of Nations. It is being formed not out of paper schemes imposed upon the peoples but out of the pooling of economic, political and military interests. It is on a basis of shipping, food, naval control, finance, and a joint military strategy that the substance of the league is being brought into existence. These common needs and dangers are generating an extraordinary community of ideals. The revolution in Russia and the intervention of America marks the transformation of the war, the fulfilment of its better promises. For that impulse to unity which common perils and common necessities have forged is beginning to demand some community of political forms in the constituent nations. Just because the hope of internationalism is so much brighter than ever, so the danger of a Central Europe dominated by the Prussian autocracy has become more intolerable. It would remain an insoluble lump in a world that was growing towards federation.

However pressing the immediate problems of the war may be, no one can afford to lose sight of this much greater prospect which is opening before us. The alliance to which we belong embraces practically the whole world except the enemy and his allies. The alliance is creating a machinery of joint control over innumerable human necessities. It will have to act at the peace conference as a kind of constituent assembly of the world. Obviously this political and economic machinery is not to be abandoned when peace is established because peace will not only have to be negotiated but administered and supervised. Common economic questions will persist after the war and will require a cooperative solution. We are creating institutions now which are called for by the emergency, but will be maintained when the acute danger has passed. They are the nucleus of internationalism.

April 28, 1917

ASSUMING WE JOIN

This piece expresses Lippmann's regretful acknowledgment that Wilson had failed to assimilate the lesson of "The Defense of the Atlantic World." [*A.S., jr.*]

Just as reaching your twenty-first birthday throws no light on how to act in order to reduce the cost of living, so discovering that our isolation is over is no indication of a policy. Yet each day men appear in print to say that such and such an alliance is necessary, that troops must be dispatched to some point in Europe or Asia, "because our isolation is over." It does not follow. You might as well argue that John must vote for Mayor Hylan because John has a vote.

There has been an important change. Before the war the area of our interest lay in the Americas, the Pacific, and eastern Asia. The United States was in contact with European diplomacy whenever that diplomacy affected those regions of the globe. As a result of the war the areas of interest have been enlarged, and America is intermittently in contact from Brest to Vladivostok. These new contacts, their depth, their purposes, their obligations are the substance of what we call "the end of American isolation," and the definition of these meanings is the significant task. For granting that "isolation" is over, we have still to find out what it is that has begun.

"It has come about by no plan of our conceiving," says Mr. Wilson, "but by the hand of God, who led us into this

86

way. We cannot turn back. We can only go forward with
lifted eyes and freshened spirit, to follow the vision." But
this is a little like saying to a person aged twenty-one, "You
have reached maturity. You cannot turn back. Go forward
and follow the vision." To which the new voter will reply if
he is worthy of his vote: "What vision, and whither?" As a
practical matter the vision is appropriated by those who have
a particular project in mind. The vision is what they think
ought to be done, and one of the most serious aspects of the
new dogma of non-isolation is that it so easily becomes a
form of fatalism. The old dogma at least had the virtue of
landmarks. It told us a little of where we were and why. The
new dogma can easily become just a general drift, and that,
I think, is what it has become within the last year. Having
learned that we must "participate," we are forgetting to spec-
ify. We are resolved to take part in world affairs, but in our
exhilaration we are inclined to omit the inquiry as to what
part.

Mr. Wilson's Fourteen Points and his other principles were
a vague attempt to define that part. But they did not operate
at any significant point, and in the actualities of Europe they
are only a memory and a catch cry. Yet we continue to "take
part." We are about to join a League in which we take part
continuously and regularly, but the part we are to take is
shrouded in utter mystery. Does anybody know what the
American representative at Geneva is to stand for? Yet that
is the crucial question. It underlies all the mumbling and
stuttering about "reservations," for reservations are nothing
but a left-handed way of setting some limits and fixing a few
guide posts by which participation is to be directed. They are
purely negative. They will tell what our representative must
not do. They will not give him any lead as to what he ought
to do. Within whatever limits the Senate may fix, the American delegate will go to Geneva with a mind that is not only
open but empty. No doubt he will be instructed to work for
justice and peace. But he will be a remarkable man indeed

if those instructions help him much. For such words are hollow vessels into which almost anybody can pour almost anything he chooses.

A nation, determined to participate but undetermined as to what it wants, is gullibility itself. Its role will be that of reinforcement for the Powers which can most effectively secure the attention of its representative. And the experience of Paris shows that the high motive of not wanting anything in particular easily degenerates into the complacency of not wanting anything very much. Italy and Japan, France and England were ready to wreck the Conference for a port, a bit of land, a sum of money. They were insistent and they prevailed. But Mr. Wilson, who wanted "nothing" but a peace that could last, could risk nothing and therefore could not be insistent.

At bottom neither he nor anyone else took his altruism very seriously. He had not convinced himself, he had not convinced the American people, that his so-called idealism was as vital an American interest as any strategic frontier in Europe or concession in Asia. He had said many times, but he had never digested the idea, that a stable peace in Europe is the first and most important line of defence for the American democracy, that a democratic settlement there meant more to the security and prosperity of Americans than anything else in the world. But such considerations were not decisive. American idealism at Paris was that of Lady Bountiful, a luxury of the comfortable and well-to-do, not part of the serious business of life.

Now the reason that sophisticated European democrats based such extravagant hopes on American intervention was not because of Mr. Wilson's words. It was because they saw, more accurately than anyone who directed American policy, that the substantial realization of Mr. Wilson's program was a vital American interest. They hailed him, because for the first time within memory it happened through a fortunate series of circumstances, that the real interests of a great

Power coincided with the hopes of the European democracies. They assumed that he understood this, and that in standing resolutely for the American interest, he would concurrently be supporting them in their struggle against the jingoes and the military cliques.

But in the test, the American program was treated like so many other ideals, as something distant, unrelated, and of no material consequence. Calling ourselves disinterested, we behaved as if we were uninterested, and furnished the world with the extraordinary spectacle of a nation willing to send two million soldiers overseas, yet unwilling to project its mind and conscience overseas. Naturally, American prestige declined steadily at Paris. When Mr. Wilson began, Europe believed that the Wilson program was an American program, a thing as vital to us as Alsace-Lorraine was to France. But in the course of time the European statesmen discovered that Mr. Wilson's program was really nothing more than his gratuitous advice in a situation he did not thoroughly understand.

If America were intending now to withdraw from all further European responsibilities, the analysis of Mr. Wilson's defeat at Paris would be of merely historical interest. But under the Covenant we engage ourselves to participate in all the intricacies of the whole world, and it is of the utmost importance that we should try to understand why in our first great experiment in participation, the results are so little like the promises. Assuming that we join the League, assuming that the League operates from the Treaties of Versailles, what is to come next? It is a question of aims and of methods, and the two cannot be separated, for the method will in the end determine the result.

September 3, 1919

POLITICS

THE PALMER LETTER

On January 10th the Washington correspondent of the New York *World,* Mr. Louis Seibold, published a letter written by Mr. Wilson as President-elect to Representative A. Mitchell Palmer. The letter explains Mr. Wilson's objections to the so-called Bryan plan for limiting the President's tenure to a single term of office. The letter was confidential at the time it was written, but its publication now is not an "exposé." The New York *World* is perhaps the leading Wilson paper in the East, and we may assume that the administration allowed Mr. Seibold to print it. As a political move it is obviously intended to check any Democratic opposition which might crystallize around the "one-term" plank of the Baltimore platform.

But the letter has a greater interest than this, for it helps us to look into the President's mind just before he took office. The earlier tone is in it, the tone of the "New Freedom" and the gallant fight in New Jersey, the tone of faith and enthusiasm for popular government, pitiless publicity, and plain speaking. Mr. Wilson believed there were to be no more nominating conventions, that in 1916 candidates would be chosen at a nation-wide primary. His faith did not halt there. He believed that as President he would do away with the power of patronage to dictate a renomination.

I absolutely pledge myself to resort to nothing but public opinion to decide that question [i.e., a second term]. The President ought to be absolutely deprived of every

93

other means of deciding it. He can be. . . . It is intolerable
that any President should be permitted to determine who
should succeed him—himself or another—by patronage
or coercion, or any sort of control of the machinery by
which delegates to the nominating convention are chosen.

Presumably Mr. Wilson meant to take his appointments
out of party politics. His words seem to indicate that he had
in mind some kind of civil service reform which would reduce
the President's patronage. No such reform has taken place,
of course, and while there is no ground for saying that
Mr. Wilson has used patronage for his personal ends, he has
unquestionably allowed it to be used for the purposes of his
party. The deserving Democrats were not confined to Mr.
Bryan's friends. On the very day when the Palmer letter was
published Mr. Wilson allowed it to leak out that a Tammany
politician might supplant an efficient and well-tried Postmaster in the city of New York.

There is consequently not a little irony in the idealism of
this letter. But curiously enough the letter explains why
Mr. Wilson has become a practical politician. He is speaking
of the President's function:

He must be Prime Minister as much concerned with
the guidance of legislation as with the just and orderly
execution of the law.

In other words, Mr. Wilson determined to depend upon
his party to carry through tariff and currency legislation. But
in depending upon his party Mr. Wilson had to hold his party
together, and the glue that consolidates parties is patronage,
"pork," pensions. Mr. Wilson could not be Prime Minister
and a reformer in the civil service and budget. The price of
his legislative success was the abandonment of his ideal that
he must decide all questions by a resort to "public opinion."
Mr. Wilson chose to pay the price. The price was Mr. Bryan,
Tammany, Roger Sullivan, a good deal of administrative dis-

organization, and a very large number of exceedingly weak partisan appointments.

The Mitchell-Palmer letter belongs to Woodrow Wilson's romantic period, to the time when the polished catchwords of orthodox political theory were still the substance of his thought. Party government, public opinion, the fine slogans of Whig statesmanship, looked like the clear, disinterested notions that we should all like them to be. They were uttered with the naivete of the high-minded, and in comparison with them the truths of politics seem cynical and brutal. In those days Mr. Wilson could believe that a great party might be controlled by reasoned judgment and splendid motives. He no longer believes this. He could believe in a President leading a party with no power but the force of his righteousness. The test of reality is a ruthless test.

January 15, 1916

TAKING A CHANCE

The other night I sat up late reading one of those books on politics which are regarded as essential to any sort of intellectual respectability. It was a book that might be referred to in the Constitutional Convention at Albany. As I read along I was possessed with two convictions about the author. The first was that he had worn a high hat when he wrote the book; the second, that he had no teeth, which made him a little difficult to understand. And all through that hot and mosquito-ridden night the disintegration of his vocabulary went churning through my head . . . "social consciousness . . . sovereign will . . . electoral duties . . . national obligations . . . on moral, economic, political, and social grounds . . . social consciousness . . . sovereignty . . . electoral . . . social . . . sovereign . . . national . . . sovereign . . ." Each word was as smooth and hard and round as a billiard-ball, and in the malice of my sleeplessness I saw the toothless but perfectly groomed man in a high hat making patterns of the balls which were handed to him by his butler.

As the night dragged along, the callowest prejudices came to the surface and all fairer and reputable judgment deserted me. I heard myself say that this ass who plagued me couldn't possibly have any ideas because he didn't have any vocabulary. How is it possible, I asked, to write or think about the modern world with a set of words which were inchoate lumps when Edmund Burke used them? Political writing is asphyxiated by the staleness of its language. We are living in a strange world, and we have to talk about it in a kind of

96

algebra. And of course if we deal only with colorless and vacant symbols, the world we see and the world we describe soon becomes a colorless and vacant place. Nobody can write criticism of American politics if the only instruments at his command are a few polysyllables of Greek and Latin origin. You can't put Bryan and Hearst and Billy Sunday into the vocabulary of Aristotle, Bentham, or Burke. Yet if you are going to write about American politics, can you leave out Bryan and Hearst and Billy Sunday, or even Champ Clark? The author I had been reading did leave them out completely. He talked about the national will of America as if it were a single stream of pure water which ran its course through silver pipes laid down by the Constitutional Fathers.

I tried to recall any new words which had been added to the vocabulary of social science. Boss, heeler, machine, log-rolling, pork-barrel—those were the words which meant something at Washington or in Tammany Hall, but my author would no more have used them than he would have eaten green peas with a knife. Anyone who did use them he would have regarded as a mere journalist, and probably a cocksure young man at that. Then I remembered that the diplomats had made current a few fresh words within the last generations—hinterland, pacific penetration, sphere of influence, sphere of legitimate aspiration; they had meaning, because nations went to war about them. But the real contributions, curiously enough, have come not from the political theorist, but from novelists, and from philosophers who might have been novelists.

H. G. Wells and William James, I said to myself, come nearer to having a vocabulary fit for political uses than any other writers of English. They write in terms which convey some of the curiosity and formlessness of modern life. Speech with them is pragmatic, and accurate in the true sense. They are exact when exactness is possible, and blurred when the thought itself is blurred. They have almost completely abandoned the apparatus of polysyllables through which no direct

97

impression can ever penetrate. They do not arrange concepts, they gather percepts, and never do you lose the sense that the author is just a man trying to find out what he thinks. But the political writer who gave me the nightmare never admitted that he was just a man. He aimed at that impersonal truth which is like the inscription on monuments.

He regarded himself as a careful person. His method was to retrieve in qualifying clause whatever he had risked in assertion. So he achieved a compendium of things-that-can't-be-done, a kind of anthology of the impossible. His notion of getting at the truth was to peal it, like Peer Gynt's onion, though Peer Gynt had the sense to be surprised that there was nothing to an onion but the layers.

My temper grew worse as I reflected on the hypnotic effect of books done in this manner, on the number of men whose original vision is muffled by verbal red tape and officialism of the spirit. The true speech of man is idiomatic, if not of the earth and sky, then at least of the saloon and the bleachers. But no smelly or vivid impression can win its way through these opaque incantations with which political science is afflicted. They forbid fresh seeing. An innocence of the eye is impossible, for there are no words to report a vision with; and visions which cannot be expressed are not cultivated. No wonder, I thought, political philosophizing means so little in human life. Its woodenness is the counterpart of a wooden politics, its inhumanity is the inhumanity of a state machine. The language is callous, unmoved and unmoving, because it aims to reflect rather than to lead the life upon which it comments. Dead speech is good enough for thoughts that bring no news, and it is to the timidity of political thought that we must ascribe its preference for a dead language. In these tomes over which we yawn at night there are occasionally ideas which might shake the world. But they do not shake it, for they are written for people who do not like to shake it. They are hedged with reservations, fortified

98

with polysyllables, and covered over with the appalling conceit that here is truth—objective, impersonal, cold.

I generalized rashly: That is what kills political writing, this absurd pretence that you are delivering a great utterance. You never do. You are just a puzzled man making notes about what you think. You are not building the Pantheon, then why act like a graven image? You are drawing sketches in the sand which the sea will wash away. What more is your book but your infinitesimal scratching, and who the devil are you to be grandiloquent and impersonal? The truth is you're afraid to be wrong. And so you put on these airs and use these established phrases, knowing that they will sound familiar and will be respected. But this fear of being wrong is a disease. You cover and qualify and elucidate, you speak vaguely, you mumble because you are afraid of the sound of your own voice. And then you apologize for your timidity by frowning learnedly on anyone who honestly regards thought as an adventure, who strikes ahead and takes his chances. You are like a man trying to be happy, like a man trying too hard to make a good mashie shot in golf. It can't be done by trying so hard to do it. Whatever truth you contribute to the world will be one lucky shot in a thousand misses. You cannot be right by holding your breath and taking precautions.

August 7, 1915

BRANDEIS

Wilson's nomination of Louis D. Brandeis for the Supreme Court had produced a bitter reaction from some of the most eminent leaders of the American bench and bar. Marshall's apothegm from *McCulloch* v. *Maryland* is, alas, misquoted. What Marshall actually wrote was: "We must never forget that it is a *constitution* we are expounding . . . intended to endure for ages to come, and consequently to be adapted to the various *crises* of human affairs." Evidently the quotation marks were misplaced. [*A.S., jr.*]

One public benefit has already accrued from the nomination of Mr. Brandeis. It has started discussion of what the Supreme Court means in American life. From much of the comment since Mr. Brandeis's nomination it would seem that multitudes of Americans seriously believe that the nine Justices embody pure reason, that they are set apart from the concerns of the community, regardless of time, place, and circumstances, to become the interpreter of sacred words with meaning fixed forever and ascertainable by a process of ineluctable reasoning. Yet the notion not only runs counter to all we know of human nature; it betrays either ignorance or false knowledge of the actual work of the Supreme Court as disclosed by two hundred and thirty-nine volumes of United States reports. It assumes what is not now and never was the function of the Supreme Court.

The significant matters which come before the Supreme

Court are not the ordinary legal questions of the rights of *Smith* v. *Jones*. If they were, the choosing of a Supreme Court Justice would be of professional rather than of public interest. In our system of government the Supreme Court is the final authority in the relationship of the individual to the state, of the individual to the United States, of forty-eight states to one another, and of each with the United States. In a word, the Court deals primarily with problems of government, and that is why its personnel is of such nation-wide importance. But though the Court has to decide political questions, it escapes the rough-and-tumble of politics, because it does not exercise power for the affirmative ends of the state. What it does is to define limitations of power. It marks the boundaries between state and national action. It determines the allowable sphere of legislative and executive conduct.

These are delicate and tremendous questions, not to be answered by mechanical magic distilled within the four corners of the Constitution, not to be solved automatically in the Constitution "by taking the words and a dictionary." Except in a few very rigid and very unimportant specific provisions, such as those providing for geographic uniformity or prohibiting the enactment of bills of attainder, the Justices have to bring to the issues some creative power. They have to make great choices which are determined in the end by their breadth of understanding, imagination, sense of personal limitation, and insight into governmental problems. It is a commonplace of constitutional law, insisted upon by students like David Bradley Thayer, a commonplace to be kept vigilantly in mind, that Justices of the Supreme Court must be lawyers, of course, but above all, lawyers who are statesmen.

To generalize about periods and tendencies in the history of the Supreme Court is to omit many details and qualifications, but that the great problems of statesmanship have determined the character of the Court at different periods in our history there can be no doubt. In the first period, barring a negligible opening decade, the Court under Marshall's great leadership dealt with the structure of government. It gave legal expression to the forces of nationality. Marshall also laid down what may be called the great canon of constitutional criticism by insisting that it is a "Constitution that we are construing, a great charter of government with all the implications that dynamic government means." After Marshall the ever-present conflict of state and national power absorbed attention until the Civil War. Then followed a third period in which national power was ascendant, a period of railroad and industrial development, of free lands and apparently unlimited resources, a period in which the prevailing philosophy was naturally enough laissez-faire. It was a period of luxuriant individualism. The Fourteenth Amendment was made the vehicle of its expression, the quality of the Court was exemplified in the sturdy personalities of Justices like Brewer and Peckham. "Liberty of contract" flourished, social legislation was feared, except during the sound but brief leadership in the opposite direction by Chief Justice Waite.

The period of individualism and fear is over. Occasionally there is a relapse, but on the whole we have entered definitely upon an epoch in which Justice Holmes has been the most consistent and dominating force, and to which Justices Day and Hughes have been great contributing factors. It is the period of self-consciousness as to the true nature of the issues before the Court. It is the period of realization that basically the questions are not abstractions to be determined by empty formula, that contemporary convictions of expediency as to property and contract must not be passed off as basic principles of right. It is this new spirit which led Justice Holmes to say that it was the Court's duty "to learn to transcend our own convictions, and to leave room for much that we hold dear to be done away with, short of revolution, by the orderly change of law."

At present the important field of judicial interpretation is practically restricted to two provisions of the Constitution:

the Commerce clause and the Fourteenth Amendment. Around these center the contending forces of state and national action. The Fourteenth Amendment in a word involves an application of the "police power," which extends "to all the great public needs." And so it covers the whole domain of economic and social and industrial facts and the state's response to these facts. The principle of law—that the state cannot exercise arbitrary or unwarranted power—is undisputed. The difficulty is with the application of the principle, and the application involves grasp and imagination and contact with the realities of a modern industrial democracy. Under the Commerce clause we are dealing not with abstract legal questions but the pervasive facts of life, for, as the Supreme Court itself has said: "Commerce among the states is not a technical legal conception but a practical one drawn from the course of business."

To the consideration of these very questions Mr. Brandeis has given his whole life. To their understanding he brings a mind of extraordinary power and insight. He has amassed experience enjoyed by hardly another lawyer to the same depth and richness and detail, for it is the very condition of his mind to know all there is to be known of a subject with which he grapples. Thus he is a first-handed authority in the field of insurance, of industrial efficiency, of public franchises, of conservation, of the transportation problem, of the inter-relations of modern business and modern life.

But his approach is that of the true lawyer, because he seeks to tame isolated instances to as large a general rule as possible, and thereby to make the great reconciliation between order and justice. Mr. Brandeis would extend the domain of law, as he only very recently put it before the Chicago Bar Association, by absorbing the facts of life, just as Mansfield in his day absorbed the law merchant into the common law. This craving for authentic facts on which law alone can be founded leads him always to insist on establishing the machinery by which they can be ascertained. It is this which has led him to create practically a new technique in the presentation of constitutional questions. Until his famous argument on the Oregon ten-hour law for women, social legislation was argued before our courts practically *in vacuo,* as an abstract question unrelated to a world of factories and child labor and trade unions and steel trusts. In the Oregon case for the first time there were marshalled before the Supreme Court the facts of modern industry which reasonably called for legislation limiting hours of labor. This marked an epoch in the argument and decision of constitutional cases, and resulted not only in reversal of prior decisions, but in giving to the courts a wholly new approach to this most important class of present-day constitutional issues. As advocate Mr. Brandeis has secured the approval of every constitutional case which he has argued—argued always for the public—not only from the Supreme Court of the United States but from the courts of New York, Illinois, and Oregon.

We may be perfectly certain, then, that Mr. Brandeis is no doctrinaire. He does not allow formulae to do service for facts. He has remained scrupulously flexible. While, for example, he has made us realize that there may be a limit to the efficiency of combination, yet he has insisted that the issue must be settled by authoritative data, that such data must be gathered by a permanent non-partisan commission. So Mr. Brandeis helped to give us the Federal Trade Commission. He sees equally clearly that there are limits to the uses of competition, and no man has spoken more effectively against the competition that kills or more vigorously for the morality of price maintenance.

The very processes of his mind are deliberate and judicial —if we mean by deliberation and judicial-mindedness a full survey of all relevant factors of a problem and courageous action upon it. He has an almost unerring genius for accuracy, because his conclusion is the result of a slow mastery of the problem. Events have rarely failed to support his judgments. In the New Haven situation, for instance, the conclusions which Mr. Brandeis had reached and for which he sought quiet acceptance a decade ago were finally vindicated. So of all his public activities—the adoption of a sliding scale in franchise returns, the adoption of a savings-bank insurance, the settlement of industrial disputes, the regulation of conditions of labor, the conservation of our natural resources—in each problem there have been three stages: thorough investigation by and with experts; education of the public to the results of such investigation; and then political action with informed public opinion behind it, either by legislation for the government or by changes in the structure of one of the great groups of the state, such as the trade union or employers' organizations.

Mr. Brandeis says of himself: "I have no rigid social philosophy; I have been too intense on concrete problems of practical justice." A study of his work verifies this analysis. It is true he has a passion for justice and a passion for democracy, but justice and democracy enlist a common fealty. It is by his insistence on translating these beliefs into life, by his fruitful intellectual inventiveness in devising the means for such translation, that Mr. Brandeis is distinguished. One who has brought the agency of a vitalizing peace to the most anarchistic of all industries, the garment trades, and has done it not by magic but by turning contending forces into cooperative forces, has that balance of head and heart and will which constitutes real judicial-mindedness.

It is said of him that he is often not amiable in a fight. There is truth in the statement. The law has not been a game to him, the issues he has dealt with have been great moral questions. He has often fought with great severity. He has rarely lost. His great fights have been undertaken in the public interest. In the course of his career he has made enemies, some of whom were malicious, others honestly convinced that he had wronged them. A number of charges have been made against him, no one of which has been proved, though no one can question that Mr. Brandeis's enemies have spared no pains to prove them. His friends who are in a position to know the details of his career believe in him passionately. They are delighted that so able a committee of the Senate should have undertaken the work of running down every insinuation. They believe that no man's career can stand as much scrutiny as his. They want the insinuations crystallized, examined and disposed of, so that the nation may begin to employ this man who has at once the passion of public service and the genius for it.

February 5, 1916

UNTRUSTWORTHY?

Opposition to the confirmation of Mr. Brandeis as Justice of the Supreme Court among unprejudiced people has finally narrowed down pretty much to one point. Even though the charges against him have not been established, many people cannot dispossess themselves of a lingering doubt as to his record. If he is not to be suspected why has so much suspicion fastened upon him? The answer is plain. Mr. Brandeis has been a rebellious and troublesome member of the most homogeneous, self-centered, and self-complacent community in the United States. This community has condemned him, not necessarily because in the New Haven and Shoe Machinery cases he was a caustic and successful critic of the management of their favorite corporations, but because an attack made by him seemed to come from an enemy within the gates. It created in their minds an impression of disloyalty. Hence it was that lawyers who had been opposed to Mr. Brandeis in litigation for many years would testify that his reputation was that of being "untrustworthy," but would when challenged be unable to reproduce out of their own personal experience any confirmation of the charge. It was a special community that had found Mr. Brandeis untrustworthy—the powerful but limited community which dominated the business and social life of Boston. He was untrustworthy because he was troublesome. He was disloyal, if at all, to a group. All the smoke of ill-repute which has been gathered around Mr. Brandeis originated in the group psy-

107

chology of these gentlemen, and because they are men of
influence it seemed ominous. But it is smoke without any fire
except that of personal or group antagonism. Whenever a
supposed conflagration is investigated it is found, as in the
Shoe Machinery case, not to reflect on Mr. Brandeis's character and fitness.

The force of the hostility to Mr. Brandeis in Boston is
consequently broken by its intensive character. The fifty-one
signers of the petition opposing Mr. Brandeis's confirmation
did not represent fifty-one individual investigations and ver-
dicts derived from different sections of the community. It
represented substantially one investigation and one verdict
which had been repeated so often that it ceased to require the
confirmation of facts. Among the petitioners there were a
few "outsiders," but the overwhelming majority were men
more closely connected with one another by economic, social,
and family ties than existed in the case of any other similar
community in the country. For the most part they transact
the same kind of business in the same neighborhood; they
belong to the same clubs; they are bound together by a most
complicated system of relationships by blood and marriage.
They come of a proud line and are jealous of a noble tradition; but they cannot expect to escape the penalty of uniting
so much mutual intimacy with so much exclusiveness. The
penalty is that of being peculiarly subject to group influences
and judgments. They form an essentially ingrowing community. Very few outsiders make more than a superficial impression on their business and social behavior, and the insiders act and react most intensely on one another. For this
reason they count for very much less than their intelligence,
education, and economic power entitle them to count in
American public affairs. Ordinarily a community of this kind
can lead its own exclusive life without provoking criticism;
but when it acts aggressively in public practically as a unit,
its members challenge public attention and should not resent

public scrutiny. The contra-Brandeis petitioners started on a deadly errand. They undertook to destroy the reputation of a man, to prevent a public servant from using his great abilities to the best public advantage. They have exhibited only their own disqualification to draw an indictment.

March 11, 1916

THE CASE AGAINST

BRANDEIS

The Brandeis hearings are closed, and all that any supporter of Mr. Brandeis would ask is that people might read the testimony. His opponents have had every conceivable opportunity to present every bit of evidence, rumor, and suspicion that could be found to throw an unfavorable light upon him. They have been able to draw upon great legal ability to formulate this case. In the nature of things they have had the assistance of the newspaper headlines, for a "charge" is "news" and a refutation is dull. They have had all the tactical advantage of the offensive. The advocates of Mr. Brandeis have not done what they might so easily have done, started a counter-attack upon Mr. Brandeis's enemies. They have not tried to develop their case in a sensational way. Had they felt less sure of themselves, they could, for example, have put President Lowell, Mr. Taft, Mr. Root, on the stand and cross-examined them mercilessly to show that no one of these gentlemen has any exact knowledge on which to base his suspicions. They have not done this because those who followed the testimony knew that the case against Mr. Brandeis had collapsed by its own weight.

The final decision is with the Senate, but since a number of newspapers in the East have already summed up against Mr. Brandeis, it is perhaps not amiss to emphasize some of the crucial points in the case. What might be called the theme, the *leitmotif* of the charges, is that Mr. Brandeis has frequently been guilty of double-dealing. He is supposed to be a man who is at once violently partisan for his client, and yet disloyal to him. He is supposed to be without the "judicial temperament," and at the same time inclined to be on both sides of a case. Those who attacked him seemed unable to agree on whether he is a ruthless partisan, or a man who is not partisan enough. But they concentrated finally on the belief that he is not the absolute partisan of his client.

Their favorite example is, of course, the Shoe Machinery case. We shall not here analyze the facts all over again. They were published at some length in the issue of March 4th, and no one has questioned them. Certain misconceptions, however, cannot be smashed too often. Thus, Mr. Brandeis did not draw the objectionable clauses in the leases. They existed before he was associated with the corporation. When he appeared in 1906 before the Massachusetts legislature to argue against prohibitory legislation, he did so by agreement with the Shoe Machinery Company and shoe manufacturers, and with the understanding that there would be a voluntary change in the leases. As early as 1906 he was counsel for a large number of shoe manufacturers, and no one thought there was anything improper in the relationship. He was still on good terms with the United Shoe Machinery Company. When the company failed to live up to its agreement that it would change the leases, Mr. Brandeis resigned. Four years later, when Mr. Brandeis advised a group of shoe manufacturers he did so without pay—in fact he contributed $2500 out of his own pocket—and he used no confidential information. This last point was admitted by Mr. Sidney Winslow, the President of the United Shoe Machinery Company.

Next in importance is the Lennox case. Late in 1907 the firm of P. Lennox and Company was in difficulties with its creditors. James Lennox, son of Patrick, one of his creditors, and his counsel called on Mr. Brandeis for assistance. He advised an assignment for the benefit of the creditors, and urged Mr. Lennox to talk it over with his father. Mr. Brandeis

then agreed to act as trustee for the creditors under an assignment to liquidate the assets. All agreed. The assignment was
made to Mr. Nutter, who is Mr. Brandeis's partner. These
were the terms on which the firm was employed, a matter
proved by the fact that the compensation received was paid
not by any individual but out of the trust assets. The amount
was approved by the court of bankruptcy. But Mr. Patrick
Lennox failed to turn over his individual property, which was
covered by the assignment. Mr. James Lennox refused to
assist the trustee in the business unless he received $500 a
week, which Mr. Brandeis's firm regarded as excessive. Mr.
Nutter then advised Mr. Lennox to hire separate counsel.
About six weeks after the assignment, the claim was first
made that Mr. Patrick Lennox was not a partner in P. Lennox and Company, that the firm was not insolvent, and that
the assignment had been fraudulently secured. The Lennoxes
were welching. The creditors demanded their claims, and
insisted that under the circumstances bankruptcy proceedings
should be instituted. Mr. Nutter informed the counsel for Mr.
Patrick Lennox and wrote to his son James. James did not
object. Patrick's counsel said he would contest. Bankruptcy
proceedings were started, and Mr. Brandeis's firm appeared
for some of the creditors. They were fought by Mr. Patrick
Lennox. The verdict was pronounced by a jury. Mr. Nutter
and two others were appointed trustees in bankruptcy and
administered the trust until a settlement was reached. Mr.
Brandeis's firm, therefore, was entirely consistent. It was at
all times the representative not of an individual but of the
trust. It was the Lennoxes who tried to violate the trust they
had created.

Then there is the charge that Mr. Brandeis was employed
by *Collier's Weekly* to defend Mr. Glavis in the Ballinger
case. That is true, and no one has ever denied it. Mr. Glavis
was a poor man. Why *Collier's Weekly,* which had published
his article, shouldn't furnish counsel for him, may be left to
the metaphysician of honor.

There is the charge of Mr. Clifford Thorne that Mr. Brandeis "threw" the Advance Rate case. Mr. Thorne suffered under the delusion that Mr. Brandeis was counsel for the shippers, whereas the fact is that he was counsel for the Interstate Commerce Commission.

There is the Warren will case, which may be left with the admission of Mr. Moorfield Storey that he would have acted exactly as Mr. Brandeis did.

There is the charge that Mr. Brandeis was responsible for the destruction of the finances of the New York, New Haven and Hartford Railroad. The fact is that he predicted the destruction when there was still time to avoid it. He was disregarded, and his prophecy was fulfilled. To say he ruined the road is like saying that a physician who warns a man against drink is responsible for him if he becomes a drunkard.

But why is it that so many eminent Bostonians are convinced that Mr. Brandeis's character is tainted with a tendency to betrayal? One witness put his finger on the truth when he said, "We have what I may call an aristocracy of the Boston Bar; I do not use the word at all offensively; on the contrary they are high-minded, able, distinguished men. But they cannot, I think, consider with equanimity the selection of anybody for a position on the great court of the country from that community who is not a typical, hereditary, Bostonian." The sense of betrayal is not based on evidence of particular betrayals. He has attacked the United Shoe Machinery Company and the New York, New Haven and Hartford Railroad—the twin pillars of the Boston community. This is the origin of that sense of betrayal, which these gentlemen have tried so hard to reduce to evidence. He has outraged a group loyalty. That is why he is accused of double-dealing and violent partisanship—the double-dealing was in his unwillingness to abide by the free-masonry of the Boston purple; the partisanship was in the effectiveness of his attack.

March 25, 1916

THE ISSUES OF 1916

Boies Penrose of Pennsylvania and Murray Crane of Massachusetts represented the Old Guard in the Republican party; Henry L. Stimson was a surviving figure in the Theodore Roosevelt tradition of national authority. [*A.S., jr.*]

It is about a week before the conventions, and the nation is not clamoring for anybody. Woodrow Wilson is to be renominated in St. Louis; in Chicago the appeal is entirely to the politicians. It is possible of course that some form of revivalism will sweep the convention. But the indications are that the political manoeuvering of the last four or five months will continue to the end. It is a year of secret letter writing between so-and-so, of private dinners and private luncheons, and a great variety of gentlemen making special trips from this man's house to that man's. Even those of us who expect to attend the Republican convention cannot hope to see the machinery at work. We shall not be present at the conference of a dozen political managers who are planning to sit in a hotel bedroom wearing their straw hats on the back of their heads. We shall not hear the long-distance telephone messages from New York, or be able to say with any certainty why Mr. Boies Penrose and Mr. Murray Crane have come to the conclusions they come to.

But of one thing we can be absolutely certain. This is a year of catchwords. This is a campaign in which the slogans are to be as vague as possible in order that they may be as

114

broad as possible. Both parties and all candidates are making an appeal which has two qualities: it invites emotion without formulating it. The ideal is a thrilling, nerve-wracking platitude: Peace and Prosperity; Preparedness without Militarism; American Rights, American Honor; Deeds not Words; Americanism. There is a fervent desire on every one's part to proclaim his adhesion to ideas which almost nobody can dispute.

Let us suppose the Republicans come out for Americanism. Does any one suppose the Democrats will come out against it? Not much. When it comes to the task of informing the people that the flag is red, white, and blue, that the national anthem is the "Star-Spangled Banner," that honor is preferable to dishonor, that justice is greater than injustice, I for one am convinced that Mr. Wilson's rhetoric is as good as that of any Republican who could be nominated. It is a year when everyone is planning to assault the American mind with batteries of high-sounding mottoes. It is a year when the harlot words which serve any cause are to walk the streets. They will serve those who suffer with Belgium, and those who are aware how formless is our democracy, and those who fear an invasion, and those who want a protective tariff, and those who think a dead Republican is better than a living Democrat.

In one sense this retreat into grandiose abstraction is the normal result of anxiety and danger. Perhaps the most terrible of all the curses of war is the way it destroys the delicate fabric of thought and sends men scampering to their dumb attachments. In time of war whole populations will live and die for phrases which no man can define. Ideas, discrimination, and invention require a climate of assurance and liberal ease, and the bewildering complexity of danger is their mortal enemy. It is almost as true of us as of the nations in Europe to-day that the mind of the people is squeezed and frightened into an angry, inflexible, inarticulate distraction.

But the war has brought to us something more. Through the uneasiness of America there runs a sense of our own

relative incompetence. We have not been able to find a foreign policy which meets the facts of the world and squares
with the historic prejudices of our isolation. We have not
been able to summon enough forethought and cooperation
from our political institutions, enough technical ability from
our population, enough intelligent unity from our minds, to
meet the new standards of national cohesion and purpose
which Europe has set for the world. This I take it is the best
meaning which hides behind the phrases Americanism and
Preparedness.

This surely is the issue of the campaign. But it is not an
issue between the Democrats and the Republicans. It is an
issue between the facts of our time, the needs of our people,
and all those who offer to rule and lead us. No one can assert
now that one party stands for a successful solution, and that
the other doesn't. There is a group in the Republican party
represented by men like Mr. Henry Stimson, there is even
a tradition in the party, which favors a closer national organization. But the real fight is within both parties and beyond
them, and it is a fight between those who have caught the
vision and those who haven't. There are Democrats who
understand this as deeply as the best Republicans; there are
one or two members of Mr. Wilson's cabinet who have
grasped it at least as well as anyone else in public life. If Mr.
Roosevelt stands for it, as his Chicago speech showed, it is
quite certain that Mr. Penrose does not, and that the Republicans in Congress with few exceptions don't know what it's
all about.

The supreme question, it seems to me, is this: in which
party will the minority which has some sense of the problem
come to the top? And having come to the top, how long
can it stay there if it tries to follow its vision with sincerity
and thoroughness? For no matter which party wins, the real
struggle will be within it. No party as such recognizes or
agrees to fulfill the needs of America. If Mr. Roosevelt were
nominated and elected he would have to cross party lines at

once. No Republican majority conceivable would endure a real program of preparedness. To elect Mr. Roosevelt, then, is to elect him for a struggle with his own party in Congress and its local organizations throughout the country. Battleships and soldiers he may get without disruption, but the nationalization of industry and politics he will not get without destroying the party, and the political system and most of the economic prejudices of the people who would come into power with him. If the Republicans nominate him, it is because they do not understand what preparedness means, or because they do not believe that Mr. Roosevelt will do more than scratch the surface.

Preparedness is an easy word to use, but an infinitely difficult thing to achieve. It costs a price which a democracy like ours has not yet shown the smallest inclination to pay. I do not mean price measured in army and navy bills. I mean price measured in a willingness to create democratic organization at the sacrifice of sectional, private, class and personal interests. When I read the names of the men who dominate the Republican party and think of their almost unbroken record of resistance to the nationalization of industry, their record on the tariff, on patronage, on "pork," on the relation of business to government, of government to the farmer, of power to the labor union, I wonder whether the leopard can change his spots.

What do they mean when they shout for preparedness? Are they willing to unify and socialize the railroads and the means of communication, to regulate rigorously basic industries like steel and coal mining, are they willing to control the food supply and shipping and credit, are they willing to recognize labor as a national institution? Are they willing to go behind all this and create a workable, modern, scientific, federalized system of education? Are they ready to end the destruction of national vitality through unemployment, child labor, overwork, and poverty? Are they willing to do all this which is the price of cooperation for a free people? If they

117

are not, what are they talking about so earnestly? Do they mean simply a little preparedness, a better first line of military defense, and all other things left to drift as now?

That is the issue and that is the puzzle. In time of war our conservatives, turned preparedness agitators, might be willing to do these radical things without choking on the pill. But to do them in time of peace is a revolutionary undertaking. England nationalized her railroads over night because war was upon her. But to attempt that when there is no war is to arouse every prejudice and interest which fights against it. England has had to deal with labor unions as they have never been dealt with before. Can any one picture to himself the struggle which this would have meant under normal conditions? I wonder whether the defense societies have any notion of the consequences of their propaganda.

If preparedness is an issue which will raise a powerful opposition, so is an adequate foreign policy. The outstanding fact of this war for America is our relation to the Power which controls the seas. Our quarrel with Germany is a direct result of British naval policy. Our future in the Far East and Pan-America, our future in the carrying trade, in the competition for markets, is bound up with our relations to the British Empire. The peace of this hemisphere depends upon our policy in regard to the world-wide empire which touches us from Canada to the Falkland Islands and the Philippines. The supreme question of foreign policy is our relation to the British Empire; the supreme danger lies in ignoring it or challenging it; and the greatest hope, I believe, for western civilization lies in an agreement with it.

It is all very well to talk glibly about rights and honor. The problem of the statesman is: How are we to adjust the end of our isolation to the facts of British sea power? Till some one has thought that problem through to the end, and dared to face the conclusions, we have no foreign policy. Some decision we shall have to make in the next few years, and it is the most important decision of international policy since we misinterpreted Washington's Farewell Address. That a first step has been taken by Mr. Wilson in his historic speech on a world alliance is clear to any one who realizes the relation between a League to Enforce Peace and the problem of sea power.

But the statesman who has the audacity to grapple with it must be prepared for a long and bitter struggle with public opinion. There are no votes to be won, and there is no party harmony to be maintained by the President who will undertake to meet this issue. It is not only the German-Americans and the Irish-Americans who will fight it. A deep Americanism will resist it. And if I'm not mistaken the very people who would support a radical program of nationalization are the ones who would resist it most. The statesman who takes the slogans of this campaign seriously will have to struggle with vested politics and industry to secure preparedness, and with vested Americanism to secure a foreign policy. It means a period of unrest and fermentation to which no man can set an end.

These are the issues, not between the parties, but against them and within them. And those who care for the American future will keep these issues in mind. They will not give their allegiance completely to any party or either candidate. They will use these issues as tests which all the politicians must face, and if there is no satisfactory response from either faction they may have to consider whether the time has not come to challenge the party system itself.

June 3, 1916

AT THE CHICAGO

CONVENTIONS

George Ade was the Indiana humorist. Herbert L. Satterlee, the son-in-law of J. P. Morgan, was working for Roosevelt. Frank Hitchcock, who had served as Postmaster General in the Taft administration, was the manager of the Hughes campaign. George W. Perkins, an imaginative proponent of welfare capitalism, was regarded by the progressive Progressives as the evil genius of their party. Hiram Johnson was the Progressive governor of California. John Parker later became a Democratic governor of Louisiana. [*A.S., jr.*]

On the train to Chicago I met one of the most prominent of the Republican managers. He had with him, he said, a clipping from the New York *Evening Post* which set forth what Mr. Roosevelt thought of the Republican party four years ago. The substance of it was that the historic party of Lincoln had become a whited sepulchre inhabited by second-story men. The clipping was hardly needed as a reminder. The delegates had not forgotten. Whoever else may have lost sight of Armageddon, they had not. It was the central impulse of their political religion. They were perfectly willing to stand around in hotel lobbies and let ardent Progressives shout at them that they wanted Teddy. The inflexible sense of those delegates was in the refrain: "This convention will nominate a Republican."

There never was any question about it that the memory of 1912 was the decisive fact at Chicago. The platform might talk about the prestige of America. What the delegates were concerned about was their prestige back home. Four bitter years they had been cursing Mr. Roosevelt in the regular metaphors of politics; he was the "ingrate," the "Benedict Arnold," the man who "had bitten the hand that fed him." The hard, substantial, unimaginative men who had been sent to Chicago had identified the sense of their own self-respect with anti-Rooseveltism. The public opinion to which they were responsive was not that of the "American people" supposed to be calling insistently for Teddy. They answered to their friends in the organization who would have regarded them as soft and gullible fools had they permitted "T. R. to get away with it now." Optimistic Roosevelt workers comforted themselves with the thought that politicians are practical men out to win. They little knew that real character of the so-called practical man. He is not a person who forgets his prejudices and takes the long view of a situation. He is always a man who reacts to his brute memory and his immediate experience.

The practical sense of those delegates was that they had a real prize to offer, and that there was no reason why they should give it to the man who had tried to destroy them. The mass of them had no particular fervor for any candidate. They cared for the party and they wanted a good party man. The real issues of the day played a shadowy role in their minds. The orators talked about a crisis, but it was obviously the same old crisis that always exists when the Democrats are in office. So for the first few days the Favorite Sons were allowed a run for their money, or to put it more accurately, they were allowed a run because of their money.

The headquarters of the Favorite Sons were worth visiting. They had the atmosphere of booths at a tawdry world's fair. In front of the Indiana rooms there was an intolerably genial young man who barked at you to come in, seized you if you came within reach, clutched you with a moist hand, and projected you into the cigar smoke with an arm around your shoulder till he had you face to face with Indiana's most attractive offering, Mr. Jim Watson. "Meet Mr. Watson and have a cigar—newspaper man—good. Great story for you boys . . . the delegate from the Philippines has just declared for a merchant marine and Fairbanks . . . always glad to see you." Massachusetts had a red-satin and gold parlor, and before there was time to realize it, Senator John Wingate Weeks had offered a cigar. The would-be President was presiding, a great egg-shaped man. In one corner was a photograph of Weeks as an Annapolis graduate, not yet egg-shaped. On the table was Weeks in a company of naval reserves drilling on Boston Common during the Spanish War, already egg-shaped. The inference was that Weeks had always been for preparedness. He defended the port of Boston, I believe, against Cervera's fleet.

Leaving the battle-scarred veteran, I approached the Roosevelt Republican headquarters. It was a colder and more business-like place. Theodore Roosevelt, Jr., was shaking hands with Negro delegates. George Ade was talking to George von L. Meyer. The chief office boy was Mr. Satterlee, who sat at a roll-top desk with nothing very much to do. But he had decisions to make. A man brought in a statuette of Roosevelt as a Rough Rider with an American flag in his hand. The base bore the inscription "I am for peace." Inspecting it critically Mr. Satterlee approved the sculpture but changed the inscription. Make it read "peace with honor," he said, and dismissed the artist with the air of a determined executive.

Upstairs in two or three small rooms was Mr. Frank Hitchcock, who owns a card-index and has money enough to travel. No badges, and no cigars and no slogans, but perfect assurance prevailed. Mr. Hitchcock, looking tired and clean, saw us. He asked no favors and made no complaints. The invincible logic of the situation was with him. The Hughes candidacy was unanswerable, and all the clear-sighted people knew it from the start. They were not worried about Mr. Hughes's opinions on "Americanism" and "preparedness." They knew that he would not have allowed his name to be used had he disagreed with the general plan of the attack on President Wilson. They knew that when he spoke he would say all that can be said in words about the alleged issues at hand. They knew he was progressive enough to make a progressive campaign against him impossible. They knew Mr. Roosevelt had committed himself so deeply against the President, had thrown overboard so much progressive baggage, had proclaimed the crisis so overwhelmingly that he could not fight the anti-Wilson ticket. They knew that the threat of a third party headed by Mr. Roosevelt was a bluff that would not be made good. They did not yield to the delusion that Mr. Hughes could be scared out of the running, because the fact that he would run must scare out the Roosevelt opposition. They knew that the Hughes nomination would pocket Mr. Roosevelt and eliminate the Progressive party.

To be sure Hughes was not an unmixed delight. But there were politicians in the convention who had learned something from 1912, and the menace of Roosevelt and the Progressives was more vividly in their minds than the stark virtue of Hughes. They did not allow themselves to think too much of 1920. Against this logic and this mood the Roosevelt workers argued ingeniously but helplessly. They pointed out that Hughes was the cruellest boss-killer of them all, that T. R. was always good to the good bosses, and a story spread around that one somewhat pro-Roosevelt boss had said: "The Colonel used to kick me out of the front door every once in a while, but he'd see me now and then at the back door. But this man Hughes won't let me smell the lilacs around the White House." It did not avail. Nothing could have availed with those delegates. They were going to nominate a Republican and no one else.

In the newspapers, in the emotions of the spectators, in the noise of marching and shouting, the Progressives played a big part in Chicago. But in the perspective of fact, in the actual balance of power, they never counted seriously. The Republicans were polite to them, but not profoundly interested in them. They were regarded as a small collection of spoilt children who had no important influence and were neither to be feared nor insulted. Except for the fact that the Hughes nomination was in itself a concession to progressivism, the Republican convention ignored the Progressives. It followed its schedule relentlessly. It conferred when the Progressives asked for a conference. It appointed a committee which was in itself a defiance. The committee listened for hours to the astonishing fact that the Progressives wanted Teddy, and were even willing to compromise on Teddy. Having learned the fact they reported it gravely to the Republicans who had read in the papers that the Progressives wanted Teddy. They followed their schedule with the realistic sense of men who knew that confronted with the *fait accompli* the Progressives would be helpless.

The Republican convention has been described as cold. It was cold because there never was anything to grow hot about. The triumph was so easy that there wasn't anything to gloat over. But the sense of brute power was overwhelming, like that of a great monster with little brain which plodded forward and could not be stopped. It was a most representative crowd, representative of a massive and selfish and cynical demand for place. It was not the "cohorts" of a legendary Wall Street. Articulate Wall Street was demonstrating vainly for Teddy and tepidly for Root. It was the gathering together of distributed privileges, of tariff-protected manufacturers, business lawyers, and pillars of society from all over the union. It was the quintessence of all that is commonplace, machine-made, complacent and arbitrary in American life. To look at it and think of what needs to be done to civilize this nation was to be chilled with despair.

This brutal fact flowered up into flamboyant oratory. I shall not soon forget the nine and a half hours I sat wedged in, listening to the nominating speeches and subsisting on apple pie and loganberry juice—hours of bellow and rant punctuated by screeches and roars. I think there were fifteen nominations plus the seconding orations. It was a nightmare, a witches' dance of idiocy and adult hypocrisy. DuPont for instance, and his wonderful grandfather, and the grand old state of Ohio, and the golden state of Iowa, and the flag, red, white and blue, all its stripes, all its stars, and the flag again a thousand times over, and Americanism till your ears ached, and the slaves and the tariff, and Abraham Lincoln, mauled and dragged about and his name taken in vain and his spirit degraded, prostituted to every insincerity and used as window-dressing for every cheap politician. The incredible sordidness of that convention passes all description. It was a gathering of insanitary callous men, who blasphemed patriotism, made a mockery of Republican government and filled the air with sodden and scheming stupidity. The one note of freedom in those roaring days was during the demonstration for Roosevelt, when the sun suddenly appeared after days of rain. There was enough humanity left to cheer the sun.

To go from the Republican to the Progressive Convention was to find again the open generosity of a better America. The mass of the delegates there were the most warm-hearted crowd I have ever seen. But from the first it was evident where their hopelessness lay. In 1912 the cant phrase which dominated them was "service." This year the word was "leadership." They have no creed, none whatever. The passion which had been diffused through their "covenant" had been sucked out and concentrated on Theodore Roosevelt. They clung to him as a woman without occupation or external interests will cling to her husband. They clung so hard that they embarrassed him with their infatuation. They loved too much. They loved without self-respect and without privacy. They adored him as no man in a democracy deserves to be adored. They took a creed from him which subsequent events showed was not their real creed.

They trusted their leaders, but their leaders never trusted them. The delegates never understood what was happening, and it was never fully explained to them. What happened was this: the men who controlled them tried to use the Progressives as a threat and a bluff to force Theodore Roosevelt on the Republicans. I believe that for a few hours they thought the bluff might work. But it was always a transparent bluff, for it was obvious that Roosevelt did not intend to make it good if Hughes were nominated. Everybody seemed to realize the emptiness of the threat except the naive Progressive delegates.

The first division amongst them was over the question: Should Roosevelt be nominated early so as to make him a real threat? The "conservatives" prevented this; why I do not know. For obviously if the bluff was to have even a tinge of reality it must be made before the balloting at the Republican convention. The real reason, I imagine, was the feeling of men like Mr. Perkins that Mr. Roosevelt should be spared the pain of having made an empty gesture.

By Thursday at least it was plain as day that no matter what the Progressives did, Roosevelt could not be nominated. The problem then was this: Should the Progressive party kill itself, or should Roosevelt be made to bear the onus of killing it? That was all that was left to think about, and on that the "radicals" and "conservatives" divided. The "coterie," as it was called, retained its control and the nomination was delayed. On Saturday morning came the telegram suggesting Senator Lodge. The Progressives were humiliated. On the man to whom they had given their love they turned their anger. Lodge was an unbelievable suggestion, a slap in the face to every Progressive. They were bewildered at the sheer folly of it, unable to understand what had happened to their leader. It was not only a stupid suggestion in a political sense;

it seemed to show a temperamental bluntness, as if a class blindness had descended upon him.

They tabled his suggestion with resentment, and then nominated him. The spirit of that nomination was to strike back at Theodore Roosevelt. It was a nomination made in order to make trouble for him. There was no mistaking it, and in that spirit, I think, he understood it. Once they had thrown the burden on him, they felt better. The convention recessed, and the leaders had about two hours for telephone communication with Oyster Bay in order to devise an answer. In the meantime Hughes had been nominated.

When the convention gathered at about three o'clock the answer was known to most of us in the press section and on the platform. The delegates did not know. They were held in suspense, teased along, a Vice-President was nominated, campaign contributions were solicited, and everything was done to make it look as if there would be a campaign. There are three explanations of this tragic farce. One is that the radicals were in control and determined to make the inevitable refusal more uncomfortable. Another is that they intended to go it without Roosevelt. The third is that they were pulled along gently to the reading of the telegram and the hurried adjournment to prevent a smash.

As it became evident from hints thrown out and from the general evasiveness of the men on the platform that the Progressive party was lost, a very curious and a very significant thing happened. The aggressively nationalistic and military tone, the Bismarckian creed which the party had taken from its leader began to disappear, and the old cries for social justice and popular rule were heard again. Hiram Johnson mentioned the interests of children, and it sounded strange. John Parker, the most poignant figure at the convention, begged them not to destroy a party which offered the only hope to liberal southerners. In the last hours there was a momentary flare of the real soul of the party. When the end came, there were tears and anger and a bitterness at the cold brutality of it all. Mr. Roosevelt had been nominated defiantly. He declined skillfully but without a note of comradeship for the men and women who had adored him. There was a great destruction of faith, and to my mind an unnecessary and inhuman treatment of a very human and trusting band. It was unnecessary to fool them, it was unnecessary to make an empty bluff, it was unnecessary to use them, it was unnecessary to be uncandid with them. Unnecessary, because even by the coldest calculation, the men who used the Progressives were poor politicians who should have known from the very start that Theodore Roosevelt would not be nominated by the Republicans.

June 17, 1916

THE PUZZLE OF HUGHES

Many of us are very busy inventing theories about why we are not cashing in now on the legend of Hughes the fearless, the just, the wise, and the heroic. That is the human interest of this campaign—to find out why a man of rare courage and frankness, of balanced mind, a man of experience in politics, should be wandering around the country trailing nothing but cold and damp platitudes. The puzzle is to explain the evolution of a distinguished man into an undistinguished candidate.

For it is impossible to pretend that Mr. Hughes is a good candidate. In fact, if we had to judge him merely by what he has been saying since he was nominated we should have to grant that he is a Republican of the 'nineties, superstitious about the tariff, philistine about business, frock-coated about labor, and with a regular Union League attitude toward the Democrats, national honor, and prosperity. As a candidate Mr. Hughes has been the perfect representative of a convention that spent a whole morning enjoying speeches by Joe Cannon and Chauncey Depew. From Mr. Hughes's campaign you would hardly know that a great war was opening a period in human history if it weren't for repeated references to the fact that Europe is going to be so efficient that our tender business men must be protected against competition.

He is the nominee of a party that has at present only one principle to its name—a desire to beat Mr. Wilson. On whom is Mr. Hughes counting? On the Republican organization, the Roosevelt Republicans, the homeless progressives, the upper-class pro-Ally vote, the pro-German vote, the anti-Democratic suffrage vote, the anti-Carranza Catholic vote. What have these people in common except a desire to punish the President? Mr. James R. Mann, a Republican leader in the House, wished to warn Americans off armed ships in order to avoid war with Germany; Mr. Robert Bacon, defeated candidate for the senatorial nomination in New York, would have liked a war for the sake of France. Mr. Roosevelt thinks Mr. Wilson has been a poltroon before Germany; Mr. Bernard Ridder thinks the President takes his orders from Viscount Grey. One group of Republicans wishes to stop "pork" and "ineptitude," and so it is trying to give the Republicans control of the Senate in order that Penrose may write the tariff bill, Warren of the army posts may control appropriations, and William Alden Smith, landlubber of the *Titanic,* be chairman of the Committee on Naval Affairs. Mr. Nicholas Murray Butler would like to save the country from progressivism, and Governor Johnson would like to save it from President Butler.

Mr. Hughes was not nominated as candidate of a party or leader of a cause, but as a drag-net for all possible anti-Wilson votes. The politicians calculated that if all the people who do not like the President were collected the party could win. Mr. Hughes's task as a candidate has been to keep enough people from liking Mr. Wilson. All the colors in the rainbow of politics are represented in the Hughes following. Mr. Hughes trying to be very efficient as a candidate, one hundred per cent efficient, has mixed the violent contrasts, and the result of course is a dull gray.

But when all this is granted, as I believe it must be by the warmest Hughes admirer, the puzzle still remains. Why has the hero of the insurance investigation, the merciless and accurate enemy of corruption, been willing to stultify himself as a candidate? For an infinitely better Hughes exists, as any one can see who will study his career. Those who know him best claim he would be a much abler President than he is a candidate. If we are to get at the truth of that, the most important truth before the American people to-day, we have to cut through the fog of the campaign and develop a theory as to how his mind is working.

Mr. Hughes seems to me to act like a man who has been stunned so that his brain for the time being has lost its fighting edge. He appears to be frightened and anxious and unable to make dangerous decisions. There is a striking similarity between his vacillation now and that of Mr. Wilson struck in the midst of a family crisis by the blow of the European war. Mr. Wilson seemed to be unnerved for a while, incapable of making up his mind, and liable to all sorts of foozles. He recovered extraordinarily, as Mr. Hughes undoubtedly will. But at the moment Mr. Hughes acts as if he were too worried to think, too confused to face issues, too depressed to lead. Inside of him there appears to be the kind of strained bewilderment and conflict which clog the intellect and enfeeble the will.

To explain that, we have to look I think to personal interests which lie deeper than politics. The fact is that this is the first great crisis of Mr. Hughes's public life when he has staked everything on success. The ambition which flared up in 1908 he has pushed away from himself again and again until at last it has broken through. For years Mr. Hughes has been telling himself and others that a Justice of the Supreme Court must give up ambition. "I hope," he said in 1912, "that, as a Justice of the Supreme Court, I am rendering public service and may continue to do so for some years, but the Supreme Court must not be dragged into politics, and no man is as essential to his country's well-being as is the unstained integrity of the Court." No one has ever given better reasons why a judge should not run for office. Yet here he is running for office. You and I may think his former scruples about the Court unworthy of democracy. That is not the point. The point is that Mr. Hughes had the scruples and expressed them with great emphasis. The sharpness with which he expressed them only four years ago shows how he had wrestled with that question and that he thought he had disposed of it. Those scruples are not altogether dead. Mr. Hughes has the kind of conscience that could not allow them to disappear altogether. In his effort to be an efficient candidate he has had to stamp on them violently, but it is the nature of conscience to keep on hurting a man even when he does not realize it.

An important element of his character plays into this hesitancy. Mr. Hughes is not a sociable man in the popular sense, nor a lover of publicity and crowds. In small groups he is humorous and companionable, but his contact with people is spontaneous only when he feels much at home. His feeling reaches the common life at few points, as is so often the case with men who are intensely concentrated in their work. His energy has gone into technical study for which only a small minority have any active understanding. To touch the world at many points and like it is foreign to him. The best work of Hughes has to be done in solitude, at his desk, with a marvelous power of close attention. But campaigning and being popular is a disorderly life, a haphazard, superficial way of living. The instinct of his soul is to be thorough, expert, intense, and stumping the country is just the worst condition for the fluent working of his mind. I have heard him say that the reserve which hedges the Supreme Court, coming after the blatant publicity of the governorship, had meant the world to him. For Justices of the Court are allowed to think, unmolested by distorting headlines, unfair attacks, and inquiries into the habits and motives of their souls.

He has given up that quiet so congenial to his mind for the hubbub of a campaign which may after all bring him defeat. Only a superman could fail to recoil, wonder about the choice he has made, and want too much to win. The dignity and peace of his life are at stake in this election. He is making one of the great gambles of American politics. On the bench he shared with Mr. Justice Holmes the distinction of being the leader of his profession. Defeated as the Republican candidate this year, the sacrifice would be appalling and complete. I know there is a convention that men like Mr. Hughes are not subject to human motives. Yet we may be sure he is human enough to have felt deeply the shock and risk of his decision to leave the bench.

Now, a man who has just gone through such a personal crisis is more likely to hesitate, to play safe, to trust the good old formulas, to cling to the party, than to strike out for himself with the assurance that even if he loses he wins. In New York Mr. Hughes could strike out because he was bigger than his office. He could let go the full energy of his mind, knowing that he represented a cause which could not be beaten. To-day he represents a conglomeration of antis standing for no cause for which he can work without reservation.

He inherited the case against Mr. Wilson; he did not make it. It was Colonel Roosevelt, and he alone, who laid out the lines of the attack on the President. It was in the Roosevelt bones to be against Woodrow Wilson. The Colonel is a red-blood, does not distrust soldiering and empire, belongs by tradition and temperament to the aristocratic group which always comes to the top in time of war. But Mr. Hughes has nothing in common with this; there is nothing of the "heroic" mood about him. He is severe, prosaic, pedestrian, respectable middle-class, and it isn't mere impertinence that has caused the American people to display such unmitigated interest in his personal appearance. The mood which Roosevelt embodied, the campaign which Roosevelt sketched, Mr. Hughes had to take over, and it fits him as little as the uniform of a Rough Rider. If Mr. Hughes dared to let his intellect work, he could not help being much more moderate in his assaults on the President. A just judge could not escape realizing that there is a very great deal to be said for Mr. Wilson. But the queer fact that Mr. Hughes inherited anti-Wilsonism, had it thrust upon him, and had to live up to it, puts him in the position of a lawyer called in at the last moment to argue another man's brief. Had Mr. Hughes led the attack he might have developed a powerful indictment, but it would have differed in substance and tone from what is really a hand-me-down from Roosevelt.

Mr. Hughes to-day is a man who has repressed a profound scruple, has risked a career for which he was peculiarly fitted, has entered a kind of life which he does not enjoy, has made himself the exponent of a party without principle and of a mood which is not his own. Why then did he accept the nomination? It is no answer to say that a man must not refuse to run for the Presidency. Several men have refused. Mr. Hughes has the sort of conscience which would violate a tradition only when some other great moral issue seemed to demand it. What was the issue that called Mr. Hughes from the bench? It was not Mexico and not the tariff. It was something which has never been mentioned in the campaign, and yet seemed to Mr. Hughes a compelling reason for acceptance. The very afternoon when he resigned and sent his telegram to the Republican Convention he explained his action by saying that our system of government could not be worked without two strong parties, and that he was the only man who could unite the Progressives and the Republicans. He felt profoundly that the nation needs to be governed by the Republican party welded together and strengthened. To him the Progressive rump was a calamity, not because he hasn't some sympathy with progressivism, but because he believes in the dogma of two parties and because three parties mean Democratic rule. The call came to him as a way to save the country by redeeming the Republican party.

At first it seems a little strange that Mr. Hughes of all men should care so much about parties, because the truth is that he never can live happily with his party. Believing in the two-party system as an ideal, he is the sort of man who always tends to wreck the party he is in. When it comes to the concrete task of keeping an organization together, Mr. Hughes is too uncompromising and too honest to pay the price. In the political sense he has almost no gratitude, and parties are cemented by gratitude in the shape of pork, patronage, and deals. Mr. Hughes believes theoretically in a great unified organization; elect him, and if he keeps to the instincts of his soul he will fight pork and patronage and deals till the party is torn to pieces. The very quality which has made Mr. Hughes a marked man in American politics is at war with Mr. Hughes's theory about what politics ought to be. He is not a party man, but he believes passionately if abstractly in two parties. The paradox is that he cannot practise the administrative efficiency he preaches without disrupting the organization he left the bench to unite.

This conflict in Hughes between philosophy and practice runs deep. His general theories are the good old American theories, for he seems to have had a most conventional education which filled him full of unanalyzed dogmas about government, business, labor. Side by side with them there have grown up convictions about things he has learned from intense though limited experience. Where he has studied the facts he is almost always realistic and modern. He knows what corruption is because he dissected it. He knows about administrative inefficiency because he fought it. He knows about the distinction between federal and state action, about the police power under the Constitution, because as a judge he had to deal with these matters. But about the struggle between capital and labor, about international politics, he is commonplace and uninteresting, saying merely the thoughtless things which every gentleman of his age and class says if he doesn't stop himself. His is a mind which is original and powerful only after great effort. He has nothing of Mr. Roosevelt's genius for brilliant intuition or Mr. Wilson's extraordinary power to learn quickly. On the subjects Mr. Hughes knows about there are few men to equal him for grasp and thoroughness, though one never feels even in his best work that creative quality which shines through the investigation of a man like Mr. Justice Brandeis.

An example is Mr. Hughes's fight for the direct primary. Most progressives of the time believed it was the cure for boss rule. Mr. Hughes, at war with the bosses, picked up the direct primary as a club. In the heat of the fight he had no time to think through the meaning of the remedy he was proposing, or to foresee that the direct primary complicated matters instead of simplifying them. He had not that quick penetration and sure political instinct which could look beyond what happened to be the accepted theory of the people he trusted. Mr. Hughes, unlike Mr. Wilson, really has a single-track mind. Whenever he has to act without long and careful preparation, he acts according to rule. "Proper" and "correct" are words that occur most often in his speeches.

This need for intense effort is responsible also for what often looks like his capacity for making much out of little. He has a mind like a microscope, and when he has looked hard and long at a thing it takes on an importance for him which often seems out of perspective. His fight against racing, for example, was far less a crusade against vice than it was an attempt to enforce the spirit of the law because it was law. Mr. Hughes came close to law-breaking when he was governor and fixed on the race tracks as an issue. He might have selected something totally different, though an evangelical bias no doubt played a part. There were greater evils in New York for a courageous man to fight; the race tracks happened to hit the center of his deep and narrow vision.

This is the defect of a virtue which is his finest quality. It might be called the instinct of workmanship. He has the passion of a good watchmaker, of a master craftsman for doing particular things particularly well. He has little aesthetic interest, none of the brooding of Lincoln, or the epic size of Roosevelt or the liveliness and width of Wilson. But he has in rare measure the passion of the good workman in persisting at a dry result. His judicial opinions do not shine with the gallant genius of Holmes, but there is something assuringly trim and shipshape about them. In a larger view

136

of democracy the appearance of this quality in public life is a renewal of hope that popular government is not necessarily crude and that the expert mind can win its way to the top.

If Mr. Roosevelt's mood was heroic, that of Mr. Hughes is workmanlike. The reason he dislikes the Democrats is because the sense of the craftsman rebels against the amateur. Mr. Hughes is far less concerned about national honor and prestige than he is with a feeling that the task of government has been in the hands of undisciplined men. He is annoyed at what he calls vacillation and ineptitude the way a good housewife is aroused by a clever but sloppy cook. The vision which drives him is of a nation inspired by his own instinct of workmanship. How it is to be so inspired, Mr. Hughes has not yet had time to find out, for workmanship, unlike heroism, cannot be achieved by temporary exaltation. Uncertain as to how to accomplish his end, he is filled with a personal conviction that the love of work well done shall seep through the government and take hold of the nation.

This central virtue has certain offshoots which cannot be ignored. It is only too easy to identify the man well trained to govern with the man who has happened to govern. Republicans often make this confusion. Having been in power a long time, representing those classes of the community which control large affairs, they very easily imagine that Republicans are a little better born, that Democrats are congenitally defective, that the mass of the people has few resources to draw from, and that the first crudeness of a party long out of power is a sign of intrinsic inefficiency. I don't suppose Mr. Hughes really believes this, but he often talks as if he did, and it is not altogether certain that he doesn't think a little too highly of people who happen to be Republicans. Certainly he has not been candid about his own party, for it is plain as day that Penrose, Gallinger, Smoot, Warren, Smith, and Fordney are no lovers of efficiency.

Nor is it clear that Mr. Hughes distinguishes between the technical efficiency of a Republican lawyer and the social efficiency of the statesman whose sympathy is as wide as the nation and deep as the labor upon which it rests. If Mr. Wilson has done nothing else, he has gone far toward restoring confidence in the possibilities of our government. The radical and the humble have felt a response from Washington they have never known before. The generous, idealistic, peace-loving people of America have felt they were represented in Mr. Wilson. Let Mr. Hughes come in with anything that resembles a plutocratic reaction, and the cause of efficiency will receive a staggering blow no matter how good Mr. Hughes's appointments may be. For efficiency will never be a popular cause in America until it is tied securely to radical liberalism. If Mr. Hughes as President should blunder about labor and the progressives as he did in California, he will merely give efficiency a bad name. Let him take warning from the failure of an efficient constitution in New York, smothered under a popular vote which distrusted the men who framed it.

In a time when there were one or two complicated problems before the people which required expert treatment there would be no doubt that Mr. Hughes measured up to the office. But we are not in such a time, and that is why there is doubt of his fitness. We are in a time of unimaginable complications, of unexpected crises. It is a period of extreme uneasiness beneath the surface when the government must have the willing confidence of the people in order to move successfully. The President of the United States in the next four years will have to be a very nimble-minded and versatile man, a man capable of quick intuitions, and with the power to guess rightly almost on the spur of the moment. There will be few questions he can study thoroughly. He will have to be able to pick ideas in a hurry, keep close to the deeper currents of popular feeling, and have no fear of adventure.

September 30, 1916

THE PROGRESSIVES

Meyer London was a Socialist congressman from New York; Jeanette Rankin, the first woman to serve in the House of Representatives, was the only person to cast votes against the declaration of war in both 1917 and 1941. Henry Cabot Lodge and Elihu Root were key figures in the Republican establishment. [*A.S., jr.*]

Progressives have the opportunity to carry their victory to the floor of Congress, for it appears that neither party has an effective working majority in the House. Under such conditions ten independents who knew how to cooperate could do much to reform the Congressional system. If they will lay their plans carefully before the new Congress assembles, they ought to be able to prevent the organization of the House on the old lines. There never was a better chance to force a reform of the rules. Then too, under a more liberal procedure, this group could exert great influence on legislation. Unless we are greatly mistaken, it will find the President not at all unfriendly, and a basis of cooperation might even be established. If the genuine progressives, both Democratic and Republican, the trade-union members, Miss Rankin, and Mr. Meyer London fail to organize such a *bloc* they will be throwing away the splendid beginning which began with the election. The way to go about it is to start now organizing an independent caucus, consult with those who have studied the rules of Congress, and select a floor leader of parliamentary experience.

Hiram Johnson in the Senate will be a perpetual symbol of the problem that the Republican leaders must solve. He represents dramatically the thing which defeated Mr. Hughes. Without him, and the kind of Republican who will follow him, a regenerated party is at present unthinkable. Yet it is no less difficult to imagine the party after it had assimilated its Hiram Johnsons. For the sources of feeling which he draws upon are after all far closer to the Wilson Democracy than they are to anything important in the Republican party of the East. With the Penroses there can of course be no permanent understanding, but is it any more conceivable that the people who vote for Johnson or La Follette will work smoothly with Republicans like Mr. Root or Senator Lodge? If Colonel Roosevelt is the great fact which the Republicans must assimilate in the next four years, Hiram Johnson is a symbol of the popular feeling which both the Colonel and the Old Guard will have to assimilate.

November 18, 1916

HONOR AND

ELECTION RETURNS

Until the returns came in from California, it was generally assumed that Hughes had been elected President of the United States. David Lloyd George was just about to become Prime Minister of Great Britain. [*A.S., jr.*]

Towards ten-thirty on election night many prominent people began to issue statements about the defeat of Mr. Wilson. Not content with registering their pleasure in the victory which seemed to be theirs, they stamped violently and joyfully on the prostrate loser. It was wretched sportsmanship. It was a sin against that spirit of live and let live without which a democracy like ours is unworkable. And it was unintelligent. It was unintelligent not because the later returns reversed the result, but because all the talk about yellow streaks, too proud to fight, and national honor has now become feeble political melodrama.

Eighteen million men and women voted in the election. They were certain to divide more or less evenly. No one in his senses ever supposed there would be a difference of two million votes between the candidates. The less popular was sure to poll many more votes than there were human beings in the United States when the nation was founded. And yet prominent Republican newspapers and ex-Presidents talked for months as if Americanism and national honor could be won or lost in a few pivotal states. The reason those premature rhapsodies sound so queer now is that we have had a demonstration of what it means to make simple spiritual values depend on the complex movement of a diversified people. If on Tuesday night we had cast off the motto "too proud to fight," are we to assume that by Thursday night we had adopted it? If by midnight we had erased the yellow streak, did we paint it in by daybreak?

Obviously not. No one who knows politics thinks that the votes of eighteen million people are determined by any such single reason as Mr. Roosevelt assumed. He knows perfectly well that if there are 8,508,000 Wilson votes and 8,090,000 Hughes votes, it does not follow that there are 8,508,000 people too proud to fight and 8,090,000 red-blooded heroes. Anyone who watched the Republican campaign knows that the methods used to win votes entitled no one to conclude that they fitted the neat formulae announced on election night. The last ten days of the Republican campaign were an effort to create a stampede by threatening the ignorant with the danger of a panic. Suppose this had been even more successful than it was. Just how would this result indicate that the American people wanted intervention in Mexico or less vacillation as against Germany?

Or consider the talk about the fibre of our people having been weakened. Has Ohio less fibre than Indiana or Pennsylvania? Is Vermont the home of heroes and New Hampshire a poltroon by sixty-three votes? Is North Dakota fat and materialistic, South Dakota lean, athletic and the soul of honor? Why do Arizona and New Mexico, why does the town of Columbus itself, find Wilson's Mexican policy less intolerable than certain northern newspapers? Why do so many polls of militia regiments on the border show a majority for Wilson? Now it would be just as much out of order for one of Mr. Wilson's supporters to say that the result was "national" approval of all he has done. The winner has the votes to elect him. How he got them all no human being can say with certainty. The point is that the motives which go to the making of majorities or minorities in a republic the size of ours are infinitely more complicated than any partisan will admit.

It is a sign of political immaturity to treat a nation as if it were an individual with a conscience, a sense of honor, a single financial interest, a single head, a single heart, and a single life. Actually a nation is a mass of communities and classes and groups tied together for some purposes, antagonistic for others, indifferent to many. It consists of people growing up, growing old, passing on in the business of life. To make fixed entities out of Britain, Germany, America, and talk as if they were changeless as pieces on a chess board is to live among those fictions which obscure the necessities and the true costs of politics. Mr. Lloyd-George was guilty of such a fiction in the famous interview when he compared Britain to a prizefighter and said it did not matter how long the war lasted. Because he thought of his country as a single immortal person and lost sight of the mortal agonies of everyday life in the trenches, he uttered a remark that was revolting to every humane person.

It is a dangerous thing to forget that a nation consists of a large number of people, and that men may disagree without becoming villains. Whoever forgets it is certain sooner or later to feel a little silly.

November 18, 1916

CHICAGO—DECEMBER

FIFTH

Theodore Roosevelt's Progressive Party of 1912 still clung to life after their leader had humiliated his followers in 1916 by proposing that they nominate Henry Cabot Lodge for President. Gifford Pinchot, Harold Ickes, James A. Garfield, Raymond Robins, William Allen White and Chester Rowell were Progressive militants. [*A.S., jr.*]

They are at it again. Not content with the thrashing they got at Chicago, with the humiliation they endured during the campaign, the Progressive Republicans have started right in to repeat the same circle of disaster. Those who believe in signs will note that the thing begins again in Chicago. When I refer to Chicago, I am not thinking of the conventions. They merely consummated the obvious. I am thinking of the meeting held last January at which the Progressives committed themselves to anti-Wilsonism and thereby made themselves politically helpless. Once they had declared that the defeat of Mr. Wilson was a question of national honor and salvation, their threat of a third ticket was ludicrous, and their fighting power nil. For if to throw out Wilson was the paramount issue, how could the Progressives refuse to support any one who promised to throw him out? And since the Old Guard with its dull brain had figured out that the

Progressives plus the Republicans were a million votes stronger than the Democrats, what on earth was the use of their conceding anything to the traitors of 1912?

Luckily for the progressive cause, there was a sufficient number of people who did not follow their leaders. These people were not obsessed with anti-Wilsonism, and by their votes they have managed to keep progressivism alive. They did it by showing that the progressive vote was not a negative prejudice, not a personal antipathy, that it sought positive ends, that it could not be unbalanced by echoes of the war, above all that it was incalculable. The rank and file was wiser than its leaders. By its long hesitation, by its refusal to commit itself till election day, it kept the party leaders guessing, and won a recognition commensurate with its strength and importance. By letting the Wilson Democrats know that the progressive vote could be won by progressive principles, it forced the Democrats to bid for it. It enabled the progressives in the Democracy to push their own reactionaries to the background, and committed President Wilson deeply to a progressive attitude. And yet, though the progressives reelected Wilson, they did not mortgage their souls to his party. A vote that has shown it can form a new party in sixty days, can abandon that and elect a former opponent, is a dangerous and incalculable political power.

Dangerous and incalculable is what the Progressives must be if they are to make their way against the hardened organization of the old parties. They must be elusive, surprising, hard to catch, and impossible to hold. They must scorn the entanglement of prejudice, and for the sake of mobility cast aside all those antique generalizations about the intrinsic virtues and vices of either party. The moment they begin to say that "permanent progressive advance through the Tweedledum party is impossible," or that the "Tweedledee party can best secure," they are lost.

This is what Messrs. Rowell, Gifford, Pinchot, Robins, Garfield, White, and Ickes are now saying. They have issued a statement—date line Chicago, December 5th—announcing that the Democratic party is "impossible," that the Republican party can "best secure," and won't the Old Guard please create an Executive Committee of ten reactionaries and six Progressives in order to promote social justice. I know what I would do if I were Mr. Penrose. I would say: "Certainly, you poor lambs, the new era has begun. We begin with patriotism, floods of it, crises, emergencies, national honor. We go on to recognize together the basic ineptitude, vacillation, and sectionalism of the Democrats. For the next three years we work ourselves up into a state of hysteria to prove that at all costs the Democrats must be beaten. Then we meet in convention. You get a plank urging a minimum wage for women workers in Alaskan restaurants. A few of you are put on the campaign committee. All of you are allowed to make speeches and contribute money, and whether you like it or not you will have to support the Republican ticket. But if you ask me for my candid opinion of you, as between man and man, I don't mind saying that you are too simple to play politics, and too good to play poker."

November 16, 1916

IN THE NEXT FOUR YEARS

> The spirit of the nation is a great force, but it is one which cannot be always on the alert, and, while it sleeps, the part of noble institutions is to keep watch. *F. S. Oliver on Alexander Hamilton.*

A successful President to-day is not a man working through noble institutions to dear ends, but a virtuoso trying by main force and personal authority to grind out a few crude results from a decadent political machine. For the first year or two of his term, perhaps under the pressure of an electoral campaign, a determined man can extract from Congress a few good pieces of legislation. Even then he has to buy this legislation at the expense of administrative efficiency. But when he has paid his price, exhausted the coercion of patronage, the institutions through which he works crumble in his hands. In the end he is left, as Woodrow Wilson is to-day, alone, the one source of energy in the government, and with a responsibility that is beyond human power to fill.

There is an old saying that a good man can make any machine work well. It is not true of the American government as it is now organized. The concentration of all vitality in the Presidency has become something like a disease in which there is feverish activity at the center, a cold inertia in all the parts. We expect of one man that he shall speak for the nation, formulate its needs, translate them into a program. We expect that man to instill these purposes and this program into a parasitic party system, drive his own party to enact them, and create an untainted administrative hierarchy through which to realize his plans. We expect him to oversee the routine, dominate group interests, prepare for the future, and take stock of possible emergencies. No man can do it. We do not live in a world where individual genius alone matters. We live in a world in which intelligence must be collective, in which leadership itself requires a division of labor.

As the thing works to-day, if the President is absorbed in a foreign complication everything else comes to a dead stop. The affairs of the American people have to run on a single track, because the one responsible national officer has a single-track mind. It is no fault of Woodrow Wilson's. It is the fault of the institutions with which he is surrounded. It would be folly to suppose that any man could at one and the same time formulate the end of American isolation, play a part in the organization of world security, take charge of military reform, solve the railroad problem, prepare for the world-wide economic problems of the coming peace, know how to deal with food riots in New York, lay out our relations to Mexico and Latin-America, and keep the vast administrative organization of the government keyed up. Merely to meet crises as they are thrust upon him is an inhuman responsibility. Actually to lead the people towards a richer cooperative life, to intensify the war against poverty and ignorance and class rule, to integrate and democratize industry, to make education national and modern is something for which no one can be adequate. The President is burdened with the task of a benevolent despot and then denied the authority and resources to make even a despotism effective. In the system of checks and balances, it is the checks alone which seem to have much vitality.

As compared with the other great states of the world, the United States to-day is in point of organization one of the most backward and intellectually one of the most timid. Whatever else the war has done, it has at least taught England and Germany and Canada and France that large-scale operations can be planned and executed, that modern nations must think in very large sums of money, that the old scruples and dogmas of legalism and laissez-faire are old men's bogeys. These immutable laws of private profit and of "human nature" are shaken to the ground, and Europe is putting into effect the most drastic kind of collectivism. On its administrative side socialism has won a victory that is superb and compelling. In their severest trials the progressive nations have discovered that the old unorganized, competitive profiteering is unsound and wasteful. The very plans which were supposed to wreck human society have been adopted as a means of salvation. But the United States trundles along without nationalized railroads or shipping, its mineral resources unsocialized, its water power exploited, its fundamental industries whipped into competition, its food distribution a muddle, its educational system starved, its labor half organized, badly organized, and unrecognized in the structure of society.

In Europe the task of the democracies will be to capture the vast socialistic machines and operate them for the peace of democracy. In America the task is roughly speaking to create the administrative collectivism and at the same time strengthen and clarify popular control. It is a grim collectivism which Europe has established. It is dominated by a class and operated in the main by a bureaucracy. It has scant respect for liberty, it works through fear and compulsion. We shall have to establish much the same machinery, while we preserve the spirit and purpose of liberalism.

In reelecting Woodrow Wilson America defeated a sally which promised neither to modernize the machinery of the nation nor to favor its popular aspiration. That President Wilson is a good democrat, that he is unafraid of the power of wealth and social position, that he is an enlightened inter-

149

nationalist has been demonstrated again and again. A genuine liberal may disagree sharply on many things he has done or failed to do, but beneath any disagreement there would remain a profound conviction that he has the will and the courage, though he may for lack of assistance frequently be without the knowledge and the means to do his part in making the world a juster and more humane home for men.

The translation of this faith into action is in overwhelming measure still to be done, and no matter what other problems of war and peace the next four years bring, the basic task of the President is to inaugurate the machinery of a democratic collectivism. It will mean, of course, in the first instance a still greater abandonment on Mr. Wilson's part of the whig doctrine with which he entered politics. It will mean a sharper personal conversion to the scale and motive of modern cooperation. Then it will require the assembling of like-minded men in his Cabinet and in the bureaus, for democratic collectivism is unworkable except through delegated authority, and authority delegated is intolerable where the officials are blind to the deeper purposes they are asked to execute. It will mean something still more spectacular. It will mean a war against that Congressional system which makes good administration impossible and turns almost all legislation into petty interference or sordid snatching. Congress will not reform itself. It will be reformed only from the outside by a President speaking for the nation.

When Mr. Wilson announces a sound and drastic social program and carries the fight to Congress for legislation to enact it and freedom to administer it, he will be acting on the faith, however dimly uttered, by which he was reelected.

March 3, 1917

AND CONGRESS

The unfortunate "Gum-shoe Bill" was William J.
Stone of Missouri, chairman of the Senate Foreign Relations Committee. [*A.S., jr.*]

This last session of Congress has been an ominous exhibition. From first to last it was calculated to destroy all confidence in the machinery of representative government, and
the filibuster at the end was only the spectacular climax of a
session which will cause the soberest man to fear for the
safety of the Republic.

It showed the legislature of a supposedly democratic people degraded to that level from which violent convulsions
ensue. There is no magic in the forms of democracy. Like all
other instruments of life they have to face the test of experience. If they cannot perform the business of a nation, if they
cannot meet its needs and deal energetically with its perils,
nothing will save them. The shibboleths and the shells may
exist as they did in Mexico under Diaz; the reality of representative government will disappear. The fact is the Congress
of the United States has ceased to work. Were we a people
without a measure of political stability, were the danger we
are in as acute as that of France or Britain, representative
government would be swept away at this moment. In the
most deadly peril of fifty years the machinery of free government has broken down.

This last session was the final stage in a process of decay.
It was garrulous, wasteful, amorphous, frivolous and foolish.

It wasted money like a drunken sailor and time like a bab-
bling idiot. It could not think, it would not imagine, it could
not organize, it could not act. It squabbled over trifles,
grunted and squealed and rooted, and left the country in
chaos. It spoiled whatever it touched, obstructed everything
it was asked to assist, attended to everybody's business but
its own. It conducted raiding parties against the treasury,
against administration, it died with the curses of a nation
upon it, a soiled and debauched thing. The spirit of the Congress was incarnate in the chairman of its committee on
Foreign Relations. To have permitted a man like "Gum-shoe
Bill" to head its most important committee was to call down
the contempt of a people. Stone is the type of senile and
slinking politician whose rise to power is sheer disaster. He
is the kind of man who should not be trusted in any important
relationship. He is the leader of the committee which deals
with America's destiny in the world.

He is only a product, to be sure. He is the kind of thing
which the basic evils of our congressional system throw up.
He is a product of that false separation of powers which has
made Congress irresponsible and left it without leadership,
of that absurd mechanical arrangement of the session which
fixes the time of Congress by the clock instead of by the work
it has to do, of that malignant usurpation of administrative
functions which has made Congress primarily a market of
patronage and pork and petty favors and sheer dishonesties,
of that system of rules which kills debate on policies and
opens it wide to rant and irrelevancies, which makes seniority
the test of power, which puts a premium on the art of staying
in office, and divests Congress of interest and responsibility
in the nation's affairs.

Among Americans who have watched Congress closely,
who have dealings with it on any public matter, the legislature
of this nation is cordially despised. There isn't a decent public servant in Washington who doesn't breathe a sigh of relief
when Congress adjourns. There isn't an official interested in

his work who can't work better when Congress is gone. It is regarded by the best officials we have, not as a coordinate and cooperating branch of the government, but as an illimitable nuisance to be evaded and avoided wherever possible. So deep has this gone that the President has uttered publicly his derision of the methods of an institution which ought to be his constant partner.

His real feeling was displayed even before his statement after the adjournment. It was revealed in his unwillingness to have Congress on his hands in the trials which lie ahead. The long delay in going to Congress for authority to act against Germany was dictated undoubtedly by a desire to have Congress out of the way, to secure the necessary power at a minimum of indiscreet and meddlesome talk. He waited till the last week, he fought against a special session because he feared he could not sustain the dignity and interest of the nation while Congress was in session. He miscalculated time. Perhaps if he had gone sooner, the filibuster would have been broken, but the fact that he did not trust Congress remains. No one is better acquainted than Mr. Wilson with the real nature of Congress, no one is more deeply anxious to face the prospect of war with Germany relying on the full strength of representative government. He has been forced in this last month to show by his acts that he considers the Congress of the United States as composed and organized to-day an incompetent adviser and assistant.

No mere reform which introduces cloture into the Senate rules will make Congress a decent instrument of democracy. The evil is far deeper, arising in the last analysis from the Constitution itself. We have tried to construct a government in which leadership is divorced from responsibility, a government in which those who make the laws have no organic relation to those who execute them, a government in which head, heart, and limbs are separate bodies without internal connection. And because no government is workable on that principle we have seen the growth behind the legal govern-

153

ment of a party system which lives as a parasite upon the government, is fed by pork, held together by patronage, which has created out of the separation of powers a perilous confusion of powers. The thing has broken down at last, as all observers knew it would, and we are now in a situation where only the most revolutionary changes in the congressional system can save representative government in America.

March 10, 1917

THANK YOU FOR NOTHING

H. H. Asquith had served as Liberal Prime Minister of England from 1908 to 1916. [*A.S., jr.*]

> The Power that governs the earth is not the Power of Life but of Death; and the inner need that has nerved Life to the effort of organizing itself into the human being is not the need for higher life but a more efficient engine of destruction. *The Devil in a play*

> Without the aid of women England could not carry on the war. *Mr. Asquith in Parliament*

So that's accomplished, and another statesman has had an idea drilled into his head. But Mr. Asquith's education has come pretty high when you think of it. Women have died, have worked themselves sick, have spent their youth and their ardor for many bitter years to teach the Asquiths what they might so easily have known long ago. It has come high. It has deprived an empire of two generations of women's leadership. It has diverted into propaganda an energy that would have served England well. The conversion is now de-

155

scribed as a triumph! A cynic would call it a monument to the density of statesmen.

The directing classes in the modern world have to be frightened, bullied, shocked before they stir themselves out of their office routine and their dinner party program to a recognition of the simplest and most obvious things. It takes a threat of strikes to win recognition for labor, a world-wide convulsion to attract attention to the needs of oppressed peoples, the agony of war to convince Mr. Asquith that women belong to the modern industrial state. Without a terrible jolting they go on dithering about the rights of free contract, law and order, and women's sphere, though all the heavens cry out that they are talking nonsense.

Now New York in this emergency has got to spend the energy of its very best women teaching the same kind of American man the same lesson. The suffragists have to go through the summer and autumn, organizing, pleading, traveling, planning in order to break a path for light in the conservative darkness. They have to fight bogeys, fictions and slanders, fence with shadows, and bore themselves without mercy over dull people. And some day Mr. Root, Mr. Stimson, Mr. Wickersham, a number of editors, and some Tammany Hall politicians will make the great discovery all over again, and another step in human progress will have been accomplished.

If the prospect makes suffragists a little sour, if it tests their good nature a little too severely they must be forgiven, for any one with any sense of the immensity of the task before mankind can hardly fail to grow impatient at the price that has to be paid for the bare preliminaries of reconstruction. They are wrung from the governing minds of the modern nation at a ruinous cost.

April 7, 1917

LEONARD WOOD

General Leonard Wood, who had been commissioned in the Army Medical Corps in 1886, was a close friend of Theodore Roosevelt's and had worked with him in organizing the Rough Riders in the Spanish-American War. Later he served as a colonial administrator in Cuba and in the Philippines. From 1910 to 1914, he was Chief of Staff of the Army. His truculent nationalism made many look on him as TR's heir, but he was far to the right of Roosevelt on domestic issues. After 1920 he served as Governor General of the Philippines until his death in 1927. [*A.S., jr.*]

There were no end of Caesars after Julius as there are Roosevelts after TR is dead. The name is a magnet of affection and of votes, and whoever can carry the name can carry some of the affection and some of the votes. There is consequently a tussle for the name. The leading contender is Leonard Wood, and there are strong arguments to support him. If the Roosevelt of 1914 to 1918 is considered by himself, if the many previous Roosevelts are put out of mind, Leonard Wood may justly claim the bulk of the estate. He has some of the mannerisms, and at least one of the impulses of Roosevelt.

His managers have naturally made the most of the friendship and the resemblance. They have tried to ride Wood to power behind the fiction that whatever you found in Roosevelt you would find again in Wood. But the closer you examine

157

the real Wood behind the pseudo-Roosevelt the more the fiction fades. For while Roosevelt was the voice of a multitude, Leonard Wood is the unmistakable voice of a faction. As you unwrap the campaign coverings you find a Robert Lincoln to an Abraham; a president of a sleeping car company to the great emancipator.

The first wrapper that comes off is the exuberant praise given Wood by Roosevelt himself. That cannot stand in evidence, for Roosevelt praised other men just as highly at one time or another. Of Hiram Johnson he said, for example, in 1912, that he was fit at the moment to be President of the United States. Then, too, Roosevelt was no Warwick. Among all his titles to fame one title will always be conspicuously absent. He will never go down in history as a successful chooser of good Presidents. The case of Mr. Taft settled that. The nomination of Henry Cabot Lodge in 1916 confirmed it. In fact, it was a fairly good rule of thumb always to vote for Roosevelt when you could, and never to vote for his candidate when you could avoid it.

Leonard Wood's grievance also has to be discarded. The treatment Mr. Lansing received did not make him a great Secretary of State, nor does Leonard Wood's treatment indicate qualifications for President of the United States. He has a grievance. He was not used during the war up to the limits of his abilities, and lesser men were given greater responsibilities. The grievance resulted from the fact that Leonard Wood could not be the first under Wilson, and neither he nor any one else knew how he could be used as a second. He was a prima donna capable only of singing soprano in a piece when there were no more prima donna parts left. It was unfortunate. It was even tragic. It will not make him a good President. And however answerable Mr. Wilson may be for the decision to keep General Wood out of France, the General's inability to disentangle his zeal for military preparedness from his feud with the Commander-in-Chief remains a part of the record.

158

Into the same discard with the Roosevelt inheritance and
the grievance must go the advertisements of his publicity men.
They are energetic if not objective, and they spare no ad-
jectives. Finally you come to the official biographies, to *The
Career of Leonard Wood,* by Joseph Hamblen Sears and
to *Leonard Wood, Conservator of Americanism,* by Eric
Fisher Wood. There we must pause and ponder. For these
volumes are not likely to err unfavorably to the General.
They are genuine documents by fervent admirers and they
are written to supply the reasons why he should be the next
President. I do not propose to go behind the facts as stated
in these two books, except where they are supplemented by
the Encyclopedia Britannica and by the writings and speeches
of the General himself.

I take the facts and let rhetoric go. It is not important
that Cape Cod, where Leonard Wood lived until he was
nineteen, looks to Mr. Joseph Sears like "a doubled-up arm
with a clenched fist as if it were ready at any moment to
strike out and defend New England against any attack that
might come from the Eastward"; nor that Mr. Eric Fisher
Wood has discovered that four out of the twenty-two heads of
families on the Mayflower were ancestors of the General; nor
that he finds in the General "hereditary traits—medical, patriotic and executive" upon which he "has built up his ear-
nest and efficient character"; nor that a Cape Cod sea captain
said that when Leonard "did get into a fight, his face sort of
lit up"; nor that he is "five feet, eleven inches tall, weighs 195
pounds and has a 44-inch chest"; nor that, so far as Mr. Eric
Fisher Wood knows, the only thing that Leonard Wood did
at the Georgia Institute of Technology was to organize and
coach "the first football team the Institute ever had . . . His
team in the first season defeated the champions of the South,
and lost only one game during the two years he was its captain . . . Starting with that impetus and proud of his initial
reputation the Georgia Tech has always since then maintained
a fine football record." These things have to be endured in a

biographer as gallantly as Assistant-Surgeon Leonard Wood endured the thirst and the fatigue of the desert in his pursuit of the Apache Chieftain Geronimo.

In the pursuit of a President you traverse the sands of ir-relevance right up to the close of the Spanish-American war. There is nothing in the biographies before that time to indi-cate the education of a statesman. A limited schooling, the Harvard Medical School in the early eighties, a brief period of practice as a surgeon in Boston, several years of Indian fighting in the southwest, time at army posts, service as the Doctor Grayson to President McKinley, and then Colonel of Rough Riders: it is not until Santiago de Cuba fell that Leonard Wood arrived on the scene as a man with a bent for administration. He was made the Military Governor of San-tiago and then promoted to the Governorship of Cuba. He held that post till 1902 when the first intervention ended. The first concrete evidence of Leonard Wood's statesmanship is to be found, if anywhere, in Cuba from 1899 to 1902.

It happens to be the only concrete evidence. It is true that he was later appointed Governor of the Moro Province in the Philippines, and that he pacified the native tribes. But Presi-dents of great nations are not made nor even revealed by policing savages in the tropics. It is true also that General Wood was Chief of Staff from 1910 to 1914, but no one claimed then or has claimed since that Presidential qualities were conspicuous. It is to the Cuban governorship that the biographers turn, and rightly. The task of reorganizing that island was one of the moderately big undertakings of recent colonial experience, and Leonard Wood has his place among the empire builders.

How high a place it is difficult fairly to estimate. In the opinion of his biographers only the sky is the limit of their praise. They naturally dwell upon the sanitary improvements, the road building and the public works, the improvement in the administration of justice, and the modernizing of jails, asylums, hospitals and schools. That Cuba became a vastly

160

better place to live in under the American occupation is certain, and the credit is Leonard Wood's. But we are looking for evidence of his statesmanship, of his constructive ability in the moulding of institutions. It is not enough to show that his instinct for order and for cleanliness caused him to pacify and cleanse the island when he had behind him the unlimited authority of the intervention. His biographers know that this work in itself is not enough to mark a Presidential figure. They are not content to claim that Leonard Wood "cleaned up" Cuba. They insist that "Leonard Wood knows how to build for permanency. It [Cuba] is the only Latin-American republican government which has ever endured for more than three or four years." Thus Mr. Eric Fisher Wood. It is rather interesting that the biographer picked three or four years as a measure of permanency. For the Cubans took over the government on May 20, 1902. Revolution broke out on the 28th of July, 1906, a little over two months margin of permanency. Neither of the biographers seems able to remember this second intervention which occurred a little over four years after Leonard Wood left Havana. Says Mr. Sears: The Cubans "received their country at the hands of the Americans with new laws, with a republican form of government, with their own kind for rulers elected by their own people, and began an existence that has now been running long enough to prove that the work was so well performed for them as to make the impossible possible—the rotten kingdom, a clean republic; the decayed colony, an independent proud democracy. It is a piece of work unparalleled in the annals of history." Mr. Eric Fisher Wood seems equally incapable of remembering that there was a second intervention. "Today, fifteen years later," [*sic*] he writes, "the Republic of Cuba still continues to function efficiently, a proof that Leonard Wood knows how to build for permanency." The record is that the second intervention began on September 29, 1906, and that the last American troops were not withdrawn until April 1, 1909. Leonard Wood did not participate in the second intervention.

Why was a second intervention required, in spite of the fact that Leonard Wood had left Cuba an independent proud democracy four years previously? I quote the *Encyclopedia Britannica*'s article on Cuba written by Mr. Francis Samuel Philbrick, "formerly Scholar and Resident Fellow of Harvard University, and member of the American Historical Association":

> In material prosperity the progress of the island from 1902 to 1906 was very great; but in its politics, various social and economic elements, and political habits and examples of Spanish provenience that ill-befit a democracy, led once more to revolution. Congress neglected to pass certain laws which were required by the constitution, and which, as regards municipal autonomy, independence of the judiciary, and congressional representation of minority parties, were intended to make impossible the abuses of centralized government that had characterized Spanish administration.

In other words Leonard Wood left Cuba with a "constitution" but without a political code and without an institutional life. The second intervention corrected this fatal defect, and only since then can it be said that there is an approach to "permanency." The regime set up by Leonard Wood's intervention lasted four years and two months; the regime of the second intervention has lasted eleven years. This does not destroy the credit that belongs to Wood for what he really did accomplish, but it does make rather thin the claim of his biographers that his work is "unparalleled in the annals of history," especially when that claim is put forward with careful silence about the revolution which followed this unparalleled performance.

Leonard Wood cleansed the island of Cuba. He did not build a structure that endured. By his own standard of "deeds not words" the record contradicts the claim that he is a statesman who has built institutions. That does not mean that he does not stand fairly high among military administrators. The qualification "military" is necessary. For Leonard Wood has never governed a free people. In all his life he has never done a big piece of work where he had to rely upon the consent of free men. Whatever efficiency he has exhibited has always been based ultimately upon military force, and has been displayed among men who could not disobey. "His administration in Cuba," says Mr. Eric Fisher Wood, "has been likened to a curious mixture of old town-meeting republicanism and absolute autocracy: he never used his authority for the sake of using it as the Spanish Governors had so often done, but when it was the last resort he set his jaw and used it to the limit."

That happens to be the doctrine of the benevolent despot, and it is in terms of that doctrine that the whole campaign for Leonard Wood is made. Consequently no one can prove that the General is qualified to administer the affairs of a self-governing people because his whole experience is in the administration of dependent peoples. How well he has ruled subject peoples is, as we have seen, open to dispute. It is not open to dispute that Leonard Wood has held no single office under democratic conditions. He is trained to administer when he can command; he is, if you like, a successful colonial governor; he is, if you insist upon it, a Cromer or a Kitchener or a Roberts. Has any one seriously proposed a Cromer or a Kitchener or a Roberts for prime minister of England?

It may be that Leonard Wood has in him unsuspected abilities as a statesman in a republic. They have never been exhibited in action. The whole of Leonard Wood's claim to be President among the American people rests not on deeds but on words. Words about his relation to Roosevelt, speeches about preparedness, magazine articles about Americanism, talks to audiences in various parts of the country. There are no facts available about his deeds as an American statesman. He has not governed a California as Johnson has, or an Illinois as Lowden has; he has not been a cabinet officer like

163

McAdoo, or an administrator by voluntary cooperation like Hoover. He proposes to jump from the government of dependent peoples and subordinate soldiers straight to the most difficult political office in the whole world. He cannot make the jump on a record of deeds. He is in fact trying to make the jump on a record of words.

The record of his words about preparedness. He was, after Roosevelt, the foremost propagandist for military foresight at a time when such a propaganda was needed. It was no fault of his that the political setting made him the agitator instead of the executive of preparedness. But unless you choose to regard the Plattsburg camps as conclusive and outstanding evidence of Presidential qualities, the fact remains that more than any other candidate conspicuously mentioned, the man who pretends most to despise words, has little but words to recommend him for the office he is seeking.

Wood is a successful agitator with a following. It is a comparatively small but fervent nucleus of people who have responded to his words and his quality. They are people with much money and great zeal, and they are truly convinced that they have a cause and a prophet. The arguments about Cuba are afterthoughts. The directing impulse was born in the period of American neutrality when the country was drifting dangerously without military preparation. Leonard Wood was one of the first to see this. For the ulterior objects of this war he cared nothing in particular, but for war, efficiently and triumphantly conducted, he cared a great deal. Roosevelt and he focussed and organized sentiment chiefly among the upper strata of society in the big cities, in the colleges and among the intellectuals. The mass of the people they did not convert,—that was done by the President with his democratic formulas. But the inner sect of the war party was Wood and Roosevelt, and that sect is Wood today.

At certain stages of the war, this sect may indeed have made a decisive and saving difference. That is a question for the historians. The significant thing now is what that sect has become. It has been deeply affected by an unhappy experience in the war. Its members were not employed actively or long enough to consume their energy, and they have been ever since in a state of balked impulse. Their frayed nerves were easily infected with the fiercest phases of the war psychology, and they have boiled and fretted and fumed. The hatreds and violence, which were jammed up without issue in action against the enemy, turned against all kinds of imaginary enemies—the enemy within, the enemy to the south, the enemy at Moscow, the Negro, the immigrant, the labor union, —against anything that might be treated as a plausible object for unexpended feeling.

This sect has been called conservative. It is not that in any accurate sense of the term. It is far too reckless to be called conservative. The word must be reserved for men like Lord Robert Cecil and Mr. Hughes. The sect has been called reactionary. That also is inaccurate for the last thing this sect has in mind is a return to the easy-going, decentralized, unregimented America of the nineteenth century. It has been called capitalistic. It is not capitalistic, if that means that it is interested in the administration of capitalism. The sect is radical jingo with the prejudices of the Junker rather than of the great industrialists. It really is incapable of distinguishing between the military government of an occupied country like Cuba and the civil government of the United States. It is a mystical sect of innovators who propose to exalt the federal government into a state of supreme and unquestionable authority. They are not finicky about law or principle. If the biographers of the General are a fair sample, they do not know much about law or principle. They have the mood, if not the courage, of the coup d'état. They have backed every attack on civil liberty. They propose to "save" by a searching of hearts and a use of force. They are the moving spirit in the performance at Albany, and Speaker Sweet has had what amounts to a blessing from the Conservator of Americanism.

The real Wood nucleus is, however, too small to win an

election. It is not too small to run a campaign. It has money
and conviction. What it lacks is votes, and these it is now
seeking earnestly and painfully. The problem for the sectari-
ans is: how to transfer their own zeal to a majority of the
electorate? Their own response to the General is electric. His
force and his recklessness and the conqueror in him have
attracted about all the people in America whose fears find an
answer in his strength or whose recklessness finds expression
in his. The rest is hard going. The bulk of the people are either attracted to other men, or they are prosaic and not easily
inflammable.

To them the General has addressed his recent speeches and
articles, with every once in a while a stimulating word to the
sect. Thus the General's pronouncements fall into two classes.
You may call them the original and the derived, the personal
and the expedient—those which express the General's impulse, and those which are meant to catch the Republican
vote. The two classes of statements are distinct both in subject matter and in rhetorical emphasis. In the first class you
hear the leader of the sect, the real hero of the biographies,
the mystical patriot, the conqueror. In the second, and more
recent, class of public statements, you hear the mumbling of
the amateur Republican trying his level best to remember and
repeat the Republican catchwords of 1920.

To illustrate the temporary eclipse of the vivid Wood in
the vote-getting Wood take these two utterances on the subject closest to his heart—the subject of war and peace. The
first was made before he was a serious candidate, April 24,
1919. He was speaking to wounded soldiers in a hospital at
Detroit. Talk that any covenant, he said, will protect the
world from future war, is "idle twaddle and a dream of mol-
lycoddles." That was from the heart. Compare it with his
reply of February 11, 1920, when questioned by Senator
Borah:

I believe we should accept the League of Nations as
modified and safeguarded by existing Lodge reservations.

> . . . I am in favor of and shall continue to be in favor of
> the well-established foreign policy of this government
> which conserves and promotes the interest of our own
> country . . . One aim . . . has always been the promotion of
> the peace of the world.

As the Colonel might have remarked, when the elections are
at hand the weasels go to work.

Clearly the twaddle and mollycoddle vein is authentic. To
it belongs the General's statesmanlike contribution to the
problem of how best to deal with the revolutionary immigrant.
"My motto for the Reds," he said last December to the Colorado Farmers Congress, "is 'S.O.S.'—ship or shoot. I believe
we should place them all on a ship of stone, with sails of lead
and that their first stopping place should be Hell." In the
same class belong his more amiable exhortations to women
voters about their babies, to the citizens at large about the
way to preserve the national stock, about how to create democracy by means of training camps, and just how to assay
the percentage of patriotism in your neighbor. Any student of
the higher literature of Prussianism in any country will recognize at once the choice of subjects and the emphasis.
Power and prestige based on the dogma of the inheritance of
acquired characteristics (Leonard Wood has "hereditary traits
—medical, patriotic, executive") as preparedness for war regarded as a permanent and beneficial institution, accompanied by a lack of real interest in social and economic questions, except as they affect the supreme power state. Mutatis
mutandis, it is all in Houston Stewart Chamberlain, only for
him the magic word is Germanic. "And tortured one poor
word ten thousand ways."

I have called this the authentic Wood. It corresponds accurately to the experiences of his life. Where Roosevelt, the
American statesman, boasted of the many racial strains that
were in him, Wood, the bearer of our White Man's burden,
permits and encourages his biographers to boast that his is the
pure blood of a chosen people. The essential difference be-

167

tween the two friends is revealed right there, the one exuberantly catholic and national, the other intensely sectarian and factional. Roosevelt at his greatest sought to speak for a church that was at least as universal as America; Wood in his most genuine moments is a member of a quarrelsome tribe.

But an appearance of catholicity he must have to secure the office he seeks. And so in recent months he has taken to himself, besides Mr. Frank Hitchcock, a perfunctory platform of views. They have no personal flavor whatever. They have none of the emphasis and none of the emotional tone that pervades the rest of his thought. They are worn like civilian clothes. But they are all tabulated in eleven articles of faith which prove the perfect Republican orthodoxy of the General.

They are (a) that we must go slow in paying the war debt and we must not tax excess profits; (b) that we must regulate privately owned railroads equitably, properly, "etc."; (c) that in foreign affairs we should be "strong, dignified, and conservative," but must protect American interests and trade; (d) that we should have "a small but excellent army and ever-ready navy"; (e) "a well equipped diplomatic and consular service"; (f) "suitable working conditions" and "an honest day's wage for an honest day's work," just how not stated by the General; (g) a protective tariff; (h) "we" should develop "a suitable merchant marine," the "we" undefined by the General; (i) economy and a budget; (j) respect for law and order; (k) no class legislation, "but" that the government be maintained under the constitution, "each department functioning strictly within its own limits."

It will readily be seen from this that the boldness and plain speaking of the General have temporarily been suppressed in the interests of his campaign for hard-boiled Republican delegates and one hundred per cent Republican business men. The General remains a terrible lion to the voteless, a brave advocate of causes that do not enter into the duties of a President, an evangelist of the spirit, but on the excess profit tax, the tariff, the Lodge reservations and the other articles of Republicanism, he is as regular as Warren G. Harding himself.

I do not wish, however, to leave the impression that Leonard Wood is morally a timid man. He is cautious at the moment, both about his platform and about resigning from the army. He has, it is true, nothing whatever to say that can be called his own on any concrete question of modern statesmanship. Nevertheless, there are energies within him, energies that do not exist in canned goods politicians like Harding. The energies of Leonard Wood are banked down just now to facilitate the scramble for delegates. But they are there. They are energies of ambition and of domination greater, I believe, than any that have appeared in American political life within our generation. They are energies that a military career of a spasmodic kind has whetted but not satisfied or organized. The energies of Leonard Wood are fiercer than his intellectual equipment can employ or control. The intemperateness of his speech and recklessness of his manner are the visible signs of a nervous system overstrained by long frustration and incomplete exercise. The energies of Wood are pent; when they issue they follow the patterns of his experience which are to use force, to ship or shoot, to act as the conqueror does among inferior peoples. There is no composure in the character of Wood. There is instead the titan's and romanticist's uneasiness in an apoplectic soul. This looks superficially like strength, and is easily mistaken for it.

March 17, 1920

THE LOGIC OF LOWDEN

Frank O. Lowden had served two terms in the House
of Representatives and was elected governor of Illinois
in 1917. Though particularly identified with the interests of the farm belt, he was a humane and likable man
with broad interests and tolerances. The "Johnson" mentioned in the piece is Hiram Johnson of California, the
candidate of what remained of the Progressive Republicans. Lowden declined nomination for Vice President
in 1924 and thereafter interested himself in the Car-
negie Endowment for International Peace and other
virtuous and semi-virtuous causes. He died in 1943.
[*A.S., jr.*]

There is a logic to Lowden, once you grant the premises.
He comes from the middle of the country, he stands in the
middle of a road, in the middle of his party, about midway
between Wood of New Hampshire and Johnson of California.
He has risen from a farm to an estate, from obscurity to moderate fame, perhaps not quite the darling of the gods but
surely one of their favorite sons. They rejoiced over him at the
start, worried over him a while and watched him solicitously,
and now smile again. He entered politics when Cannon and
Lorimer were powerful. He was of the Old Guard at Chicago
in 1912, and yet not of them altogether. He voted for Taft
without making an enemy of Roosevelt. He stayed with the
party and he will always stay with the party. He does not
secede himself, but he does not excommunicate those who
do. So Roosevelt could write to him in 1916: "I earnestly

170

hope you will now assume a position of leadership. What I
most desire is that you shall help bring the Republicans far
enough forward to enable us to hold the Progressives far
enough back to keep a substantial alignment." He is thus the
candidate of peace without victory for those who stood at
Armageddon and battled for the Lord.

It is a series of events in the past that emphasize the candidacy of Lowden today. His most intelligent supporters regard him as a kind of liquidator of situations which happen
to control American public life today and may continue to
control them for a short time after the election. The first of
these is the grim memory of the politicians that Johnson se-
ceded in 1912, and ratified only with nullifying reservations
in 1916. The second is the eight years of Republican famine
under Wilson plus the recollection of the seven years turbu-
lence under Roosevelt which have combined to create a nau-
sea at strong men, moral heroes, crusaders, saviors, and
supermen. The third is the condition of the voters, more composed than they were a few months ago, but still jumpy and
yawning for a rest. The people are tired, tired of noise, tired
of politics, tired of inconvenience, tired of greatness, and
longing for a place where the world is quiet and where all
trouble seems dead leaves and spent waves riot in doubtful
dreams of dreams.

Lowden is the noiseless candidate in this campaign. I have
watched him appeal to the voters. He tells them that he will
talk only of prosaic things, and he does. He assures them
that he won't bother them much and he will not. He promises to relieve their taxes, to see that the government is un-
obtrusive, and that it will run itself without too much cost
and without too much friction. He does not invite them to
look to Washington for salvation, or to stake much hope
upon politics. He invites them to go about their own business
with the sense that though the government is a necessary
institution which ought to be run inexpensively and well, it
is not the chief instrument of destiny. His own campaign lit-

171

erature names in the first of five reasons why he is "outstanding Presidential timber" the fact that "many have called him a second McKinley."

There is nothing highfalutin' about Lowden. He is not burning with moral zeal or with personal ambition. He has a diminished conception of the office which he seeks, and if he represents any "movement" it is the movement away from overshadowing personalities in the White House. Wood and Johnson arouse fierce passions, inquisitor and crusader, hot blue blood, and hot red blood. They are the turbulent spirits of the Republican campaign: Johnson the expansive, pioneering courage of continental America, Wood the angry ambitions of a receding caste in the first crude manifestation of world power. Both represent an idealization of the American purpose and, therefore, at this moment a somewhat highly flavored version of it. But Lowden is unmistakably the typical member of a going concern, the experienced guardian and manipulator of established American custom in the relation between business and politics. That is the logic of Lowden. His premise is the American social system, modified from time to time by the reformer, but never captured by him. In that system the progressive is free to permeate if he is content also to be permeated. ". . . help bring the Republicans far enough forward to enable us to hold the Progressives far enough back" for what purpose? "To keep a substantial alignment."

The philosophy of a substantial alignment is the premise of Lowdenism. Historically it is a real premise, no matter how unreal it may prove to be in the years to come. The philosophy when it is articulate, says that in a country so vast as this the differences between sections and between classes are so numerous that organized government would be unworkable if all local interests and all class interests were clearly represented in political action: that without the selecting and neutralizing and binding peace of the two party system the American constitution would be infinitely confused. The philosophy asserts that without the coercion of a national partisanship over all factional differences national unity could not have been created and national administration organized. This philosophy accords usefulness to the political machine for which the ordinary reformer does not make allowance. That function is the fusing of localism by the attachment of local leaders to a national organization in which they have a vested interest. The power of that machine is the power to enforce conformity by blockading political advancement of those who do not work with it and through it. In its higher reaches this philosophy insists that no particular reform achieved by a destruction of the machine is valuable enough to warrant the destruction; that to capture the machine from within is legitimate, to secede and break it and try to supplant it is dangerous and in the end vain.

Now among the convinced machinists there are, of course, immovable and corrupt men mixed with shrewd and generous men. The usual opposition of temperaments and interests occurs within a political machine as within any other human group. There is a right, a center, and a left wing, and all gradations between. There are the usual bourbons who will never learn, and finally destroy the institution if they govern it. There are those who work from within to readjust it to new necessities. And there are those in the center who, recognizing the need of fresh adjustments, devote themselves to hauling the bourbons along while they hang on to the coat tails of the reformers. Lowden belongs to this center, to the right center in all great questions of statesmanship, to the left center in questions of routine and partisanship. The center, mind you, is the center of the Republican party conceived as one of the two indispensable organs of government. I am not discussing whether that party as a whole is too far to the right to govern America successfully after a world war. I am not discussing it here because the consciousness that there is such a question is not part of the premise on which the Lowden campaign proceeds.

The Lowden campaign is not based on any diagnosis of the social system. The Wood campaign is. The picture, it seems to me, is frenzied and misleading, but it is a picture. There is a conscious social theory behind Wood, as there is behind Johnson and Hoover. The attention of these men is fixed upon the country; the attention of the Lowden campaign is fixed upon Congress and the departments and the mechanism of parties. It is fixed on these primarily. The impulse behind the Lowden campaign is that an election is decreed by law for this year, that a man must be elected to the office of President who will do the job well. The job is conceived as the administration of the government at Washington, not as a moral purification, not as the redemption of America from perils, not as gawdsaking in any form.

It is characteristic that while Wood is the hero of a large number of biographies, while Johnson is personally known and loved by multitudes of people, there are no biographies of Lowden and he is comparatively little discussed. He is not a household name as yet. He has not been extensively and intensely analyzed. The talk about him is not curious and eager talk. He is not a natural subject for American publicity. He rarely says witty things; and he has almost no gift of phrase. To find out about Lowden you have to inquire among people who have known him. I have found no substantial disagreement among his friends and his critics.

He was born in 1861 at Sunrise, Minnesota. As a little boy he followed his father's prairie schooner into Iowa. He taught school when he was a young man, and worked his way through Iowa State University. He seems to have been extraordinarily winning, and many stories are told of the way in which his genius for making friends presided over the opportunities which were offered to him. Frank Lowden was the sort of student whom everyone accepts as a coming man. He has been a good deal of a regular fellow in his time, and at sixty the marks are there. But the underlying texture is homespun—however much it may have been overlaid.

174

He came to Chicago in 1885 and worked as a law clerk; he studied law at what is now Northwestern University; his quick professional successes corresponded with quick social success. In the early nineties there were plenty of silver spoons offered in lieu of the one he had lacked at birth. He seems to have been a lawyer engaged primarily in the organization of what are loosely called "trusts." He made money. In 1896 he married into the social set to which he had been adopted. He married the daughter of George M. Pullman. I mention it because it is always mentioned in connection with Lowden, not because I can trace any specific result of the Governor's relation to the family which sacrificed its name to one of the outstanding horrors of a hurried civilization. He has been accused, of course, of a corporate bias, but that bias, such as it is, is the bias of his time and his group, and not specific to the sleeping cars. The Wood supporters in South Dakota charge that a tax commission appointed by Lowden reduced the assessed valuation of powerful public service corporations including the Pullman Company. The charge was made by Mr. William H. Malone, the former president of the State Board of Equalization. This board was elective. It was abolished in the Lowden reorganization of state affairs. Said Mr. Malone:

> The Pullman Corporation was favored with a reduction of $17,802,284 from the 1918 figure established by the old board of $33,802,284 to the 1919 figure fixed by the Lowden Commission of $16,000,000.

The Lowden reply is as follows. It comes to me in the form of a personal letter from Mr. Frank H. Scott of the firm of Scott, Bancroft, Martin, and Stephens:

> Governor Lowden does not own any stock or securities of the Pullman Company; Mrs. Lowden owns less than one per cent of the stock of the company; the entire Pullman family owns something less than six per cent, including Mrs. Lowden's interest.

In the investigation referred to (i. e., by a joint
committee of the Legislature) each person who had made
any charge that the Governor had interested himself for the
Pullman Company, was put upon the stand before the
investigating committee. The charges collapsed utterly. The
State Board of Equalization had for years been looked
upon as one of the most iniquitous factors in the
government of Illinois, and for years governors of the state
had desired to see it abolished. Governor Lowden, months
before the charges were made or before any question of
raising the Pullman taxes had arisen, instructed Mr.
Woodward to prepare the bill abolishing the Board and
establishing a Tax Commission of three members. Certain
members of the Board concocted a scheme to defeat the
bill by raising the Pullman Company's assessment and then
following that by statements that the Governor, through
the State Director of Finance, had threatened to present a
bill abolishing the Board if the taxes were raised. As I
have said, the fact was that the bill was prepared months
before the question of raising the Pullman assessment had
been broached. Governor Lowden immediately demanded
an investigation by a joint committee of the Legislature.
That the matter was a plot was so clearly exposed that the
Legislature, the majority of whose members had been
opposed to the bill abolishing the Board, immediately
passed it by an overwhelming majority.

Men with established fortunes who have political careers
ahead of them do not behave as these charges allege. They
are not credible charges, for they involve an undue simplifi-
cation of the economic interpretation of politics. What determines the point of view of Lowden is not Pullman money or
any strong-box full of securities. He is determined by the prevailing views of an established order of business and politics
in which he has been a favored person. The determinism is
by no means complete. The history of Lowden shows a steady

modification of the normal views of his environment by the interests of a personal career. To put it very bluntly Lowden has all that money can buy, and he seeks now the things that money does not buy. His later career is marked by the growing independence of an independent fortune and conspicuous political success.

It was not always so. Lowden's apprenticeship in politics began with the first McKinley campaign. He was offered patronage by McKinley and declined. But his political associations from the Republican convention of 1900 through the gubernatorial contest of 1904 when he was defeated for the nomination, through three terms in Congress, through the convention of 1912 to his election as Governor in 1916 are without evidence of independence of the dark forces of American politics. Lowden went to the top through the usual channels, a rich man and a favored man accepting the standards of his time.

The change comes after his election as Governor. Lowden braced up. Lowden reformed. Lowden made himself one of the very best state governors in America. Again and again I was told in Chicago by friends and opponents that they had expected nothing and that he had done extremely well.

The thing he did was to persuade the legislature to adopt a radical reorganization of the business of the state, by consolidating about a hundred and twenty-five separate boards and departments into nine departments, with a real budget and with a centralized purchasing agency. Of course, extravagant claims have been made. I have heard Lowden orators talk as if these reforms would solve all social wrongs from the high cost of living to industrial unrest. I heard the Governor in Detroit make rather over-enthusiastic claims. And it is well to take with caution the figures as to tax reduction.

That, however, is not the significant aspect in a definition of Lowden as a Presidential candidate. The scheme is not his scheme. It is the result of expert investigation started before he was Governor. It embodies ideas that are the common property of administrative reformers. The thing which is Lowden's is primarily that he could take up an idea so unpleasant to the politicians of all parties, and yet persuade and compel them to accept it with a minimum of friction. There lies his strength. That would be his strength in Washington. He has shown extraordinary skill in dealing with our kind of representative government. He has the patience and the good fellowship and the modesty to find his way tolerably well through the existing confusion in America between legislature and executive. No other man mentioned, Wood, Hoover, Johnson, starts with much prospect of good feeling between the White House and the Capitol. Lowden has that prospect, a very heavy factor, indeed, in the logic of his candidacy.

But, of course, internal good feeling on Pennsylvania Avenue is not the whole of statecraft in this age. And when you examine Lowden's external relations the outlook is different. He has shown in Illinois that he can in some of his appointments be quite class-blind. His dealings with labor in Illinois show tolerance and good will and consideration but little more can be said for them. On state business he is a well-informed enthusiastic man; on all the wider questions of diplomacy, and economics, even on the wider aspects of his own administrative reforms, he is meager. Because he is meager he bends to every wind of doctrine that blows in the circle of his associates.

He has had the red hysteria mildly, and because he is fundamentally uncritical and alien to the world of ideas, his oratory is full of stock prejudice and canned platitude. They are part of the going concern. But the homespun saves him. Real contact with the Prussian spirit in America is doing to Lowden what it will always do to the balanced American, to the American who is not exalté. It is resurrecting the good humor of free men. Lowden may have said and done foolish things in the recent excitement, but he did them as a member of a crowd and because he is gregarious, not because they are organic to him. And he has done some wise things re-

178

cently. In the last few months when so many Americans have been frightened into violence, Lowden has been a good deal the candid friend of local big business. He has reminded Chicagoans of the familiar idea about sitting on the safety valve.

He has done it as one of them, and that too is part of the logic of Lowden. He is one of the insiders who know when they have had enough, know when to yield, know when not to stand pat. He believes, as Roosevelt said, in a substantial alignment; he is shrewd enough and sufficiently professional in politics to know when the strain and stress are too great. He will feel the pressure rather than understand it, and he will feel it concretely not as the incarnation of an ideology. He will go only a very little way with the reconstruction, but when he has reached the end the first thing that occurs to him will not be to ship or shoot. He is a clean opponent and a tolerant human being.

No volcanic ambitions dominate him. He is a normally satisfied man, without restlessness and with a capacity for contentment. He is not fiercely avid of power nor of fame, and he is under no delusion that he is the savior of America. He is a leading candidate this year because the turn of the calendar brings the campaign at a time when old situations are still controlling and newer alignments not quite formed. The logic of Lowden is excellent on the premise that the present mood of public discussion is a true reflection of what the next President must face. On no other.

April 14, 1920

MCADOO

W. G. McAdoo was a lawyer and promoter who made his mark when he built the first tunnel under the Hudson River. He took an active part in the 1912 campaign, became a brilliant Secretary of the Treasury during World War I and married Wilson's daughter. However, Wilson himself cherished hopes of renomination in 1920, and his son-in-law did not benefit from presidential support. In 1920 McAdoo's reputation was at its zenith. At the Democratic convention in 1924 McAdoo, his name somewhat tarnished by the backing of the Ku Klux Klan, led for many ballots; but the convention in desperation eventually turned to John W. Davis. In 1932 McAdoo delivered the vote of the California delegation to Franklin D. Roosevelt and insured his nomination. He served as senator from California from 1933 to 1939 and then became chairman of the American President Lines. He died in 1941. [*A.S., jr.*]

If the Republicans do not nominate a man who can interest the people now voting for Johnson, and if the Democrats nominate McAdoo, it will be a hot summer for the Republican candidate; and about September fifteenth Mr. Will Hays will begin to sleep badly. For McAdoo is a little like Lloyd George. He knows not only what the owners of votes are thinking now, but what they will be excited about a few weeks from now. He has the political sense: he mobilized his war psychology before most people, and he demobilized it before the rest. He has the gift, which Roosevelt had and

180

Wood lacks, of feeling with, but just ahead, of the mass of the voters, in short the gift of popular sympathy. He is possessed by what he feels, and men possessed in politics are infectious. Of all candidates he has incomparably the greatest sensibility to the prevailing winds of public opinion. Johnson, who is no mean politician himself, is by comparison immovable because more elemental; Wood is torpid and Lowden contracted and Hoover detached and deductive, but McAdoo is swift to note and swift to tack.

He picks his course quickly, moves fast upon it, and with great audacity. It may not be quite true, as one interviewer claims, that Secretary McAdoo made eight or nine important decisions one day going down in the elevator of a building in Washington, but it is somewhat in the direction of the truth. He is an agile man. He does not hesitate or brood or procrastinate or reflect at length. Instinctively he prefers the bold and the decisive to the prudent and tepid course, for he is a statesman grafted upon a promoter. The man described as the entrepreneur in the economic textbooks is, I think, the basic McAdoo, the kind of man who really likes enterprise more than profit, organizes ideas, and anticipates wants. That kind of man is first "sold" himself to an idea and then "sells" others. What he is determined to do he is passionately determined to do, once he falls into his stride. He said in 1915, when addressing the Chamber of Commerce of the United States at Washington in advocacy of the Shipping Bill:

> Since I have come to Washington there is one word in the English language with which I have become more familiar than any other, because it is the one word that is used most. I say that advisedly. I use it myself too much, and every time I use it I get ashamed of myself. You can talk to any man about anything and the first thing he says is, "I am afraid of so-and-so and so-and-so." He is afraid of something. Where is the courage of the American nation? Where is that virile power that has made this Ameri-

can nation great? Has it disappeared? I do not believe it. We are not afraid of anything, my friends, so long as we walk the path of rectitude and justice as a nation, and we intend to do that; and if this shipping bill passes all this talk about getting into international difficulties is mere twaddle.

There are, I imagine, things of which McAdoo is afraid but they are not the usual spooks which terrify public officials. He is not afraid of responsibility, nor of dinner table gossip, nor of Congressional investigation, nor of private life, nor of the editorial writers, nor of experiment. Above all he is not afraid of words. He is remarkably free of the clatter made by rusty old tin can words like reactionary, radical, socialistic.

I believe there is no intelligent banker, business man, or citizen of this country, who understands the Federal Reserve system and its workings, who does not thank God for the great law which created that system, whether it be socialistic or whether it puts the government into the banking business or not. *October 13, 1915, before the Chamber of Commerce of Indianapolis*

He had fought for that system and had helped to make it, he was for it, he was "sold," and he was prepared to thank God for it, and make a monkey of any one from Senator Root down who had opposed it. When McAdoo is under way he treats them rough, as almost any Republican candidate would quickly discover. He will not stand on ceremony. If he thinks miners are underpaid, if he knows that mine operators are overpaid, if he sees the government muddling, he will not hesitate to call the public's attention to the statistics of profits which exist for public use in Senate document No. 259, 65th Congress, 2nd Session.

In that famous instance he did no more than quote figures which over a year and a quarter had been public property, but he will not play an insider's game as insiders play it. He has not the normal reticence and inhibitions of finance and

politics. By experience as well as temperament he is an outsider who knows the inside wires. He is disposed at critical
moments to tell more than is usually told, even at the risk of
inconveniencing a few people and of scandalizing many. Mc-
Adoo is distinctly not a safe person in the ordinary use of the
word. He is less safe than most devout progressives because
he is so clever and so sophisticated. He has a devilish knowledge of the tender spots, and a willingness to touch them occasionally.

What restrains him is not etiquette, nor the sentiments of
the best people, nor fear of novelty, nor the compulsions of
routine and tradition. He is not organized by a class feeling,
nor by a set of profoundly imbedded general principles. He
is organized by a remarkable sense of what a governing majority of voters wants and will receive. He is aware of himself and of the political possibilities. He is bold to seize the
possibilities, but prudent not to overstep them. He is not a
gambler and not a fanatic and not an evangelical reformer.
He is a projector of concrete programs, and a promoter who
can reveal to people that those programs embody what they
already desire, and he is an administrator of the first order.
McAdoo is a man who makes his way in the world, not by
conformity but by initiative, not by pull or regularity or even
by genius, but by his wits. He is the kind of man who is self-
made several times over. He is big at any rate in two dimen-
sions. He has length and breadth if not depth.

The defects of his virtues are revealed rather clearly in the
statement he issued some months ago about the finances of
the government. There was a cry at that time to the effect
that posterity should pay a larger portion of the costs of the
war. The cry has served as General Wood's financial religion
ever since, although on second thought people are beginning
to think differently. McAdoo was caught by the gust.

> I think the present generation could with perfect
> propriety hand on to posterity the ultimate settlement of
> that part of our debt which remains unliquidated.

And therefore he proposed a highly ingenious scheme of funding and postponing, coupled with a plan to buy Jamaica, the Bahamas, Barbados, Nassau, British Honduras, and the Bermudas with British obligations. In public office such a stunt would probably not emanate from McAdoo, for he has the faculty of surrounding himself with excellent men. The proposal was prestidigitated out of private life, but it illustrates one aspect of the free play of his mind. It originated in a superficial public opinion of which he was acutely aware, and it was fertilized by a clever imagination. But it was not governed by sustained conviction about the enduring obligations and needs of a democratic people. It was facile and it was bold, but not calculated to produce the profoundest confidence.

I have deliberately selected what seems to me the worst example I can find. It is probably not typical, but it is an exaggerated symptom to be noted. Mr. McAdoo has been a truly distinguished public servant. When the smoke of manufactured opinion clears away, his administration of the railroads will probably be regarded as a piece of heroic and successful intervention in one of the worst crises of the war. There are not many who can estimate the work of any Secretary of the Treasury, and I am not one of them. But I have heard observers who were detached, had a chance to know, and knew how to know, rate McAdoo very high among Treasury officials. There is really no question of the practical competence of McAdoo. There is no more question of it than there is of Hoover's. Both are remarkable organizers and remarkable executives.

The doubt about McAdoo is really the obverse of the doubt about Hoover. Personally Hoover is extraordinarily fine and sensitive, but politically he has shown himself to be secluded and unaware. Lacking stimulation from the mass, he deduces opinions from a few stock ideas, in any political situation where his energy is not focussed by a specific task. McAdoo is less intricate personally, but infinitely more sensitive to the stimulus of popular feeling. When he misjudges that feeling, as of course he must occasionally, or when the important thing is not popular feeling but the governing ideas of a situation beyond the scope of immediate practical application, then McAdoo is likely to be quite conventional and rhetorical and flat, and to cater. His speeches on foreign affairs, especially in the early stages of the Treaty, are of this order. On the Fourth of July, 1919, for example, he was arguing for the Treaty: "Separate the League of Nations from the Treaty and it would be utterly impossible to enforce the Treaty . . ." That was the time July, 1919, when nobody had read the Treaty and everybody liked it because it was hard on the Huns. A year later Mr. McAdoo was saying something to the effect that God won the war but the devil won the peace. There had been the beginning of a radical change in public opinion. A beginning was enough. A hint is enough for McAdoo, but he needs the hint.

Thus in recent interviews he has been courageous and straightforward on contentious questions affecting civil liberty, Russia, the Palmer injunctions and the whole paraphernalia of the Red hysteria. He has talked the way free men are supposed to talk about these things. But he was not among the first to protest, because he is not fundamentally moved by the simple moralities. He is liberal but worldly, he is bold but immediate, he is brave but not selfless. He would win many skirmishes, and make brilliant dashes, and achieve some victories, but for the long strategic campaigning of democracy, it is hard to tell about him. It would all depend, I imagine, as indeed ultimately it always does, on the spirit and intelligence of the rank and file.

June 2, 1920

CHICAGO 1920

Philander C. Knox, who had served as Attorney General for McKinley and Roosevelt and Secretary of State for Taft, was now senator from Pennsylvania. William C. Sproul was governor of Pennsylvania. Irvine L. Lenroot was senator from Wisconsin. James W. Wadsworth was senator from New York. Reed Smoot of Utah, Boies Penrose of Pennsylvania and James Watson of Indiana were more of the Republican Old Guard. Mrs. Robinson was Theodore Roosevelt's sister. [*A.S., jr.*]

It was true, of course, that it mattered a great deal what was decided and who was chosen at Chicago. But a more compelling fact is that Chicago was too hot, the Coliseum too crowded, the hotel lobbies too nerve wracking, and the prices too high, for an enduring interest either in the future of the world or even in the assured victory of the Republican party. One delegate blurted it out on Thursday evening:

There aren't three hundred delegates in this convention who care enough personally about the result to perspire all Sunday and pay twenty dollars a day in order to start Monday morning looking for the right candidate. Saturday night is their limit, and they will vote for anybody who can win by Saturday night. All they ask is to be told by somebody, who acts as if he knew, the name of the man who is going to win.

It has been called an unbossed convention. It was in fact a convention hopelessly astray until it found men to boss it. Being unbossed consisted in having no purpose or will except the will to get out of Chicago. It happened that one set of bosses showed the uninstructed delegates the quickest way to achieve that object. Had they not shown a way, the delegates might easily have stampeded some other way if that was also the way home. Thus when the Old Guard, speaking through the neo-classic Mr. Lodge, seemed to be hurrying matters, the delegates were satisfied; whenever Mr. Lodge and his friends proposed delay there were howls of protest, and a glimmer of insurgency.

Harding was chosen, not because the convention was in love with him, but because his was the first name seriously proposed to end the deadlock. Had he failed to secure a steadily mounting vote in the ballots on Saturday morning, had it looked like another deadlock lasting over until Monday, Harding would have faded. A drift towards some one else, perhaps Sproul or Knox, would have set in at once. But by the clever manipulation of sixty or seventy votes on Saturday morning so as to create the illusion of an irresistible tide, the clique was able to start a rush to Harding which was really a rush for the next train out of Chicago.

It was a coup by master politicians who knew just what they wanted at a time when all other groups wanted the impossible. Wood was impossible, Lowden was disqualified, Johnson was impossible, Hoover was inconceivable, and as for Lenroot, Knox, Sproul or Coolidge, no powerful group wanted them badly enough on Saturday. The dark horses were waiting for Monday or Tuesday. Each expected to win as Harding won, by sheer fatigue from a deadlock, but all of them miscalculated the endurance of the delegates.

That the deadlock was deliberately prolonged in order to reduce the resistance to Harding, there can be no doubt. The way big batches of votes were distributed in the early ballots shows that to have been the case. Not accident, but design

kept Wood and Lowden neck and neck on the ballots of
Friday in such a way as at one and the same time to raise
false hopes among their followers, and yet convince the
uninstructed delegates that neither could win. Take New
York: On the first three ballots Wood had 10, 19, 23 votes
respectively. On the fourth he went down to 20. On the fifth,
sixth, seventh and eighth he had 24, 23, 24, 23. Did these
votes represent conviction or a plan? If we assume that the
New York delegates were voting for a definite candidate then
there was an open-minded gentleman on the delegation who
was for Wood on the fifth, against him on the sixth, for him
on the seventh, and against him on the eighth. I suspect there
was no such gentleman. I am inclined to doubt whether Senator Wadsworth could name the delegates who were for
Wood and for Lowden on each of the ballots. I am inclined
to suspect that the 88 votes of New York were distributed
so as to tease Wood and Lowden, prevent a combination
Friday night, and compel a deadlock. I am inclined to think
the same thing happened in certain other delegations. It was
this perfect control of a few powerful states which created
the nucleus for the stampede of the delegates who in all
senses of the word were uninstructed.

The master minds who worked this ingenious mechanical
play had a rather simple idea. They were, as Senator Lodge
insisted in a voice magnified by the electrical apparatus out
of all proportion to his body, against the autocracy of Wilson,
against despotism, dynasties, tyrants. To the public, whether
in the galleries or among the delegates, these phrases meant
the isolation of Wilson, his stubbornness, the dismissal of
Lansing, his jealousy of advice, his self-sufficiency. But to
men like Smoot, Lodge, Penrose, Watson, the phrases had
a longer history. They were associated quite as definitely with
Roosevelt as with Wilson, quite as certainly with the Roosevelt dynasty as with the Wilson. The audience may have been
thinking of McAdoo, but the clique was thinking no less of
Wood and Johnson, the Bull Moose, 1912 and 1916. The
name of Roosevelt was uttered with Lincoln's in every speech,

but the determination to have none of Roosevelt was as fixed as ever it was eight years ago and four years ago. Under cover of what they called Americanism and constitutional government the elder statesmen were determined to restore the party to what it was before the White House became the source of all authority.

So the candidacies confronted a mass of delegates seeking no one in particular, a clique of experienced politicians in control of certain critical delegations, and a suffused distrust of the great man in any form. To make an impression was not an easy thing. Lowden, Wood, Johnson and Hoover, each had his own approach, and the failure in each case was instructive.

Lowden came the nearest to success because Lowden most nearly fitted the specifications. In fact, Lowden, while not the choice of the clique, was nevertheless the choice of very powerful sections of the party. He collected delegates in the regular way, made no dire threats, and after Harding's miserable performance in Ohio and Indiana was regarded as more likely to win in November. He would probably have been nominated, but for the revelations in Missouri. The Lowden affair was a mishap, as it happened, a most convenient mishap.

Wood appeared before the convention as the heir of Roosevelt. Now to the mind of the romantic people who boomed him, and the affluent amateurs who endowed him, this fact was supposed to be an enormous asset. It was in fact a fatal liability. The men who had twice rejected Roosevelt living were not the kind to accept a reduced replica known to have an inveterate fondness for kitchen cabinets and personal government. Wood embodied all the qualities these politicians had most hated in Roosevelt, and none of the force which they had feared.

For Wood went to the convention without any of TR's great popularity. He seemed to be popular with the family and he bore a superficial resemblance to one aspect of Roosevelt. His impulse in that convention was not that of the popular hero, but of the gilded amateur trying to manipulate delegates and push his way through by main force and awkwardness. The politicians knew, even if Mrs. Robinson didn't, that, as a substitute for Roosevelt, Leonard Wood was papier maché.

Johnson came to Chicago with a considerable popular squall behind him. But he had to face the results of the hysteria and the reaction among the well-to-do and powerful. The delegates and the galleries were proof against progressivism in any form, not merely stolidly proof as in 1916, but violently proof. What was Johnson to do? How was Johnson to remain true to himself and yet make himself acceptable to that crowd? The scheme which Johnson adopted was silence on domestic issues and extravagance about the League. The League was the only thing he talked about in Chicago because opposition to the League could be found equally among standpatters and progressives. Into his hatred of the League he sluiced all the emotion that could not conveniently exude into a domestic program. This hatred of the League he identified with Americanism, and for argument against the League he appealed in Chicago almost entirely to the simplest kind of national egotism. But Mr. Lodge and his friends needed no lessons in egotism from Hiram Johnson. They forbore pledging the party to ratification, a pledge, curiously enough, which seemed to satisfy the irreconcilables. Thus in one neat stroke Johnson was deprived of any excuse for a bolt. I do not mean to imply that Johnson could have been nominated by that convention. That was never possible. But it was possible for him to affect the result decisively. He affected it not at all. It was not necessary for Johnson to be manoeuvred into ineffective silence. The trap was devised by Johnson himself as a result of his concentration on one issue. The masters of that convention handed him one all day sucker and then left him to make the most of it.

The strategists for Hoover started with another scheme. Where Johnson was irreconcilable on one issue, Hoover was pictured as irreconcilable on no issue. Judge Miller actually told the convention that the Treaty plank was identically Mr. Hoover's about an hour after Mr. Wheeler of California had said it was identically Senator Johnson's. Strange as this may seem, it is not strange to any one who heard expounded the political philosophy of Mr. Hoover's managers. They were believers, they said, in the two party system; in that system they were personally devoted to the Republican party, so devoted that they would be loyal to any candidate on any platform. They then added that Mr. Hoover was a great man, and that lots of people wanted him to be President.

A more perfect reason for ignoring Mr. Hoover entirely could not have been framed. The politicians were not looking for a great man as everybody but a political ingenue understood. What was going on at Chicago was politics for politicians' reasons to politicians' ends. The only fact about Mr. Hoover that at any time could have interested the politicians was that the Hoover vote really mattered in the election. But the strategists, all of them successful business men and intensely practical about everything but the job before them, proceeded to open as wide a chasm as they could between Hoover and the Hoover vote. They first eliminated as thoroughly as they knew how all trace of the Hoover Democrats; they then eliminated as thoroughly as possible all recognizable difference in principle between Mr. Hoover and any other candidate who was being considered. They even got to the point of eliminating the verbal differences over the plank about the League. Thus equipped with no issue, no votes and no threat, they started to "negotiate" in a fast game with nothing to negotiate with except the undoubted excellence of Mr. Hoover. Ten and a half votes cast on the tenth ballot, some of them by men who had voted for Harding on the critical ninth ballot, were the result, together with the querulous complaint of one of the chief negotiators that the delegates would not take Hoover seriously.

Of course they wouldn't. Why should they take any progressives seriously when the progressives were scattered about among Johnson, Lowden, La Follette and Hoover and even Wood? When the stakes are the control of the party, what reason was there for listening to the independents who can unite on no platform, on no strategy, and on no man?

Much will be written in the next months about the impudence of the Old Guard. It is waste of energy. What is more, such preachment is totally unreal. The Old Guard is at least true to itself. The game played by the progressives at this convention is in my opinion not one bit superior in morals to that played by the Old Guard, and it is infinitely less effective. The Old Guard can at least sink personal ambitions in a common purpose. It does not believe in fairies. It knows what it wants. The progressives do not know what they want. They just want to be a little nobler and a little cleaner, provided they do not have to stay out in the wilderness too long. They went to Chicago to play a game which only a professional can play because only a professional will take the time and the trouble to understand it. They trimmed, they evaded, they imagined they were boring from within, they tried to control a great party by making themselves as indistinguishable as possible from those who really control. They forgot that the virtues of the chameleon are purely defensive.

They did not deceive the Old Guard, but themselves they deceived mightily—preposterously as anyone can testify who looks at the result and heard their optimism. They cannot now, and they never will be able to play poker with Penrose. Their humiliation must have taught them that. May it also have reminded them of the multitude beyond, its patience strained. Beyond conventions and parties there is a living world in the midst of a transition which human power may perhaps guide, but cannot prevent. It is not written in Heaven that the Republican party is indispensable, nor is it now more than a gambler's chance whether moving men will accept either party as its instrument. Only a short time is left in which to recognize that the whole meaning of the progressive movement, its sole function in this generation is to supply temperate leadership to a people which is preparing to march. A few more such demonstrations of vanity, innocence, timidity and futility as this at Chicago, and the progressives will be annihilated by the clash of extremes.

June 23, 1920

IS HARDING A REPUBLICAN?

Clarence Day, an amiable satirist, later became celebrated as the author of *Life With Father*. [*A.S., jr.*]

If an optimist is a man who makes lemonade out of all the lemons that are handed to him, then Senator Harding is the greatest of all optimists. He has been told by his friends and his critics that he is colorless and without sap, commonplace and dull, weak and servile. Right you are, says the Senator. You have described exactly the kind of man this country needs. It has tried Roosevelt and Wilson, and look. It can't stand the gaff. I am nothing that they were. I am no superman like Roosevelt and no superthinker like Wilson. Therefore, I am just the man you are looking for. How do I know that? I am distinguished by the fact that nothing distinguishes me. I am marked for leadership because I have no marks upon me. I am just the man because no one can think of a single reason why I am the man. If any one happens to think of a reason then I shall cease to be that normal man which these abnormal times demand.

Just what is Mr. Harding trying to say anyway? Presumably some idea is lodged in his brain and panting for utterance beyond the normal human impulse to find a good reason for his own candidacy. For the sake of good appearances in history, I suppose that Mr. Harding is not exalting his defects as do the preternaturally wise animals in Clarence Day's *This Simian World*. He can't just be the one-eyed man who

194

is against two-eyed men, or the tortoise who thinks the hare leads too fast a life. Some other idea is sprouting on that front porch in Marion.

That idea, probably, is that the Presidency has grown too big for any man, and that the time has come for decentralizing its power. There are conceivably two ways this might be done. One way would be to think out a plan for adapting responsible cabinet government to the congressional system. It is a way that would require an abnormal lot of thinking. It would require also a quarrel with Congress. For until Congress disgorges its petty control over the details of administration, Congress will not be fit to take upon itself major control of executive policy. But Congress at present is so much concerned with the things that do not belong to it, that it has no opportunity to be concerned with the things that do. The relation of Congress to administration is like that of a general staff so tremendously interested in the second lieutenants that it ignores the lieutenant-generals. The result is that the general can't command the lieutenants, and the lieutenants' hair is forever standing on end while they try to obey the swivel chairs. Mr. Harding's remedy for this is to sack the general and find someone who will be content with four stars and will keep his mouth shut.

There is something in it. If you can't think of any way to redistribute the functions of government, then all you have to do is to find a President who will be so weak that power will leave him. That is the inner meaning of Mr. Harding's nomination. He was put there by the Senators for the sole purpose of abdicating in their favor. The Grand Dukes have chosen their weak Tsar in order to increase the power of the Grand Dukes. And if he is elected the period will be known in our constitutional history as the Regency of the Senate.

What will this accomplish? It will reduce the prestige and the power of the White House. Will it create a better balance of prestige and power in the whole government? Hardly. The gentlemen who intend to benefit by Mr. Harding's abnormal

195

normality are a group tiny enough to meet in a hotel bedroom. They are not the elected Congress of the United States.
Their rise to power would mean not the restoration of a
balance between executive and legislature but the substitution
of government by a clique for the lonely majesty of the President. Dangerous as is the plight we are in, it has at least the
advantage of visibility. The President may be an autocrat, yet
every one knows where that autocrat lives. But the government of a clique, an invisible, self-invited collection of friends,
would be just nothing but the return of exactly what every
decent person has fought against for a generation.

That the glory of the normal should be presented to a
weary nation as the purest Republican doctrine according to
the Fathers is one of those paradoxes which Mr. Chesterton
says, always sit beside the wells of truth. It is in fact primitive Democratic doctrine. That doctrine has always been that
anybody could govern, that leadership was dangerous, excellence somewhat un-American, and specialized knowledge
somewhat sinister. The Republicans from Hamilton's time on
have always professed belief that ability mattered, and that no
system of government could succeed in which the best men
were not preeminent. They may have had some queer notions
about what constituted the best men, but they have at least
done this republic the service of refusing to accept the idea
that anybody could do anything. They have not in theory at
least stooped to encourage the democratic vices. Mr. Harding
does. I hate to say it, but he is in ultimate theory a great deal
closer to Mr. Bryan than he is to any great Republican from
Hamilton to Root. For Mr. Bryan has that same simple faith
that any deserving fellow can do anything, which Mr. Harding
has now brought forth from the caverns of his mind.

July 21, 1920

UNREST

QUIET, PLEASE

The Industrial Workers of the World, founded in 1905, were still active both in labor agitation and more especially in the nightmares of the business community. [*A.S., jr.*]

It is rumored that a certain number of American statesmen are acquainted with the fact that the war was certain to produce severe unemployment this winter. You might think this knowledge would have cast a slight shadow over the congratulation which the Democratic Congress bestowed upon itself, that it might have received at least a little comment from the candidates, and some concerted thought from the states. Yet instead of adequate provision, what we seem to be witnessing is the usual drift into the suffering of the winter, amidst the appointment of hasty commissions to investigate, and the threats and shouts of the I.W.W. Public officials will feel themselves abused for not being able to do what they don't know how to do; there will be a scurry to provide beds and food; a few anemic employment bureaus will lift their timid heads.

And all the while the damning fact will remain that the problem could have been foreseen, that the first steps in its treatment are known. How then shall we explain to the men who are out of work why no adequate labor exchanges exist, why no form of insurance has ever been publicly discussed? What answer shall we make to their own simple diagnosis, which says that mayors and governors and legislatures are afraid to attack the private employment agencies or that the great mass of people are too preoccupied to care? They will point out that the cotton planters of the South were interesting to the whole nation; they will wonder why they, sitting dejectedly on park benches, are so little thought about. When their fighting blood stirs, and they say that they will be heard and felt, that they propose to sting us into recognition, shall we simply ask them to be quiet, to slink into corners, and to pardon us if we have failed to provide for what we could so easily have foreseen?

November 7, 1914

MINIMUM WAGE

The opposition to a minimum wage law for women is curiously compounded of interested employers, abstract theorists, and conservative and radical unionists. It presents a picture of the I.W.W., department store managers, Samuel Gompers, and a half dozen professional economists fighting side by side. The relation between republican France and autocratic Russia is a simple harmony compared to this group of allies so single-minded for such various reasons. We do not pretend to have fathomed the reasons, for they range all the way from the reasons of employers who like sweating, through those of thinkers who believe in laissez-faire, to those of labor unionists who wish to monopolize the interests of the workers. In this network of confused opposition the New York State Factory Investigation Commission is now hesitating. The Commission is to report to the Legislature in January, but its decision is now in the making, and there is danger that the strength of the opposition may balk its recommendations.

Against every form of opposition must be weighed the supreme fact that there are industries in this State which do not pay enough wages to support life. Even if the minimum wage did not have behind it a long record of fairly successful practice, any proposal to end such a condition would be an experiment which New York State could afford to try, and should. No other agency has yet been suggested which reaches the most deeply exploited groups of women workers, and none which proposes in direct and dignified fashion to place them within the state bulwarks below which American civilization shall not sink.

To those who complain that the sweated industries could not survive, the obvious and irrefutable answer is that industries which can't support themselves are uneconomic and should not be subsidized out of the health and sanity of their employees. If any subsidy is necessary, if the real cause of bad conditions isn't an intolerable inefficiency, then the subsidy should be public and frank. To those who fear State interference the reply is that voluntary action has failed. To those who point out that much of this sweated labor is incompetent the reply is that it must either be made competent or treated openly as a public charge. To those who realize the administrative dfficulties of minimum wage legislation the reply is that wisdom and skill are made by experience.

November 7, 1914

DEVIL'S ADVOCATES

The only interesting thing ever said in defense of human slavery was that it enables those who live upon it to cultivate a liberal life. But no one who reads the arguments of those who came to Washington in order to oppose the Child Labor bill will ever claim that the employment of little children makes pleasant human beings out of its apologists. One gentleman did say that you could "go down to the muddiest old pond and pull the whitest lily," but if Mr. David Clark, editor of the *Southern Textile Bulletin,* and ex-Governor Kitchin of North Carolina are the lilies, then the statement can hardly go unchallenged.

For example: When Mr. William Walton Kitchin, who is a brother of Mr. Claude Kitchin, was Governor of North Carolina he sent a message to the legislature urging a rigid inspection of factories, and a sufficient force of inspectors for the work. Mr. Kitchin is no radical. He was present at the hearing as attorney for the employers opposed to federal child labor legislation. Mr. Clark did not agree with the Governor's recommendation:

> Congressman Keating: Did the mill owners of North Carolina, in the effort to ameliorate the condition of the employees, support Governor Kitchin in his recommendation?
>
> Mr. Clark: I did not favor inspection.
>
> Congressman Keating: Was that because you did not have faith in the state inspectors, or because you had a good deal of faith in the mill owners? . . .

Mr. Clark: It is largely a grafter proposition. . . .

Congressman London: What do you mean by a grafting proposition?

Mr. Clark: I am not prepared to give you the facts, but my understanding is that if you pay, you get a clean bill of health.

Congressman London: You believe that your mill owners would resort to corruption in order to escape a fair inspection?

Mr. Clark: Not more than any others; not more than was necessary.

Congressman London: You mean they would resort to corruption of a government official?

Mr. Clark: Well, yes, if they were held up.

The editor of the *Southern Textile Bulletin,* having recorded his views of political morality, was led on to express himself about compulsory education. He had been complaining that the children taken from the mills would have no place to go:

Mr. Clark: When these people [the families of operatives] come from the mountains they do not believe in education. That is the reason we do not have compulsory education in North Carolina, because the isolated mountain districts would go Republican if we forced compulsory education upon them.

Shortly afterwards Congressman Dennison asked a question:

Congressman Dennison: Is the labor employed in your state generally or particularly organized?

Mr. Clark: It is not organized at all in my state.

Later ex-Governor Kitchin remarked that "the cotton mill furnishes an opportunity for light and remunerative work for the children"—that is to say, ten hours' work a day. A sort

204

of light refreshment. "Children twelve and fourteen years old can do just as good work as a thirty-year old man with the work he is doing, and help take care of the family. I think that is a blessing."

A doctor employed by a cotton mill testified that a girl of twelve may be employed in a cotton mill eleven hours a day without injury. In this exalted mood various witnesses offered many aphorisms:

If a mill operating an eleven-hour day employs children only eight hours, it would probably require additional machinery.

The cotton mill has done more than anything else in the South to save the people from the farm.

If this law passed and the younger children were taken out of the mill, the families would go back to the farms.

If this bill passed it would affect 35 children between 14 and 16 in our mill of 400 people. This would necessitate our building eight new houses to take care of the new families that would be brought in.

Nor is this the worst: Things were said in the testimony which touch the bottom of human brutality:

A roll of cotton cloth made by child labor is just as long, just as wide, just as white, and just as good as if made by adults.

There was this appeal to precedent:

Congress never tried between 1830 and 1860 to prevent interstate commerce in the products of slave labor.

And then there was this gentle thought about children in general:

You couldn't fix an age limit for child labor any more than you could tell when a pig becomes a hog.

In this crew and supporting it was to be found Mr. James A. Emery, counsel for the National Association of Manufacturers. Mr. Emery talked at length about constitutionality and states' rights. Finally he was asked to explain whom he represented. It developed that Mr. Emery was speaking in the name of 4,000 manufacturers all over the Union. Naturally there was an inquiry as to whether Mr. Emery had consulted the 4,000 manufacturers:

Mr. Emery: My opinion was asked on this measure at the last meeting of the board of directors. . . .

The directors acted against the bill, and "the information of the action of the board of directors was sent to all" of the manufacturers belonging to the National Association. In other words, the business men of the country were put on record against this bill without being consulted. Do they not find that a little humiliating? Do they enjoy the company they are keeping, thanks to the initiative of their counsel? And how do they expect the rest of us to respect their opinions and follow their organized advice when this is the way they permit themselves to be dragged in the kind of mud from which no lilies are ever pulled?

February 5, 1916

LENDING AND SPENDING

In another column a correspondent proposes an interesting dilemma, one which actually is presented in the lives of many Americans. It is the dilemma of the investor with a social conscience. Our correspondent is an active man with a business of his own, the management of which fully occupies his time but the needs of which do not demand the whole of his capital. He has a considerable sum of money to invest, which for obvious prudential reasons has been used to purchase shares in a number of different corporations. As a part owner in these companies he has a personal responsibility for their behavior. He wants them to be managed not only for his benefit as an investor, but according to a policy not inimical to the public interest or to the welfare of the companies' employees. But he has neither the time nor the opportunity to make sure that the businesses which are being carried on in part with his capital are managed as he would prefer. The resulting dilemma is very real. He has no effective way of attaching to his investment in these corporations the value of a moral act. He is practically obliged to hand over a power of attorney to their administrative officers, and to trust in them to redeem his own personal responsibility.

There is no immediate and satisfactory escape from this dilemma. Modern industry is passing through a transition. It is partly conducted by men who supply their own capital to businesses which they manage themselves, and with which they preserve an intimate personal relationship. It is partly conducted by large corporate administrative organizations, which derive capital from investors, but are managed by salaried officials. These officials are the only people who really know the business and are capable of controlling its conduct, because they are the people whose lives are absorbed by it. Our correspondent represents both of these classes in the modern industrial system. He has a business of his own which consumes most of his time, and which constitutes his primary responsibility. If that business is conducted in a manner which scrupulously safeguards not only the interests of its owners but those of its customers and its employees, our correspondent, even though he cannot properly perform his duties as a stockholder in other companies, may consider himself sufficiently assured of the reward which may await the virtuous man of business in another world. But a very genuine difficulty remains. A stockholder in a corporation is subsidizing and encouraging it with his money, but he cannot be certain that his encouragement is not being granted to a business policy of which, if he managed the business himself, he would not approve.

We do not know of any sure way of unmistakably attaching to the function of stockholding the moral value which may attach to personal business management. The shareholder does not and cannot share as the result of his holdings actual responsibility for the conduct of the business. Business will never obtain much of its needed reformation through the agency of a group of stockholders who may at the same time or at different times consist of the Kaiser of Germany, an infant aged two years, a dyspeptic at Marienbad and Billy Sunday. They don't know enough, they don't care enough; they have no sufficient means of knowing and no sufficient motive for caring. Stockholding is private property shorn of all its glamor, stripped of all its feudal graces, and crippled in all its moral obligations. It has nothing to recommend it but immediate necessity.

Many difficulties arise from the failure to keep in mind the distinction between a personally owned and managed business and one owned by people who do not manage it. Although the stockholders contribute nothing to the good management upon which a business depends for its success, they are still supposed to reap most of the rewards of good management. They are considered entitled not only to a fair interest on their investment, but to the major part of any residuary profits. They are looking not only for a fixed and secure income, but for a speculative increase in value. A man who buys shares in a corporation without participating in its management is merely making a bet upon the success of the business, and it is this fact which falsifies his relationship to his property and to the management of his property. He lends his capital to the officers of the company in the hope of having it returned to him in increasing measure. The success or failure of the management is tested solely by its ability to produce these unearned profits for the stockholders—unearned, that is, by the stockholders themselves.

One suggested method of meeting the difficulty is the conversion of stockholders into the position of bondholders— that is, the position of people who are paid a fixed interest for furnishing capital. There might be two classes of bondholders, one which accepted a low interest and a comparatively safe investment, and the other which involved a larger risk, and received, if the business were successful, a larger but still limited return. The adoption of such a method of financing business would substitute the purchase of capital by business ability for the purchase of business ability by capital; and it would have the advantage of at least making possible a juster and more beneficial distribution of business profits. The surplus which did not go to capital would for the most part be shared among the officials and employees of the company, and would serve to increase their interest in a business which would become more completely their own.

The fundamental problem would nevertheless remain, that of devising an effective method of exercising supervision and control over the chief administrative officials of the corpora-

209

tion; and as long as it did remain the dilemma of our correspondent would remain with it to plague conscientious investors. That problem is too complicated and difficult to be discussed here. Until something is done to solve it, corporate management will continue to be an uncontrolled autocracy. But the investor, powerless as he is to control, is not condemned to entire irresponsibility as to the conduct of a corporation nourished in part by his capital. He can, for instance, refuse to invest in any corporation whose management may be plausibly suspected of exploiting either the public or its employees. If any corporation in which he has invested is convicted of such conduct he can withdraw his investment and place it by preference in the stock of a corporation whose policy is more enlightened.

Assuming that he is a man of initiative and energy, he might go further. He might organize an "Investors' League," based upon the same ideas as the Consumers' League, whose members were pledged not to lend their capital to any questionably managed corporation. The plan may seem fantastic and absurd, but why should it be? The mere fact of its seeming absurdity indicates how socially irresponsible investors have always been in lending their money. Their investments have been determined either by the desire for security or the expectation of large profits. If the expectation of large profits were cut off by their transformation from the owners of the property into the owners of a mortgage on the property, they would require a new reason for preferring an investment in one corporation to an investment in another, assuming that both were equally safe. Why should not the preference be based on the comparative policy of the two corporations in the treatment of its employees and its customers? If investors are not capable of positively controlling the management of a business which they support with their capital, they are at lease capable of starving corporations whose management offends certain recognized standards of public decency.

In this as in many other respects the community will in the

future demand higher standards of the man of wealth than it has in the past. In one way or another the economic system must be made productive of a larger amount of human welfare. It could be made so almost immediately, without any fundamental changes in laws and institutions, provided employers and investors were as anxious to promote the human values involved by business as they are to make money. If they considered conscientiously the effect on society of their present methods of hiring and firing labor and of lending and spending money, and if they tried to live up to a higher standard, the present economic system could be indefinitely prolonged. So far as it is in danger, it is in danger because employers and investors ignore the plain responsibilities imposed upon them by their money power—the responsibility of avoiding extravagance, of discriminating on behalf of business with an enlightened social policy both in their lending and spending, and above all of recognizing that their employees need not merely kind and fair treatment but an increasing measure of economic independence and power. Thus the dilemma of our correspondent exists for all investors whether they realize it or not, and if they do not give it the same serious consideration which he is doing they will pay for their failure. Lending must be socialized as well as spending, and if the lenders ignore the responsibility, the community will seek other means to accomplish the result.

December 11, 1915

THE RAILROAD CRISIS

AND AFTER

Luckily the President is thinking more about how to avert a railroad strike than about "principles." For the phrases passed off as "principles" by both sides are masked words which beg the question for those who are informed and confuse it for those who aren't. There is a meaning behind slogans like the "eight-hour day" and "arbitration," but it is not a meaning which the public can get at by taking the words at face value. Like "Americanism" and "national honor" and "Prussian militarism" and the "freedom of the seas" these phrases are the narcotics and stimulants but not the food of thought.

As a statesman confronted with a great emergency, Mr. Wilson is compelled to break through the slogans which serve publicity rather than sense. The great fact before him is that the Brotherhoods have the power to call a strike which would bring such disaster and suffering to the country that it must be averted. The President knows that no matter how great the public sentiment against the men the strike could take place and would not be broken without riot and bloodshed and agony. Assume that the men were utterly wrong, assume that they deserved no sympathy whatever, it would still be out of the question for the President to coerce them. They have the power to strike and the legal right, and that fact can not be argued out of existence. You may believe in "arbitration" world without end but if one party which has the power declares that an issue is not arbitrable, it is useless sentimentality to talk about arbitration.

The President has done, therefore, what the practical situation required. He has narrowed the issue down to the very lowest point which the Brotherhoods will accept, and has asked the managers to try the "eight-hour day" with the pledge that it will be studied in operation, that if it doesn't work the government will save the railroads from "ruin." A more sensible and statesmanlike proposal has not been suggested, and no sympathy is due the management for pretending that it will be ruined when there is a practical guaranty that the federal power will not allow it to be ruined. Through improvement in efficiency and through possible increase of rates there is an ample margin of safety. And if it is shown that the trains can not be run on the schedules, the question can be reopened and readjusted. The railroads are not faced with the alternative of ruin or victory. The real alternative, as the President has shown, is between a strike and the trial of a new system subject to public inquiry and public guaranties.

Under the circumstances, "arbitration" is a catchword in the service of stubbornness. What use is it to talk of the "principle" when it will not work? If you can't arbitrate you can't. The true principle of arbitration is that both parties agree to settle their differences by arbitration, or that you have the power to compel them to. They won't agree and no one has the power to compel, so the actual result of standing by the principle is to bring on the strike which it is designed to prevent.

The railroads say they are thinking of the future and of the precedent which would be created. There they have hold of something which must occupy the inventive thought of the nation. In fact the most hopeful aspect of the whole matter is that from the President down there seems to be a clear idea that this calamity must not only be averted, but must be averted in such a way that better methods may prevail in the future.

There again the President's plan is both wise and imaginative. The proposal that the workings of the settlement be put to federal inquiry is fruitful. Once a commission is created to study the wages problem on railroads we shall have an agency capable of growth. For arbitration in the crude sense does not meet the facts. There is no hope, we believe, in creating a tribunal to deal with an industrial dispute after it has become an out and out conflict. What we need is an administrative commission continuously in touch with the wage problem. It is just as impractical to arbitrate wages when everything is prepared for a strike as it was to deal with rates through the courts and legislature. No tribunal can handle the situation after the irritation has culminated in a national conflict. Great conflicts can be prevented only by breaking up big issues into small ones and adjusting them from day to day. Blanket demands and high sounding principles are the curse of industrialism as they are of diplomacy.

The President has proposed a commission of inquiry. That commission will have to develop into an interstate railway wages board. At first it will probably be limited to investigation and publicity. When this fails to work it will be given power to declare demands "unreasonable." When this breaks down, as it surely will, we shall be forced to face the facts and give the government power to fix wages and hours. Wage-making will be added to the rate-making function of the government.

There will be great difficulties in this until the Interstate Commerce Commission fixing rates, service, wages and hours has developed a workable body of administrative law. But it is the avenue of hope. By fixing wages for all railroad employees, and not merely for the strategically organized workers, the Commission will have endless power for the skillful disintegration of labor monopoly. It can raise the wages of the unorganized; it can shift the balance of power among railroad workers. Just as the Interstate Commerce Commission has probably prevented a dangerous sectional alignment on railroad rates, so a wage board by a series of minor decisions can equalize power among the men. The monopolistic attitude of the Brotherhoods could hardly survive small and wise discriminations in the making of wages. Their coercive power depends on large general demands for horizontal increases. A continuous commission would tend to make the adjustments vertical. In this lies the promise of the future and not in the creation of an arbitrary tribunal with compulsory power after the trouble has got out of hand.

There can be no shirking of the prospect which all this opens up. When rates, service, wages, hours, have passed into government hands, private property in railroads has disappeared. The management is left with responsibility but with very little power. The stockholders more than ever cease to be "owners" and become bondholders without any assurance of return. We are witnessing not the confiscation of property in railroads but its evaporation. We are coming to a time when the only result of private property in railroads is an inefficient division of responsibility. Nationalization, which the President held up as a warning, is the goal towards which we are going by inevitable steps.

August 26, 1916

THE AVERTED

RAILWAY STRIKE

The Adamson Act established the eight-hour day for railroad trainmen. Jacob Schiff of Kuhn, Loeb and Company was a leading financier. [*A.S., jr.*]

The prevention of the railroad strike has caused bitterness, but it is insignificant when compared with what would have happened had the strike taken place. A number of well-meaning people have said publicly, and a good many more have said privately, that they would have preferred a strike. They do not know what a national railroad strike would mean, and they are guilty of a serious lack of imagination. There have been very few railroad strikes in the history of the world, and where they have occurred they have brought the nation which suffered them to the verge of civil war. No nation has ever undergone a strike comparable to the one we have escaped. English, French, Italian and Belgian experience was a foretaste, but not a measure of what an American strike would have been. No nation has dealt with industrial conflict over so large a territory, and no nation where strikes have occurred is so dependent as we are upon the railroads. Had the strike occurred, men and women would have died, violence would have been epidemic, business would have staggered, and bitterness unquenchable would have filled the land. And yet men supposedly as responsible

216

as Mr. Jacob Schiff tell us they would have preferred the disaster.

Preferred it to what? To what they call the sacrifice of the principle of arbitration. The principle needs closer examination. The Brotherhoods said they would arbitrate everything but the doctrine of the eight-hour day as a basis of work and wages. They were willing to arbitrate questions of pay and discipline, but not the basic work day. They said it was not arbitrable. Is that mere pig-headedness or is it true? Analysis will show, we believe, that the Brotherhoods were sound in their claim; sound, mind you, not necessarily in demanding an eight-hour rather than a nine-hour day, but in saying that the basic work day is a matter for legislation, not for arbitration.

An analogy may make this clearer. Every student of international affairs has learned to recognize that there is a difference between justiciable and non-justiciable disputes. That is why so many of the same people who denounce the Adamson bill denounce the pacifists who want everything arbitrated. They say quite rightly that you cannot arbitrate the admission of Oriental labor to California. Why? Because it is a question about which no principle is accepted both in Japan and the United States on the basis of which you can arbitrate. Likewise no principle has ever been worked out to form the basis of arbitration for the length of the working day. Had the Brotherhoods agreed to arbitrate, had the President appointed the wisest men in the world to handle the controversy, those men would have had to legislate, not arbitrate, on the question of the work day. The hours of labor can be determined only by one of two methods, by a trial of force or by the legislature as a matter of public policy. A calmer view of the situation will show that any board of arbitration set up to deal with this question would have been simply a little temporary legislature to make a declaration of policy which Congress alone ought to make. The decision would not have been more "scientific" or "fair" because it would have rested in the end merely on the judgment and social philosophy of the arbitrators. They would have had to elevate their theory into the "judgment of the society," and if such judgments are to be passed it had better be by Congress, which has the power to deal with the consequences.

Just because the basic work day is ultimately a matter of social policy, the Adamson bill was a small price to pay for the prevention of a terrible national calamity. What does it say? It says that after January 1st eight hours shall be considered a day's work, and the measure of a day's work for reckoning pay, that a presidential commission of three shall watch the effects at least six months and report within nine, and that until one month after the commission has reported, wages shall not be reduced below the present standard, and that overtime be paid pro rata. In other words, we are to have at least six months' trial of the principle, followed by a reopening of the question of wages, rates, economy, and the method of handling disputes.

The only difference between "arbitration" and the present method is that three or four arbitrators would have had to guess on no experience and on no principle, while Congress has guessed and provided a way for testing the result. The other difference is that a great calamity has been averted.

Congress still has to provide a better method for the future, but its organization can proceed calmly and with the good will of labor. That is an infinitely better mood in which to build than in the aftermath of violence, ruin and hatred. No essential interest is left unguarded, no one is deprived of his chance to be heard. Had the strike occurred no one would have been heard for all the din it would have set up. Congress acted in haste to prevent a disaster. It is a pity that it had to act in haste. It is a pity that in its action it failed to adopt the whole of the President's program. It is a pity that the nation is never prepared for its industrial crises. It is a pity that the social reformers who have thought about these matters are always ignored until the catastrophe is at hand.

It is a pity that we have had Colorado, Mesaba, West Virginia, Lawrence, Paterson, Akron, Calumet, and that Congress and the masters of business are still unaroused, and very little the wiser. It is a pity that the nation has not yet developed the enterprise and public spirit seriously to face the labor question except when labor shakes its fist.

September 9, 1916

AN INEFFECTIVE REMEDY

When President Wilson announced his railroad program at the end of August and asked Congress for the Adamson act, he opened a new era of intervention by the government. That the program was hastily adopted, that it had failed of adequate critical discussion, will not be denied even by those who earnestly believe that the President was right in seeking by almost any means to avert the strike, and that the means he did choose were sound in their intention. Apart from the fact that the President's action saved the country from a civil calamity, renewed the confidence of organized labor in the national government, and started an educational propaganda for a standard working day, the course he pursued had this value: it introduced the government into a great labor controversy not merely as a policeman or a pious missionary, but as the active and decisive influence. Whatever happens to the Adamson law, a principle has been set going which says that the final decision about hours and wages on railroads is not to be left to bargaining which breaks into violence, but is to be made and enforced by the federal government.

The crisis of last August showed that the labor and capital of the railroads were incapable of composing their differences alone, that the government and public opinion was so ignorant of the issues and the vast technical complication that, with the best will, it could not intervene wisely. The President expressed the temper of the country when he said that such a situation must never be allowed to appear again. But in choosing an instrument for remedying the condition he made himself sponsor for a method which is certain to prove unworkable. A law for compulsory investigation before a railroad strike is the kind of law which expresses a good intention though it ignores the facts.

It is intended to prevent the calling of a sudden strike or a lockout, in order to gain time for public opinion to crystallize. But a national railroad strike is never ordered without warning, and could not be. The crisis of August was foreseen months and months ahead, and the public had all the time it needed to form an opinion. What the public did not have was a trustworthy agent from which to take the facts or a satisfactory method of carrying out a decision. This defect cannot be remedied by an investigating body which sits and hears argument, but which has no power to enforce its judgments.

Suppose the judgment goes against the management? Whose responsibility will it be to see that the judgment is carried out? Whose business will it be to make certain that a principle established by public opinion is not frittered away in administration? Public opinion is clearly incapable of watching the details of such a vast process, and all that labor would have to rely upon would be its own power to strike. But the added delay imposed by the law, by enabling the management to mobilize strike-breakers, practically destroys the power to strike. The proposal therefore emasculates the union without substituting an adequate public agency for it.

From every point of view compulsory arbitration is preferable to compulsory investigation, for under arbitration there is at least some guaranty that the award will be carried out. But neither arbitration nor investigation really meets the issue. Neither of them recognizes the truth that it is as impractical to determine wages and hours by spasmodic investigation as it was to determine rates by that method. The country has learned from long experience that the rate problem could not be met by going to a court and securing a decision,

221

that only a continuing expert body with affirmative power to make rates could keep abreast of the enormous complexity of the question.

So it is with hours and wages. To leave their determination to private bargaining, to permit the two sides to organize into solid hostile groups, and then try to cut the Gordian knot by an active investigation or arbitration is to make trouble, not to cure it. No board of investigation or arbitration can possibly retain its grip on the problem, if it has to wait until a quarrel has developed and both sides are standing on eternal principles and claiming all sorts of "rights."

The way out is for the government to take the initiative and fix wages and hours on its own responsibility. This alone will make possible continuous contact with the problem, and eliminate the unscientific method of blanket awards, of wages and hours fixed by consideration of power and strategic advantage rather than by social needs and economic conditions. The government must take the initiative or suffer the results. By taking the initiative it can, by proper discrimination between classes or employees and by territorial alignments, prevent a solid aggregation of either management or employees. Its decisions will have the force of law. But in weakening the power to strike, the government will not be guilty of leaving the workers helpless, for the government would enforce the decision. The problem which would then be presented to labor would be that of keeping the government liberal in spirit and sensitive to the facts.

Above all, this method should appeal to the good sense of the country because it does away with the anomaly by which the rates, hours, and wages are fixed by separate methods instead of being treated as an organically related set of facts. Clearly the cost of labor and the return for service are functions of the same variable. They have a reciprocal relationship which it is unscientific to ignore, and the chaos of railroad conditions cannot be reduced until their financial administration is coordinated. With the federal gov-

222

ernment fixing rates, establishing service, with forty-eight state commissions introducing discordant local issues, with another helter-skelter investigating body leaving wages and hours up in the air, with Congress occasionally issuing decrees to meet special situations, it is hardly remarkable that we have a railroad problem.

The whole system is jerry-built, a rambling unplanned structure which breaks down continually at important junctures. It cannot be saved by adding hastily another ramshackle annex known as compulsory investigation. Unless the administration will see that the condition revealed last August is an integral part of the general disintegration of private management, it will merely confuse the question still further. By accepting the principle that hours and wages should be fixed in conjunction with rates, it will have done much to create that nationalized railroad organization which must in the near future supplant the friction and deadlock in the semi-private, semi-public no man's land of railroad responsibility.

November 25, 1916

CAN THE STRIKE

BE ABANDONED?

Elbert H. Gary, the head of United States Steel, was deeply opposed to the unionization of the steel industry. Samuel Gompers, head of the American Federation of Labor, naturally defended labor's right to strike. [*A.S., jr.*]

Several years ago the workers in the lighting plants of Paris determined to remind the people of that city of a few elementary facts. At nine in the evening, I think it was, they suddenly struck work for sixty minutes. For that hour it was hardly necessary to prove to any Parisian that modern society is cooperative. M. Bakst's most exquisite ballet, the professor at the Sorbonne lecturing on non-Euclidean geometry, the politician pleading before his audience, the conference of financiers were all interrupted with the same precision. A few thousand humble individuals had walked away from their machines.

When the lights were turned on again at ten o'clock the editors began to write their opinion of the outrage for the morning newspapers. They argued that no minority, no matter how just its grievances, had a right to interrupt so many higher things, that in accepting employment at an indispensable trade, the electrical workers were under a moral obligation to society at large, that a necessary occupation was a public trust. All the people who had been to the Bakst ballet agreed, and so did most other citizens of the town. But the fact remained that machine industry is so organized that determined minorities can paralyze it and that injunctions, legal or moral, cannot revive it. Indeed the more self-conscious men become about their place in the industrial system, the smaller becomes the minority which can paralyze that system. It is vulnerable at strategic points. At those points there are key men, and of those key men some are not easily replaced.

Because there has been a rather startled realization of how vulnerable the industrial system is, many Americans in the last few months have condoned the Garys and Palmers. On the merits they would never have condoned a man who will boast as Mr. Palmer did recently that he won a "victory" but did not reach a settlement. Because they felt that a new and dangerous power of coercion had been indicated, they were willing to fend the threat by disregarding immediate issues, by disregarding the equities, and to make an overwhelming demonstration of force against strategic minorities among workingmen. They saw revealed a power that might some day be violently abused, and they were ready to crush that power or anything that symbolized it regardless of whether it was then actually being abused. In other words they chose to treat as if it were actually here, a danger which at the moment was only potential.

That there is a potential danger seems to me undeniable. For illustration take railroads, coal, steel, millinery, and medical research. Imagine any social order you like in which these five occupations exist. Assume, as you must, the truth of Mr. Gompers's claim that under no conceivable social order can injunctions make unwilling and determined men work. Then picture a four weeks' strike in each of these occupations: On the railroads it is literally a national calamity, seriously comparable to an armed invasion; in the coal mines, it is a very costly inconvenience; in the steel mills it is far

225

less inconvenient; in the millinery shops, it has almost no national significance, and in medical research it may mean merely a much needed vacation for tired men. Lengthen the respective strikes to three months: in railroads it is absolutely intolerable; in coal it is greatly serious; in steel it is costly; in millinery it is still negligible, and likewise in medical research. Now on what theory is anyone to argue that railwaymen should exercise more power than miners, miners more power than steel workers, steel workers more power than milliners or scientists? Yet potentially they do. The President may never hear of a millinery strike, he will ignore a three months' steel strike, he will gamble on a coal strike, but a railway strike he could not palter with twenty-four hours. It is not a question of the justice of the men's claims. It is a question of their strategic position in the industrial system.

In what is usually called the democratization of industry, the power of the strategic minority is likely to increase rather than to diminish, unless new and better methods of social control are devised. For it is not possible to assume, I think, that the direct action of indispensable minorities is merely a phase of transition to some other social order in which all serious conflicts of interest are eliminated. In any system there will remain the fact that some men do work which sustains life from day to day, some do work which sustains it from year to year, while the labor of others is effective only over long periods of time. In a purely industrial republic in which each guild was highly autonomous those who created the immediate necessities would be immeasurably more powerful than those who produced for deferred consumption.

This may seem a bit like borrowing trouble. After all if we have government by minorities today those minorities do not consist of wage earners. It is not a minority of workingmen that is trying to foment war with Mexico, that bungled the peace, that failed to organize coal as a public service, that abolished civil liberty in parts of Pennsylvania and West Virginia. It was a minority of employers that wrecked the Industrial Conference. It was not a minority of workers who refused all negotiations in the steel industry, or exploited a bit of fantastic legalism in the coal industry. And yet, just as it was a mistake for the general public to treat the potential danger of coercion by minorities as actual, so it would be no less a mistake to treat it as negligible.

If the reluctant apologists for Mr. Gary and Mr. Palmer committed the fallacy of confusing what was possible with what had happened, the supporters of trade unionism would commit no less a fallacy if they treated what is distinctly possible as altogether improbable. Now the philosophy of labor as expounded by Mr. Gompers on December 13th is simply the obverse of Mr. Gary's. Both deny to the general public any right of representation. Both tell the state to keep its hands off. Both profess high regard for the public welfare, and both rely on their own inherent industrial power. Mr. Gary looks forward to an indefinite period of suppression. Mr. Gompers looks forward to an equally indefinite period of expansion. They are conflicting doctrines, but they spring from the same view of life. If Garyism won we should have despotism tempered by rebellion; if Gomperism triumphed we should hardly escape an attempt at domination by the strategic minorities.

While ultimately one would be about as bad as the other; while immediately as a kind of Hobson's choice I may think Gomperism is preferable to Garyism, the majority of people will as a matter of fact choose Garyism rather than Gomperism. They will do this because labor's power cannot be asserted without disturbing the routine of life, whereas the obstinate employer's power always seems to be asserted in favor of the tranquillity of the state. The exercise of its power by labor is almost always starkly and crudely visible, but the power of what Mr. Roosevelt described as the invisible government is invisible. So long as labor simply disturbs the routine again and again and again, so long as its only articulate philosophy is that it will continue to disturb it, so long

227

as its victories seem to be nothing but the fluctuations of trench warfare, orderly reconstruction of industry is impossible. In the name of majority rule as against the threat of minorities, the government will attempt suppression. In the name of liberty and democracy and humanity organized labor will blindly grasp powers which sections of labor will exploit.

Say the A.F. of L. leaders at Washington: We stand for liberty, and we mean by liberty that no law and no official shall obstruct us in the use of all the bargaining power that we can develop. Where this leads we do not say, and we do not inquire, though we shall be very patriotic about it. Now it is not conceivable that the salaried classes, the farmers or the merchants will be satisfied with the prospect of an endless cycle of demands, strikes, "settlements," recriminations. They will support the resistance to organized labor unless and until the program of labor has at least the promise of stability and peaceful adjustment within it. The leadership of the A.F. of L. will sooner or later have to grasp that fact. So long as its ideal is "rights," and its tactics militancy tempered by expediency, it will be faced with desperate opposition and that opposition will tend more and more to raise to power in the ranks of labor those who are militant without caring about expediency.

The plain fact is that sooner or later the strike will have to disappear from all those services on which the immediate life of the community depends. No people living in a complex industrial system will tolerate forever the possibility of great suffering because of a deadlocked dispute between the managers and employees in an industry producing immediate necessities. The demand that this threat be ended will become irresistible. The real question is when it will be ended and how. The reactionaries say it will be ended now by forbidding strikes. Mr. Gompers says it will never be ended. The statesmanship of labor would consist in saying that it will be ended on certain conditions. The formulation of those conditions is not an easy task but it is an inevitable one.

What is meant by "conditions"? At present the strike is

used to force the acceptance of concrete demands, an eight hour day, a certain scale of pay and so forth. The reactionary plan for forbidding strikes proposes simply to rob the unions of the only force they command, thus making them entirely dependent upon the good will of the employer. This means that law and order are identified with the will of the employer —*L'état c'est lui.* The result of this would be to make every strike a rebellion, and to make rebellion normal. Is there no alternative? There is, and Mr. Gompers has recognized it in practice though not in theory. He has agreed that policemen should not be allowed to strike. Yet he knows that the Boston policemen were miserably sweated men. On what theory then can he justify taking away from them their right to strike? Because there was an outcry? That is in itself no reason at all. The ultimate justification must lie in the belief that a legal process can be devised which at once safeguards the interests of the individual policeman and protects the community from such a strike. If no such process can be devised by the human mind then we have made the occupation of policemen one which no self-respecting men will enter.

What are the essentials of a legal process which would safeguard the interests of a working man sufficiently to justify the prohibition of strikes? This is immensely difficult ground but it may be worth while to attempt to formulate tentatively certain principles. We are dealing only with highly organized industries supplying goods and services on which the community is immediately dependent.

I. That after a certain fixed period of apprenticeship, no one shall be discharged or demoted except by a process agreed upon in advance for the industry with appeal to an administrative council of the industry in which employers and employees are equally represented. It should be an accepted principle that any one who has qualified as a member of an industry has thereafter a certain property interest in his job which cannot be confiscated except by a known legal process. This is in effect the introduction of the civil service principle into the great public utilities modified to eliminate the deadening effect of a too much vested interest in a job. It carries with it the principles of insurance against unemployment, illness, accident, maternity and old age.

II. That the wage system be revised so as to be based on the following elements: A basic yearly minimum rate fixed by agreement in relation to the cost of living at the last period when prices were not disturbed by the abnormal inflations of the war, for convenience the year 1913. The necessary yearly minimum income on that date in defined industrial regions to be the basic index of 100 for the calculation of wages. To this be added each month the differential between the index number at that time and the basic rate. The two together to constitute the minimum wage in that public service.

At fixed intervals the basic rate shall be subject to revision by conference, taking into consideration what the industry can afford to pay. The facts in the case shall be determined by expert investigators and shall be made public.

To that minimum wage another differential to be added for the different classes of labor to allow for differences in skill, responsibility, length of service, etc. This classification should be worked out by independent expert investigators and passed upon by an industrial council with equal representation of employers and employees. It is understood that these are minima, established without prejudice to the principle of special additional reward for services not easily subject to classification or as special incentive in conditions requiring unusual effort or initiative.

III. Periodic collective profit sharing based on the principle that any reduction in the cost of production or any general advance in prosperity shall be shared in some fixed ratio by the employees, the management and the consumer.

IV. Representation of the employees in the management of the corporation with the right of appeal to a public authority in case the management of the industry is inefficient and wasteful. This public authority to have power under established rules to discharge any official or any employee of the corporation found incompetent, corrupt, or useless, and after full investigation to order any reorganization in technique or business management or capitalization which may be required to make the industry in fact a public service.

V. All excess profits over a maximum fixed by Congress, unless they can be shown to be the clear result of socially useful initiative, rather than of external factors, to be taken by taxation or by an enforced reduction of prices.

VI. The right of appeal to an independent public tribunal for an investigation in all extraordinary circumstances, and in grievances where no routine method of securing redress exists.

VII. Complete civil liberty, not only in the state, but within the industry, as intended by the framers of the American Constitution.

On some such conditions as these the workers in vital industries could well afford to make a five or ten year experiment in the abandoment of the strike. The project ought to be regarded distinctly as an experiment and there should be a clear understanding that at the end of the period the whole thing shall be abandoned if it has not worked. This will put society on its good behavior and help the experiment be a success.

Such a proposal coming from labor would create a totally new atmosphere in the industrial world. People not affiliated with union labor would feel radically different about many things if they saw some prospect of real industrial peace ahead of them. And after all what would organized labor be doing by such a proposal? It would be entering into a vast collective bargain with the community, a bargain which safeguards all its essential purposes under a legal sanction. The only new thing in principle is this legal sanction. Labor in the vital industries would make a very satisfactory contract enforceable at law. The difference between it and any other collective contract would be that it ran for a longer period, that it gave labor infinitely greater security against the hazards of industry, and at the same time offered to the community at large security against the thing which it most fears. If the conditions are just in the sense that they provide for justice under changing conditions, if in other words they do not freeze labor in status quo, if they will give that sense of security without which the human reason cannot operate, then it is to the advantage of all that for an experimental period, the agreement shall have behind it the full authority of law.

January 21, 1920

THE CAMPAIGN

AGAINST SWEATING

Rome G. Brown was a conservative Minnesota lawyer opposed to the statutory minimum wage. [*A.S., jr.*]

> More than half the people employed in the factories and stores investigated in New York City get less than $8.00 a week.—*Dr. Howard Woolston, Director of Investigation for the New York State Factory Commission.*

It is all very well to say of a woman that "she is working for her living," but suppose she is working and not making her living. What are you to say then? You can remark that you are indeed very sorry, and leave the matter there. Or you can say with more piety than wisdom that wages are determined by natural laws which man must let alone. Or you can insist that she is being sweated; that a business which does not pay a living wage is not paying its labor costs; that such businesses are humanly insolvent, for in paying less than a living wage they are guilty of as bad business practice and far worse moral practice than if they were paying dividends out of assets.

Everyone knows what to think of a get-rich-quick concern

which asks people to subscribe to its capital stock, and then uses the money invested to pay profits. We call it a fraud. When a railroad goes on paying dividends without charging up deterioration, people speak of it not as a fraud but as bad business. But when a mercantile establishment pays its labor less than labor can live on, it is combining the evils of the mismanaged railroad and the get-rich-quick concern. It is showing a profit it has not honorably earned, it is paying a dividend out of its vital assets, that is, out of the lives, the health, and the happiness of its employees. A business that exists on labor paid less than a living wage is not a business at all, for it is not paying its fixed charges. They are being paid either by the family of the woman worker, or by her friends, or by private charities, or by the girl herself in slow starvation.

There are few left to deny the truth of these general ideas. Even the people who are fighting minimum wage legislation have not attempted to deny that a self-respecting business should pay the full cost of its labor. Nor has any serious attempt been made to impugn the damning wage statistics revealed in one state after another and clinched by the Factory Investigation Commission in New York. We know now that thousands of women are below the line which the most moderate estimate can call a living wage. Knowing this fact, we know that something must be disastrously wrong; knowing it, we must act to remedy it if we can, and no intelligent person will say that we are meddling in what does not concern us. The spectacle of paper-box, shirt and candy manufacturers and department-store keepers living on the profits of a business that does not pay its employees a living wage is so absurd that we begin to wonder what are the serious arguments against minimum wage legislation.

Fortunately Mr. Rome G. Brown knows all the arguments, serious and otherwise. Mr. Brown, let it be said, is an attorney who has fought living wage legislation in various states, and is the author of the brief filed before the Supreme Court in

234

the Oregon case. He is a kind of specialist in the business of finding fault with the minimum wage, and so no injustice can be done him or his cause by taking up the points he raises.

Mr. Brown's latest utterance is dated February 10, 1915, and it seems that Mr. Brown is no longer opposed to the minimum wage. He is opposed to the compulsory minimum wage, but he is for the ethical minimum wage. "Compulsion," says Mr. Brown, "stifles the humanitarian motive." Above all things Mr. Brown does not wish to stifle that. He does not say that six dollars a week is a good wage. What he says is that any attempt to force the employer to raise it would destroy the finer bloom of morality.

> His action ceases to be virtuous or moral when once
> you have enacted into a statute the precept of the Golden
> Rule, and when its observance is enforced under the
> threat of fine and imprisonment. Actions otherwise virtuous
> —of benevolence, of charity, of neighborly love—are
> deprived of all elements of morality when performed under
> compulsion.

And so, rather than take away from the act of raising wages all elements of morality, Mr. Brown would leave wages where they are. It is obviously high-minded of him, and exceedingly far-sighted. For here we see a leading attorney fighting step by step to preserve the quintessence of morality for employers toward that hypothetical time when they decide of their own free will to raise wages. At this historic moment, however, we are simply in the happy position of knowing that when employers abolish the starvation wage they will do so with unblemished ethical motives. There is indescribable comfort in the thought.

I am a student of Mr. Brown's writings, and his Tolstoyan aversion to any kind of legal compulsion is not new to me. He wrote a book just about a year ago in which he attacked the Minnesota statute of 1913, and pointed out that the real trouble with it lay in the fact that the wage established was

legal and compulsory. As a contrast he recommended the
Massachusetts act of 1912. Under that law the Minimum
Wage Commission may establish Wages Boards in particular
industries. On the findings of these Boards the Commission
may recommend a certain minimum wage, and publish its
finding in the newspapers. There are no penalties for disregarding the recommendation, except those which public
opinion creates. It is, in short, a use of "moral" force rather
than of legal force. It is this Massachusetts model which we
in New York are trying to follow.

Naturally we were happy to think that Mr. Brown approved our labors. The barbarous, immoral Oregonians and
Minnesotans who wish to force these reforms by law had
naturally to be fought, but Massachusetts and New York,
where the elements of morality are still strong, would find a
supporter in Mr. Brown.

> The Minimum Wage, by voluntary cooperation, includ-
> ing that of the states through non-compulsory statutes,
> is altogether, as it must be admitted, a logical workable
> measure.

He was referring directly to the Massachusetts act.

> It adds to the efforts for amelioration by purely indi-
> vidual initiative, and by privately organized cooperation,
> the encouragement and assistance of investigations and
> recommendations made under official authority. It nat-
> urally results in bringing in line with the employers of
> more humanitarian tendencies those who, from avarice,
> neglect or indifference, would remain inactive without
> some stimulating incentive.

So well pleased was Mr. Brown with these sentiments that
he embodied them verbatim in the brief which he presented
to the Supreme Court. Remember that this is the attorney
who is engaged in attacking the Oregon minimum wage law,
and think then what it means to have him hold up the

Massachusetts act, and by implication the New York one, as a model of righteousness. He says all that anyone would claim for the proposed statute in New York, and if Mr. Brown hadn't made a speech at the annual dinner of the National Retail Dry Goods Association on February 10, 1915, we should all have supposed that the chief opponent of the legal minimum wage law was an ardent supporter of the voluntary measure as applied in Massachusetts and proposed in New York.

But a few months have done much to Mr. Brown's spirit. His hatred of compulsion, his love of free morality, have deepened. Like Emma Goldman, he has come to fear not only the tyranny of law but the tyranny of public opinion. The Massachusetts statute he says now is "most obnoxiously compulsory." In that barbarous state, "when the wage is promulgated by the Commission, although there is no fine or imprisonment for the employer, if he fails to comply he is published through the state as an unreasonable recalcitrant." Mr. Brown only a few months ago described such laggard employers as men who from "avarice, neglect, or indifference would remain inactive without some such stimulating incentive." Now that New York is threatening to follow Massachusetts, Mr. Brown weeps publicly at the horror of compulsion from public opinion upon the avaricious, the negligent, and the indifferent. "Indeed the statute makes it a crime for any newspaper publisher to refuse this publicity to blacklist one who"—I thought Mr. Brown would say "who is avaricious, neglectful, or indifferent"; what he said was—"one who may be his own relative or his best paying advertiser—or even himself." It seemed to me then that he was becoming a bit finicky in his objection to even the subtler forms of compulsion. Yet we dare not ignore Mr. Brown. He is the heavy artillery on the other side. So, leaving aside his contributions to morals as not altogether inspiring, we must proceed to consider him as an economist.

"You cannot legislate efficiency," says Mr. Brown. "When

you compel an employer to pay a wage which is fixed regardless of the worker's efficiency, you are legislating a forced gratuity to the worker, no matter that the wage be measured by the cost of living or by any other standard which disregards its fair worth." There you have in compact form the objection to a legal minimum wage which is most persistent in people's minds. They say to themselves, "How can you force an employer to pay a girl *more than she is worth?*" Isn't that against all business, common sense and the laws of economics? What right has the state to legislate charity into the pay envelope? Isn't it absolutely wrong to force any woman to *receive more wages than she earns?*

The answer is that it might be wrong if there were any way of telling how much she is worth, or what she earns. We know what women workers *receive,* but no one has the least idea whether their income has anything to do with their productivity or their efficiency. If there is one thing the Factory Investigating Commission made clear, it is that wages for unskilled women's work in the sweated trades are not based upon any recognizable standard of efficiency or value.

Dr. Howard Woolston, who directed the work of the New York State Factory Investigating Commission, has pointed this out:

> Even for identical work in the same locality, striking differences in pay are found. In one wholesale candy factory in Manhattan no male laborer and no female hand-dipper is paid as much as $8 a week, nor does any female packer receive as much as $5.50. In another establishment of the same class in the same borough every male laborer gets $8 or over, and more than half the female dippers and packers exceed the rates given in the former plant. Again, one large department store in Manhattan pays 86 per cent of its saleswomen $10 or over; another pays 86 per cent of them less. When a representative paper-box manufacturer learner that

238

cutters in neighboring factories receive as little as $10 a week, he expressed surprise, because he always pays $15 or more. This indicates that there is no well established standard of wages in certain trades. The amounts are fixed by individual bargain, and labor is 'worth' as much as the employer agrees to pay.

These figures show pretty clearly that two employees in the same district making the same kind of goods have no way of standardizing wages on any basis of value. That is why Mr. Brown, talking about wages depending upon "wage-worth," is using a catchy phrase and a neat theory which in practice mean literally nothing at all. The kind of women's work to which the minimum wage would apply has no standard by which wages are fixed. Women get what they get, by the custom of the shop, by the whim of the superintendent, by arbitrary decision. No law of supply and demand, no sense of "wage-worth," determines that a "stripper" in order to earn fifteen cents an hour must paste paper on the side of about one hundred and fifty boxes, and a "hand-dipper" must coat about seven hundred and twenty pieces of cream candy with chocolate, while a hand-ironer in the laundry will earn twenty-five cents by pressing four plain shirts.

With these facts before us, suppose that we raised the wages of hand-dippers in candy manufacturing from fifteen to seventeen cents an hour, and thereby saved the girls from the most extreme hardships of poverty. By what standard would the Mr. Browns be able to say that we were paying this girl more than she is worth, that the extra cents were a "forced gratuity," or that we were interfering with the laws of supply and demand?

For what in the name of sanity are these economic laws as they appear in practical life? Mr. Brown and others talk about the value of cooperation, and how fine it is for employers to raise wages voluntarily. Yes, but why is it fine? Isn't it disastrous to tamper with the economic law, or are

239

we to understand that the economic law has no terrors when violated by the good will of the employer? Or perhaps may we assume that economic law, as Mr. Brown uses the phrase, is nothing but the will of the employer?

I am forced to believe it. I am forced to conclude from much study of Mr. Brown that whatever happens to exist is "natural" and "according to law," that any change inaugurated by the workers or by public opinion is "artificial," but that any change created by employers is merely economic law working itself out to beneficent ends.

The phrase "economic law" on the lips of men like Mr. Brown is nothing more than sheer buncombe which conceals a prejudice. It belongs to the same grade of intelligence which says, "You cannot make water run up hill," in the face of the fact that you can make it run up to the top of the highest skyscraper; which says, "You mustn't interfere with nature," and then proceeds to join oceans at Panama, deflect rivers, create lakes, move mountains, clear jungles, abolish typhoid, fly in the air, swim under the water, tunnel the earth. It is pathetic to think of what Mr. Brown's plight would be if millions of people hadn't spent their lives "interfering with nature." They have put clothes on his back, carried him in trains, protected him by fire laws, surrounded him with policemen; he has been shaved, washed, manicured; he has gone to the dentist's. He owes all that he is to invention, education, organization. The very liberty he talks about is a product of human effort, an effort to impose rational purposes upon the blind drift of things. When Mr. Brown is prepared to abolish all tariffs, all production of property, all factory laws, all laws against fraud, when he is ready to leave everything to whim and chance and accident, there will be some consistency in his thought.

In the meantime he is wasting fine words. What he calls natural law is really an amazing and damnable inefficiency on the part of employers. In these trades where women are em-

ployed and sweated we are dealing not with inexorable laws
but with thoughtless, stupid, careless, uneducated employers.
Strangely enough, they are only too ready to describe the
inefficiency of the girls they employ. Of course the girls are
inefficient. What else can one expect from the present housing,
schooling, and working conditions open to them? But for
every score against the incompetence of the workers there is
at least one score against the incompetence of the management, and it is time the general public realized that these
manufacturers and retailers who will be affected by the
minimum wage are proved by the facts to be profoundly
incompetent business men. When they cry out against "inter-
ferences," those who know the facts laugh. Those employers
who wish to be regarded as self-respecting captains of industry literally do not know how to run their own business,
and far from the state's interfering with them by investigation,
interference is more likely to prove their salvation.

The New York Commissioners unearthed the most ludicrous inefficiency. They found employers who kept their pay-
rolls in pocket-memorandum books; employers who had no
knowledge of rates paid by competitors for similar labor;
employers whose rates varied as much as fifty per cent in the
same neighborhood; whose labor cost varied as much as
from seventeen per cent to thirty-nine per cent in the same
line of work. They found seasonal fluctuations which were
violent. They found that in eleven large retail stores in New
York City 44,000 new names were added during the year
and 42,000 names were dropped. This was to maintain an
average working force of 27,000. In box and candy factories
nineteen plants employed 3,400 persons to maintain a force
of 1,700. The time lost between jobs is large. Of 1,500
women interviewed, 1,000 had lost an average of one month
in the preceding year. Obviously the labor market in sweated
industries is not a model of intelligence and foresight.

If this welter of inefficiency is the product of "natural

241

law," every civilized person will cry out for the interference of human law. It is "natural," no doubt, to slop along in the archaic manner, producing money profits at an enormous vital deficit. By the same token garbage would accumulate in back-yards and alleys, and all manner of disease-breeding foulness litter the earth. It would be "natural" to leave it there, it is artificial to remove it.

But two terrible results are prophesied: 1, the minimum wage will drive men out of business; 2, it will raise prices. Mr. Brown uses both threats, though it is a little difficult to see how a business which had been extinguished could raise its prices. The idea is, I believe, that some firms will go to the wall, and that the remaining ones will recoup by raising prices. These fears are, as we shall see later, based on theoretical guesses, rather than actual probabilities. For the moment I wish to consider a third possibility based on the experience of the brush industry in Massachusetts. Brush making, it should be said, is the first industry in the country in which the minimum wage has been fixed by a wage board. Let me tell the incident in Mr. Rome G. Brown's own words:

> One brush concern, since the minimum wage for brush makers took effect, has discharged over one hundred of its unskilled employees and has reorganized its methods of work so that its less skilled labor is done by those who also perform more skilled work; and at a total wage which is $40,000 a year less than that paid formerly.

In other words, the effect of the minimum wage has been to raise wages, eliminate a hundred of the most unskilled, and increase efficiency so much that the cost of labor is $40,000 less than it was. One would think Mr. Brown might be led to confess that this particular firm of brush makers had been a pretty inefficient organization. Not Mr. Brown. He is not in the business of admitting inefficiency among employers. This firm of brush makers, he tells us, was not uneconomical; it was unselfish. And when the state brought its brutal hand

down upon these sensitive brush makers the finer moral qualities disappeared:

> In self-defense against the arbitrary interference of the
> state with its business, it is now forced to figure its wage
> scales on a selfish basis. . . .

The result is that it pays a higher wage and saves $40,000
a year. But what some people may wish to know is whether
this particular firm, in the old days when it was on its un-
selfish and inefficient basis, was applying those natural laws
of economics about which Mr. Brown so graciously instructed
the Supreme Court.

Let us assume that the Minimum Wage act is passed in
New York. The Commission is created, and it proceeds to
establish wages boards in four industries—paper boxes,
candy, millinery, and retail dry goods. These boards, after
investigating the cost of living and the existing wage scales,
order a general raise of wages from a median of six dollars
to eight dollars. Let us assume that these industries are not
able to improve their efficiency, are not able to do what the
firm of Massachusetts brush makers did. Let us assume that
higher wages will mean no increased productivity among the
women workers. Under these circumstances, what would the
minimum wage cost the manufacturer in cutting down his
profits, or the consumer in raising prices?

Suppose that the whole cost is borne by the consumer.
Then if work-shirts cost three dollars a dozen and the labor
of sewing them is paid sixty cents, when we raise wages ten
per cent, the labor cost becomes sixty-six cents. The price
instead of being three dollars becomes three dollars and six
cents. In other words, while the worker receives a ten per
cent increase, the consumer pays only a two per cent increase.

It is estimated that to raise wages of 2,000 young women
in New York candy factories from five dollars and seventy-
five cents to eight dollars, confectioners in order to cover the
cost would have to charge eighteen cents more per hundred

243

pounds of candy. The profits in department stores average over five per cent on a year's business. But as the stock is turned five or six times annually, the yield on the investment is twenty-five per cent to thirty per cent. By raising the wages of girls under eighteen to six dollars, and of women over eighteen to nine dollars, the cost might be increased one and one-quarter per cent. If this were taken from profits instead of being added to the price, it would reduce the return to about nineteen per cent. The reason why these figures are so low is that the whole cost of labor in these sweated industries is a small fraction of the manufacturing cost: In the case of paper boxes, labor is a charge of from seventeen per cent to thirty per cent of the market price; in candy manufacture, the average labor cost is about thirteen per cent of the manufacturing expenses. By raising that charge we raise the total cost very little.

In the face of all this, what becomes of the cry that we are proposing to ruin business? It takes its place, doesn't it, beside all the other exclamations which have accompanied factory laws since the beginning of the nineteenth century? It is the cry which has accompanied every effort to clean up working conditions, protect mines, guard the life of child and women workers. Employers are always threatening a migration to less civilized countries. Yet somehow they stay where they are. A few go. In Victoria, one manufacturer in a panic moved out before the law went into effect. He moved over to Tasmania. Then Tasmania adopted the same law. In Victoria when the law was first passed in 1896 there were 3,370 factories employing 40,814 people; after fifteen years' experience of the law there were 5,638 factories employing 88,694 people.

But suppose a few employers do move out of the state— say from New York to New Jersey. How long will New Jersey tolerate their production of pauperism, disease, and degradation, and its costs in charities, hospitals, and sanatoria? Just about as long as it takes New Jersey to realize the ridiculous social cost of sweating.

Yet we are told that some employers will go to the wall. Able neither to raise prices nor increase efficiency, they will fail. To them the community must reply with simple kindliness that they belong with the landlords who own firetraps and conduct nests of disease and crime. They would better go out of business, and make way for better men.

It is often claimed that the minimum wage will become the maximum. President Wilson during his campaign gave an impetus to this argument by saying:

> If a minimum wage were established by law, the great majority of employers would take occasion to bring their wage scale as near as might be down to the level of the minimum; and it would be very awkward for the workingmen to resist that process successfully, because it would be dangerous to strike against the authority of the federal government.

Of course there is at the moment no question of a federal law. We are discussing state laws, and as regards New York a law which is to have no legal compulsion behind it. We are proposing to have a state commission of three persons select a small number of sweated industries where women and children are employed, and establish for those industries wages boards consisting of six representatives of the employer, six of the workmen, and two or three of the outside public. This conference of the trade is to study conditions and recommend a minimum wage, which is then to be published as an official recommendation. No one is legally bound by it. But even supposing he were, as in Oregon, California and elsewhere, how can the legal fixing of the least that may be paid affect the discussion of how much more shall be paid? If we make a rule that no one shall receive less than eight dollars a week, how does that prevent an employer from offering, or the workers from asking, nine or ten dollars? It is like assuming that because the tenement house law prescribes one hundred cubic feet of air per person, no one must live in more than one hundred feet.

245

But, say our critics, the tendency will be to level down to the minimum. Yes, but whom will it level down? Half the unskilled women workers will be levelled up. What ground is there for supposing the others will be levelled down? Are they, in the language of Mr. Brown, being paid more than they are "worth"? Or are they being paid what they are "worth"? Or aren't they being paid what the employer feels called upon to pay them? How will their status be changed by increasing the pay of the sweated workers?

Moreover, it is difficult to contemplate the folly of an employer who paid all his help, skilled, unskilled, experienced, and novice, anything like a single minimum standard. With no incentive left for improvement, no reward for skill, the efficiency of his plant would be a spectacle, and he would find very soon that he had been cutting off his nose to spite his face.

There is, however, no need to guess about these dark predictions. The minimum wage in one form or another has been applied for many years in various parts of the world. In Victoria it has been enforced by law since 1896; it has been applied in New Zealand, in England, and elsewhere. In the United States the trade unions have in various trades applied it. For clearly there is no economic difference between a minimum established by force of law, by force of public opinion, or by force of a strike. The economic effect is the same, and all the terrible results prophesied ought to have shown themselves. It is, I believe, an almost unanimous conclusion of students that the minimum rates have not tended to become the maximum.

For example, according to Mr. Harris Weinstock of the United States Commission on Industrial Relations, 2,458 workers in the city of Auckland, New Zealand, had their wages fixed by law. Among these 948 received the minimum, and 1,510, or sixty-one per cent, received more. In Christchurch, New Zealand, out of 2,788 under the wage law fifty-nine per cent received more than the minimum. In Dunedin, fifty-one per cent received above the legal minimum. To those, then, who assert that the effect is to level down wages, we can oppose the answer that where tried it has done no such thing.

Mr. M. B. Hammond, vice-chairman of the Industrial Commission of Ohio, from whom I quote these figures, says quite pertinently:

> Furthermore, it must be remembered that the employers' claim that such a system of wage regulation would have a levelling effect on wages is beside the mark, since at the present time in most industrial establishments of any considerable size in this country, great numbers of employees performing the same class of work are paid the same wages, irrespective of differences in individual efficiency. A few years ago when I visited certain large steel mills in Pittsburgh, I was told that in one of them where 12,000 workers were employed, two-thirds received a flat rate of $1.50 a day, and in another mill employing 4,500 men, two-thirds of the employees received $1.65 a day.

Indeed, our campaign against sweating is badly named a minimum wage campaign. The minimum wage exists, but it is so low and so irregular that it has become an infinitesimal wage. What we are struggling for is a minimum that shall be a living wage, a minimum which is yet so low that in all conscience it is little above the slave-owners' standard, a minimum which shall enable a woman who works all day long to earn enough to sustain her health, buy decent food, clothes, and lodging, and secure a little recreation.

There is one prediction persistently made by Mr. Brown and others which experience shows to be true. A certain number of the ultimately inefficient workers are displaced when the living wage standard is applied to an industry. The brush factory in Massachusetts which reorganized, saved $40,000 on its wage bill, and discharged a hundred of its least skilled employees, is a case in point. There are undoubtedly people working to-day whom no business man would keep if they could not be sweated. Child labor is the most striking example, coolie labor is another; some immigrant labor, both men's and women's, falls within the category. There are also groups of workers who are physically or mentally defective, and there are those who have not yet learned the trade and so require an apprenticeship of some kind.

We are asked what is to become of these people? The question generally assumes that we have forgotten all about them, or that in our ruthless benevolence we plan to throw them out into the street. Yet as a matter of fact it is just these marginal workers who constitute the most convincing argument for establishing living wage standards. But they cannot be dealt with wholesale.

In low-skilled occupations such as the sweated trades, no long period of apprenticeship is required. But there is a time when the young girl is so inexperienced that she wastes material and produces very little result. All sensible minimum wage laws provide for about six months' probation at something under the standard wage. There has been a tendency among employers to abuse this privilege. They have found it cheaper to take on "apprentices" for six months, discharge them, and recruit a new force of "inexperienced workers." They have generally worked this evasion of the spirit of the plan when the difference between the regular wage and the probationary wage was greater than the difference between the value of an inexperienced and an experienced employee.

Obviously these difficulties can be met by resourceful administration. An alert Commission can adjust its findings so as to eliminate gross circumvention and still make perfectly feasible a term of apprenticeship. The deeper remedy for the situation lies in the school system which turns into industry workers with so little general training and vocational adaptability.

The plan we propose carries with it a provision for licenses to be granted by the Commission in special cases where the evidence is clear that a person should be permitted to work for less than the minimum wage. This elasticity is needed for good administration, because in any human problem there are particular people who fit badly into a general rule. There are, for example, a number of workers who are crippled in one way or another and yet manage to live self-respecting lives by earning small sums. No one proposes to crush them under an iron rule, and so a human discretion is allowed to the Commission.

There are nevertheless classes of workers whose productivity is very, very low. They may be old, or weak-minded, or physically feeble, or so utterly untrained and illiterate that under American conditions they cannot be employed at a living wage. We say of them that they should not be employed. They should not be permitted to debauch the labor market, to wreck by their competition the standards of other workers.

At this point we break radically with our critics. We are against sweating. That means we are against cheap labor and for the economy of high wages. We say that it is saner and in the end less costly to take care of these industrial incompetents than to allow them to compete with the great mass of the workers.

The sick and mentally defective should be cared for by the state. The old should be pensioned. The children should be kept in school and subsidized to stay there if necessary. None of these people belong in the labor market, and the minimum wage if it keeps them out will do a most useful service.

Not enough has been made of the fact that the fixing of an American minimum is one of our best protections against indiscriminate and overstimulated immigration. Once abolish sweating and take industry off a basis of cheap labor, and you have reduced one of the great incentives to the most threatening forms of immigration. If the European is compelled to work at not less than an American standard, he will be less useful to the employers of cheap labor, and less effort will be made to bring him over.

The same reasoning applies to the employment of children. They are hired to-day because they are cheap. Make them expensive, and fewer of them will be hired; there will thus be less opposition to child labor laws. Indeed, by the transition from a sweated to a living standard there are few problems of industry which are not affected. Whenever business men abandon the old notion of all the traffic will bear and all the human body can stand and turn to an intelligent counting of vital costs, a better morale appears in the industrial world.

We are dealing in these sweated trades with industries where cooperation, pride of work, technical and social standards are most primitive. Competition has corrupted them to the point of despair, and only by the establishment of some device like the wages board can we hope to create a civilized discipline. The employers must organize to send their representatives; the workers must combine to send theirs. At these board meetings the conditions of the trade as a whole have to be analyzed, statistics have to be compiled, investigations made. Well-managed plants are compared with befuddled ones; the whole philosophy of management is opened to discussion. The educational effect of this will undoubtedly prove to be very great.

For what the minimum wage plan proposes is really a kind of legislature of the industry—a legislature in which workers, employers and public are represented. This is the Wages Board. Its findings are subject to veto or review by the Commission or by the courts. But when the disagreement is not too radical, the Wages Board becomes in practice the actual parliament of the industry. Under the Oregon plan its decrees are enforced by the state, under the Massachusetts plan by public opinion.

Its powers, like that of any legislature, are limited. It establishes only the minimum wage. But this must carry with it agreement about hours, piece work, labor conditions, manu-

250

facturing methods, use of machinery, and, in the end, profits and prices too. In short, the Wages Board is a device for stimulating in sweated and primitive trades those beginnings of economic democracy which the unions are beginning to construct in the more mature industries. Ultimately this is perhaps the greatest promise of the experiment. The management of these chaotic trades will be scrutinized by the persons most closely concerned—the people who live and work in them. Employers will begin to know what they are at, how their methods compare with those of their rivals. They will learn the difficult and necessary art of thinking about the trade as a whole in its relation to labor and the public. The workers will for the first time get genuine representation, and they should learn by direct example the value of the solidarity of labor. They will receive constant practice in formulating their needs, exerting pressure, making intelligent their demands. And this, it should be remembered, is in industries where women predominate, women who will soon be voters. No more necessary or more valuable school of democracy can be created than these trade legislatures, in which people have a chance to learn how to govern the conditions of their work.

Yet it would be absurd to assume that minimum wage legislation is a kind of omnibus for paradise. To fix a "living standard" would be a great advance over what we have, but by every civilized criterion it is a grudging and miserable thing. In those moments of lucidity when we forget our hesitancy before brute obstruction, it seems like a kind of madness that we should have to argue and scrape in order that we may secure to millions of women enough income to "live." If we had not witnessed whole nations glowering at each other all winter from holes in the mud, it would be hard to believe that America with all its riches could still be primitive enough to grunt and protest at a living wage—a living wage, mind you; not a wage so its women can live well, not enough to make life a rich and welcome experience, but just enough to

251

secure existence amid drudgery in grey boarding-houses and cheap restaurants.

We may fail to secure that. So far as the press is concerned, the issue hardly exists. It lies at the moment stifled in platitudes and half-truths about "not hurting business." From the little comment there is, we might think that a business was sound if it rested on the degradation of its labor; might think that business men were a lot of jumpy neurotics ready to shrivel up and burst into tears at a proposal to increase their wages bill a penny or two on the dollar; might think, from the exclamations of Mr. Brown and his friend John Smith, that a campaign against sweating would do no less than ruin the country.

But you cannot ruin a country by conserving its life. You can ruin a country only by stupidity, waste, and greed.

March 27, 1915

SHORTER HOURS

Oregon has a law which says that "it is the public policy of the state of Oregon that no person shall be hired or permitted to work for wages, under any conditions or terms, for longer hours or days of service than is consistent with his health and physical wellbeing and ability to promote the general welfare by his increasing usefulness as a healthy and intelligent citizen. It is hereby declared that the working of any person more than ten hours in one day, in any mill, factory, or manufacturing establishment is injurious to the physical health and wellbeing of such person, and tends to prevent him from acquiring that degree of intelligence that is necessary to make him a useful and desirable citizen of the state." The Oregon Supreme Court has declared this statute constitutional. It is now before the Supreme Court of the United States. The question is, does the police power cover such legislation or is it a violation of "liberty" under the Fourteenth Amendment? It is the first time that the court has had to deal with the working hours of men since the Lochner case in 1905, when a ten-hour law applying to bakers in New York was annulled. The court reasoned then that it had not been convinced that baking is a "dangerous occupation." Thus as matters stand now it is constitutional to limit the hours of women, but of men only in certain accepted dangerous trades. In this so-called Bunting case which comes from Oregon, the attempt will be made to secure a decision extending the right to limit men's hours in all trades.

The argument is that practically any trade becomes a dangerous trade if the hours are overlong. To prove it the state of Oregon has submitted a brief about a thousand pages long which is an exhaustive collection of all the available facts and opinions, medical, economic, moral, drawn from the whole world, which bear upon the question of overwork. It was prepared by Miss Josephine Goldmark of the National Consumers' League in consultation with Mr. Louis D. Brandeis, who was to have argued the case, but of course had to withdraw when he was nominated for the Supreme Court. At the invitation of Attorney-General Brown of Oregon, Professor Felix Frankfurter of the Harvard Law School was invited to take Mr. Brandeis's place. Miss Goldmark's brief has more than a passing interest. It is more than a bit of argument. It is really an authoritative treatise on the effect of fatigue, as applied to men as well as women. It carries on her masterly work now published under the title *Fatigue and Efficiency*. It contains more honest and illuminated research than has ever before been brought to the support of a piece of American labor legislation. For this brief is not only an argument to a court, it is a scientific demonstration of the need for shorter working hours, and it will be used for a long time by legislators, trade unionists, and by enlightened employers as a book of reference and authority. We hope in a later issue to summarize it.

April 15, 1916

THE N.A.M. SPEAKS

More ingenious use of Scripture has rarely been made than in a recent preliminary report of the National Association of Manufacturers. The document deals with the legislative minimum wage. It will repay reading by anyone who wishes to mix laughter with his tears. He will find that the discussion begins at the beginning, with Genesis, in fact, from which we learn that Jacob worked seven years in payment for each of his wives, Leah and Rachel, and six years more for the possession of a herd of cattle. Jacob's wages were changed ten times by his employer, Laban, but as to whether this industrial unrest was due to strikes or legislative minimum wage boards, the National Association of Manufacturers does not commit itself. Be that as it may, we hear next about Athens, where, significantly enough, the wholesale price of wheat was fixed in the third century, B.C.; also about Sparta, and even Thebes, where a workman could never aspire to office. There are passing but learned allusions to Aristotle, Xenophon, Pisistratus, Pericles, and Periander, as well as to Cicero and the emperor Diocletian who, disregarding the laws of economics in the year 301 A.D., fixed a minimum rate for provisions and wages.

Yet we must not linger over the scholarship of these practical men. Let us pass without comment Constantine and the emperor Zeno. Let us come at once to Jesus of Nazareth, and his parable of the laborers in the vineyard, as quoted by the National Association of Manufacturers:

St. Matthew, XX, 1–15—"For the Kingdom of Heaven is like unto a man that is an householder, which went out early in the morning to hire laborers into his vineyard.

"And when he had agreed with the laborers for a penny a day, he sent them into his vineyard.

"And he went out about the third hour and saw others standing idle in the market place.

"And said unto them: Go ye also into the vineyard, and whatsoever is right I will give you. And they went their way.

"Again he went out about the sixth and ninth hour and did likewise.

"And about the eleventh hour he went out and found others standing idle, and said unto them, Why stand ye here all day idle?

"They say unto him, Because no man hath hired us. He saith unto them, Go ye also into the vineyard, and whatsoever is right, that shall ye receive.

"So when even was come, the lord of the vineyard saith unto his steward, Call the laborers, and give them their hire, beginning from the last unto the first.

"And when they came that were hired about the eleventh hour, they received every man a penny.

"But when the first came, they supposed that they should have received more; and they likewise received every man a penny.

"And when they had received it, they murmured against the good man of the house.

"Saying, These last have wrought but one hour, and thou hast made them equal unto us, which have borne the burden and heat of the day.

"But he answered one of them and said, Friend, I do thee no wrong; didst not thou agree with me for a penny?

"Take that thine is, and go thy way: I will give unto this last even as unto thee.

"Is it not lawful for me to do what I will with mine own? Is thine eye evil because I am good?"

Here the document pauses, and remarks:

This parable is regarded by the commentators as
having established some very interesting principles and
facts, viz:

1. The right of a man to do what he desires with his
own money (if he does not do evil with it, or interfere
with the rights of others).

2. The tendency of the maximum and the minimum
wage to become the same, whenever the latter is greater
than it would be usually.

3. The fact that the length of the work-day at this
period was by no means limited to a three-hour or
eight-hour schedule.

The quotations, remember, are from a document issued in
the year 1915 by the official body of American Manufacturers. The first eleven pages out of thirty-two are devoted to
these supreme assininities.

I must confess that after such an introduction it was a little
difficult to approach the rest of the report with the entire
respect of an open mind. How, for example, was one to treat
the statement that "the legislative minimum wage has so far
been enacted mainly in the agricultural states of the West . . .
the exception outside the agricultural states being the industrial state of Massachusetts," when everyone knows that
Massachusetts does not have a legislative minimum wage at
all? It has a legal wage commission, whose findings do not
establish a legal wage because those findings have no compulsory power. Oregon and Washington, on the contrary,
have a real legislative minimum wage. But Oregon and Washington are not mentioned in this report, and their experience
is not discussed. Massachusetts is discussed, and never once
is there a hint that the author of this document knows the
difference between the Massachusetts and the Oregon and
Washington method. He simply ignores the Western states
as "agricultural," and treats Massachusetts as if its voluntary

minimum wage system were identical with a legislative minimum wage.

Nor does the author make the least attempt to distinguish compulsory arbitration in Australia from the minimum wage as proposed in the United States. They are all one to him, and all bad. Conciliation boards, arbitration courts, compulsory minimum wage by legislative fiat, compulsory minimum wage by the decree of a wage board, voluntary minimum wage by the agreement of a wage board, the maximum wage in Rome, the Statute of Laborers in 1349—no distinction is made. They are all interference with the wage contract, and they are lumped together in one foggy denunciation for the befuddlement of human reason. It is impossible to argue with the sponsors of this document. They have got themselves so tangled up in ignorance and misstatement, they are so blandly oblivious even of the difference between setting a maximum and a minimum wage, that all one can do is to give samples of their quality of mind, and leave it to the reader to determine how seriously he will have their argument.

They say, for example, that when the Australian Commission of the National Association of Manufacturers made its investigation, "it was given evidence daily of the growing dissatisfaction." But they furnish absolutely no evidence. They simply assert about Australia and New Zealand that "nowhere is more industrial unrest to be found." Nowhere, indeed! and that after Lawrence, Lowell, Paterson, Calumet, Akron, West Virginia, Butte, and Colorado.

They go on to state that in Massachusetts "practically every employee affected by the law has been discharged." That is a serious indictment if true, and pending a report from the Massachusetts Commission I am in no position to dispute the assertion. But when I read that one firm discharged seventy-five women and minor workers, I remain unconvinced until the statement is supplemented by some facts as to who is now doing the work of these seventy-five who were discharged. Another firm of brush makers reports that "it has been necessary recently to discharge some of our employees, and of course in doing this we have allowed those to go that we considered of the least value." But nothing is said to make certain that this cutting down of the force was not due to industrial depression.

Since they were looking for experience, I wonder why the first biennial report of the Industrial Welfare Commission of Washington is not even mentioned in this document. Why have the Manufacturers failed to dispute these assertions?

The sequence of it all is that there are vastly more women workers in the State of Washington to-day receiving a living wage than there were two years ago when the law was enacted; that there are more higher-paid girls than there were then; that the whole wage standard, together with the standards of efficiency and discipline, has been raised. . . .

And in the forthcoming report of the United States Bureau of Labor Statistics on the operation of the Oregon Minimum Wage Law they will be able to read that:

The rates of pay for women as a whole have increased. Wherever the wage rates of old employees were affected by the minimum wage rulings, they were benefited. Some women upon reinstatement after an absence had been compelled to accept the rate to which they were legally entitled, a rate below that received during their earlier services. The average rates of pay of minors and experienced women have increased, that of inexperienced adults decreased slightly. More girls under 18 years received over $6 after than before the minimum wage determination. Among the experienced women not only the proportion getting $9.25, but those getting over $9.25 have increased. The proportion of the force receiving over $12 has also increased, although the actual number have decreased but not in the same degree as the decrease in the total force . . .

No evidence of decreased efficiency among women affected by the wage rulings could be discovered. The numbers for whom comparable data on this subject could be secured were too limited, however, to warrant conclusions.

All the changes arising from decreased business, reorganization of departments and increased rates and earnings, resulted in an increase in the female and also the total labor cost of three mills per dollar of sales. This increased cost was not distributed equally among stores or among departments in the same stores. The female labor cost varied from an 8-mill increase in Portland neighborhood stores to a 1.2-cent decrease in Salem stores.

Business conditions reduced the number of women employed. The majority of those who remained and were affected by the minimum wage rulings were benefited in rates of pay and also in average earnings. Those to whom the minimum wage determinations did not apply sustained no losses chargeable to these rulings.

All this assertion and counter-assertion is, of course, immensely unsatisfactory. But it is necessary because the Manufacturers' Association has chosen to state on its own say-so that the law is a failure, and to ignore entirely the most trustworthy official documents which happen to be available. The Washington and Oregon reports may be wrong, but the N.A.M. has not attempted to disprove them. The arguments of the New York State Factory Investigation Commission may be biased, but the N.A.M. has not mentioned them. The N.A.M. may know all about Massachusetts. It has not published the statistics.

This at least is certain. The temper and tone of the report can inspire no confidence whatever. From the idiotic interpretation of the parable about the vineyard to the blank assertion that the minimum wage has "invariably failed," the report is a mass of undigested assertion, unsupported argument, and

260

appeals to prejudice such as one would expect from an illiterate quack, not from the representatives of supposedly intelligent manufacturers.

Hear, for example, the argument that low wages do not make for ill health:

> Low general standards of living are usually accompanied by ignorance of the laws and resources of hygiene, by no nutrition and malnutrition, and hence by lower standards of vigor and resistance to disease than where higher standards of living prevail. Obviously, then, lower standards of physical strength and resistance are due to such conditions of labor as excessively long hours of work in the unskilled and sweated industries, or to conditions inherent in the character of the employment itself.

In short, "no nutrition and malnutrition" are not due to low wages; "low general standards of living" are not due to low wages.

It is perhaps not for an outsider to presume to offer advice to the Manufacturers' Association. If this is the best it can do, the intellectual victory of its opponents is assured from the outset. But I cannot help wondering what humane and intelligent employers must think of these documents issued in their name. If I were a manufacturer I should either hang my head and blush, or get up and shout from the housetops that these spokesmen of mine were fools who were making a fool of me. I should do what I could to get rid of them at once, knowing that the manufacturers' cause will never command respect while such fifth-rate intelligence is allowed to speak for it.

July 3, 1915

261

MR. ROCKEFELLER

ON THE STAND

John D. Rockefeller, Jr. was the son of the founder
of the Standard Oil Company; his own sons became in
later years governors of New York, Arkansas and the
Chase Manhattan Bank. At this time Rockefeller was
40 years old. Frank P. Walsh, a liberal lawyer then
from Missouri and later from New York, was chairman of the Commission on Industrial Relations. [*A.S.,
jr.*]

Mr. Rockefeller seemed terribly alone on Monday when he
faced the Industrial Relations Commission. There was an
atmosphere of no quarter. A large crowd watching intensely
every expression of his face, about twenty cameras and a
small regiment of newspaper men, a shorthand reporter at
his elbow, and confronting him the Commissioners led by the
no means reassuring Mr. Walsh—except for an indefatigably
kindly police sergeant who gave him one glass of water after
another, not much was done to pamper the witness. He met
what he knew to be his accusers with the weary and dogged
good humor of a child trying to do a sum it does not understand for a teacher who will not relent.

From the first Mr. Rockefeller was on the defensive. He
began by reading the long statement which was printed that
evening in the newspapers. The statement was very carefully
prepared; much thought and labor had evidently gone into it,

262

but as a matter of style it did not sound in the least like anything that Mr. Rockefeller had to say on his direct oral examination. Perhaps we did him an injustice, but it never occurred to us to suppose that Mr. Rockefeller had written the document himself. Nevertheless, Mr. Rockefeller read the paper well.

But it was much too smooth to be convincing. When he read with warm emphasis that "combinations of capital are sometimes conducted in an unworthy manner, contrary to law and in disregard of the interest both of labor and the public," we wondered whom he had in mind. Nor were we any more enlightened as to what he really stood for when he said that "such combinations cannot be too strongly condemned nor too vigorously dealt with." He read those sentences with sincere indignation and without betraying the slightest self-consciousness. To the charge that he has enforced an industrial absolutism in Colorado, he replied with much feeling that "an attitude toward industry and toward labor such as is here implied is so abhorrent to me personally and so contrary to the spirit of my whole purpose and training that I cannot allow these allegations to pass unnoticed. . . . While it has been said that I have exercised an absolute authority in dictating to the management of the Colorado Fuel and Iron Company, it has also been said that I have been too indifferent, and that as a director I should have exercised more authority. Clearly, both cannot be true."

Yet it seemed to me as I listened to him that both could be true, and that in fact it was just such a dilemma which was the truth. For while the reality of the Rockefeller power could hardly be questioned, the use of that power appeared to have been second-hand and inadequate. For ten years Mr. Rockefeller had not seen his property; his relation to it was by letter and by conference with the officials. What he knew of it must have come to him from them, and, as he has confessed, he trusted their word. Now when we speak of the despotism of the Czar of Russia, we do not mean that he in person acts

263

despotically in every province of his empire. We mean that a despotic hierarchy exists owning allegiance to him as its titled head. We know that if the Czar wished to liberalize his government he would find himself hampered by his subordinate officials. But he has to bear the responsibility for the things that are done in his name, and because he has potential power he is blamed not only for what he does but for what he doesn't do.

This seemed to be the predicament of Mr. Rockefeller. I should not believe that he personally hired thugs or wanted them hired; I should not believe that the inhumanity of Colorado is something he had conceived. It seems far more true to say that his impersonal and half-understood power has delegated itself into unsocial forms, that it has assumed a life of its own which he is almost powerless to control. If first impressions count for anything, I should describe Mr. Rockefeller as a weak despot governed by a private bureaucracy which he is unable to lead. He has been thrust by the accident of birth into a position where he reigns but does not rule; he has assumed a title to sovereignty over a dominion which he rarely visits, about which his only source of information is the reports of men far more sophisticated and far less sensitive than he himself.

His intellectual helplessness was the amazing part of his testimony. Here was a man who represented an agglomeration of wealth probably without parallel in history, the successor to a father who has with justice been called the high priest of capitalism. Freedom of enterprise, untrammeled private property, the incentives of the profiteer, culminate in the achievements of his family. He is the supreme negation of all equality, and unquestionably a symbol of the most menacing fact in the life of the republic. Yet he talked about himself on the commonplace moral assumptions of a small business man. There never was anybody less imperial in tone than John D. Jr. The vastness of his position seemed to have no counterpart in a wide and far-reaching imagination. Those who listened to him would have forgiven him much if they had felt that they were watching a great figure, a real master of men, a person of some magnificence. But in John D. Rockefeller, Jr., there seemed to be nothing but a young man having a lot of trouble, very much harassed and very well-meaning. No sign of the statesman, no quality of leadership in large affairs, just a careful, plodding, essentially uninteresting person who justifies himself with simple moralities and small-scale virtues.

His tragedy is that of all hereditary power, for there is no magic in inheritance, and sooner or later the scion of a house is an incompetent. Yet the complicated system over which he presides keeps him in an uncomfortably exalted position, where all men can see its absurdity. It is the weak monarch who finally betrays the monarchy. It is the unimaginative, blundering, good-natured king who pays for the acts of his predecessors. Those who rule and have no love of power suffer much. John D. Rockefeller, Jr., is one of these, I think, and he is indeed a victim. The failure of the American people to break up his unwieldy dominion has put a man who should have been a private citizen into a monstrously public position where even the freedom to abdicate is denied him.

January 30, 1915

THE ROCKEFELLER PLAN

IN COLORADO

The miners employed by the Colorado Fuel and Iron Company have been offered what is called an "Industrial Representation Plan." It provides that the workers shall elect annually men chosen from amongst themselves to represent them. There is to be one delegate for every hundred and fifty wage-earners, but each camp is to have at least two representatives. The balloting is to be secret, and conducted by the employees themselves, though the appeal in a disputed election lies to the management of the company. At the meetings where the elections are held the men are to have the opportunity of airing grievances and offering advice and instructions to their representatives. To qualify as a voter a man must have been employed for at least three months.

The mining camps are classified in five districts—the Trinidad, the Walsenburg and so on. At the call of the president of the company the elected representatives of the workers are to meet an equal number of representatives appointed by the company management. These district conferences, presided over by the president or his appointee, select a number of joint committees of six men. There are to be committees on Industrial Cooperation and Conciliation; on Safety and Accidents; on Sanitation, Health and Housing; on Recreation and Education. These joint committees are to be available at any time for consultation with the management. They have also the power of raising questions within their jurisdiction. But the committee on Industrial Cooperation and Conciliation may take up "any matter pertaining to the prevention and settlement of industrial disputes, terms and conditions of employment, maintenance of order and discipline in the several camps, company stores, etc., etc." The etc., etc., is quoted. In addition to the district conference there is to be an annual conference of all the delegates and officers.

This elaborate machinery has at least the primary merit of establishing some communication between the men and the officers—and judged by conditions which existed before the strike, this is a considerable advance. Under it the management will learn much that it should hear, will be able to avoid many blunders and smooth out many petty wrinkles. If peace is the object, the plan will no doubt further it a little by ventilating some difficulties and allaying certain causes of friction.

But there should be no self-deception about the scheme. It does not establish representation nor provide for collective bargaining. The fact that the men have to choose their delegates from the employees of the company is a death blow at any genuine representation. For it means that the miner who is unfortunate enough to be elected has to represent his constituents at the risk of his job. And no good intentions of Mr. Rockefeller's can alter the fact that a miner in an obscure Colorado camp is at the mercy of foremen and mine superintendents. To ask him to fight the cause of his fellow-workers, when that cause will carry him into conflict with the men who control his employment, is to destroy at its roots the possibility of real representation. It is like asking Mr. Rockefeller to trust his interests in the hands of a lawyer employed by Mr. Frank Walsh.

The first requirement of any representative government is the safety and independence of the representative. That is why we provide, for example, that no Congressman can be held legally responsible for what he says on the floor of the House. But this plan for Colorado virtually gives the opponents whom the men's representative has to deal with a power

267

of industrial life and death over him. To be sure there is Article 18, Section III, which provides for some protection. If the representative feels discrimination he may appeal to the joint committee of the district and from that to the Industrial Commission of the State of Colorado. In practice, however, this would amount to very little protection, for the possibilities of discrimination are endless. A troublesome representative can and will be made to suffer.

Without genuine representation there can be no collective bargaining. The men have no one free to fight their case for them. In addition, the plan provides against any really powerful collective action. Article 3, Section III, states that

> There shall be no discrimination by the company or by any of its employees on account of membership or non-membership in any society, fraternity, or union.

In other words, the old-fashioned open shop. Article 4, Section III, which follows this declaration, contains the core of the whole matter:

> The right to hire and discharge, the management of the properties, and the direction of the working forces, shall be vested exclusively in the company, and except as expressly restricted, this right shall not be abridged by anything contained herein.

It is the charter of absolutism, and in the face of it any talk of "industrial representation" is a mockery. The company retains every essential of its old mastery, and the only difference is that it has been frightened into a willingness to listen to advice. No doubt Mr. Rockefeller means to use his absolute power in somewhat more enlightened fashion. But his power is supreme and unquestioned, and whatever is done will be an act of grace or of prudence. The men remain helpless. Split into small groups in distant gullies, represented by men as helpless as themselves, how in the name of sanity are they to bargain with the power of Rockefeller?

We can understand why a local manufacturer might fear to deal with a national union, but what excuse Mr. Rockefeller has for refusing we cannot see. His wealth is organized on a national scale, he employs experts to represent him, but he insists that miners in Colorado shall face his vast power organized by constituencies no larger than a mining camp. Against his power of discharge, what equivalent have they? None but the strike, and for that funds, leaders, and more organization are required. The district conferences have none of those essentials of industrial power. Whether Mr. Rockefeller intended it or not, his plan is based on the principle of first dividing the men and then ruling them.

The proposal is being submitted to a referendum of the men. We hope they will see their own interests clearly enough to reject it.

October 9, 1915

UNREST

Attorney General A. Mitchell Palmer had begun his arrest and deportation of suspected revolutionists in the fall of 1919. Big Bill Haywood, a leader of the IWW, had been convicted of sedition; he appealed his case and was currently out on bail. In 1921 he jumped bail and went to the Soviet Union. The Lusk Committee of the New York Legislature contributed enthusiastically to the national panic. [*A.S., jr.*]

Those who recall the volume of words uttered in the last few years about unpreparedness will recognize the original cause of our present difficulties. For one year we have tried to drift somehow back to some kind of peace footing. Instead we have drifted into a severe internal conflict. We are paying the price today for the complacency of having said on December second a year ago that the return to peace "promises to outrun any inquiry that may be instituted and any aid that may be offered. It will not be easy to direct it any better than it will direct itself." In these last months it has directed itself to the edge of disaster.

This was not accomplished by the comparatively insignificant people who wish to overthrow the government. It was accomplished by the office holders who have been too absentminded to behave like a government. They have refused to look ahead, refused to think, refused to plan, refused to prepare for any of the normal consequences of a war. The attack on the government is nothing as compared with the

270

paralysis of the government. Can anyone name a single piece of constructive legislation or administration carried through since the armistice? Railroads, shipping, prices, import and export policy, our financial relations with Europe, not one of them has been dealt with. To the problem of capital and labor, aggravated by the price convulsion and by the nervous fatigue of the war, what has been the constructive contribution of the government? A hall to meet in and a chairman.

Compared to those of any other nation our difficulties were small. But they were difficulties, and they required action and policy and leadership. There has been none. For the government of the United States resides in the mind of Mr. Wilson. There are no other centers of decision. Whatever thinking is done he does. If he is away the thinking apparatus is away. Because for the last year he found himself more than occupied with the treaty of peace, there has been no government at home able or willing to deal with those things that we have neglected at our peril. For this neglect a most fantastic excuse has been put forward. It is that nothing could be done until the treaty of peace was ratified.

It is pointed out that labor's productivity is low. It remains to be pointed out that the productivity of the government in respect to leadership is lower still. There has been no example from Washington to inspire hard work, prevision or prudence. The assumption has been that fate or luck would take care of us, as it did the babes in the woods. There has been no program on which men could loyally unite, no line of policy defined which they could follow, no purposes set before them to which they could apply their energies. It has been an abdication of leadership. In great matters it has been a year of waiting around. At first this was a relief after the intense strain of the war, but gradually as the results of neglect made themselves felt a panic has spread.

It has infected most seriously a large number of the established leaders of the community. They are in danger of losing their heads for they are enormously frightened. Worst of all

271

they show that they are frightened. They are doing just what leaders must never under any circumstances do: betraying their own lack of confidence. In real life, as well as in fiction, the greater the peril the cooler and more collected the leader must be. Who ever trusted a man when he twittered and chattered? While others tremble, he stands firm, unhurried, imperturbable! If for a disastrous moment he begins to wring his hands, to cry out, see spooks, to curse and pray, adieu to his leadership for the stampede and the rout are on.

The cold shiver which is passing down the backs of so many is produced chiefly at Helsingfors, Stockholm, Copenhagen, and in the close vicinity of City Hall Park. In manufacturing costs it is probably the world's most expensive shiver. Historically it is the sequel to the nightmares experienced by those who expected to hear at almost any moment that the German army had landed in New York, who saw a spy in every nurse girl and sedition in every brogue. The same people who suffered such horrors as those all through the war are now daily in the presence of imaginary soviets, dictatorships, confiscation decrees, and above all extraordinary tribunals. In their mind's eye, and this is essential to a charitable understanding of the case, they are already experiencing a sally from the tenements, followed by confiscation, the brutal dictatorship of an ignorant and alien horde, and the whole catalogue of social pestilence. In the worst cases the thing has all the vividness of an hallucination. For most of our leading citizens it is sufficiently real to have unstrung what was left to unstring after the war had finished with their nerves. Naturally it is difficult for them to understand those who are trying to retain composure without complacency. It seems as if only an incendiary could be calm when there is a fire. But that is just where bad nerves are leading them astray. The incendiary, they may be sure, is in a state of fluttering excitement. The person who remains calm, if he is fit for his job, is the fireman.

Our leaders should remember that they have no monopoly

of bad nerves, and that the example set by those who are conspicuous has enormous effect on the rest of the population. What example do they set? Are they devoted to the truth? Do they insist, as leaders should insist, on the authentic news? Do they squelch rumor and gossip and legend? They repeat them at every dinner table. Do they withhold judgment till the evidence is in? Do they judge as they would be judged? They do not. They condemn sight unseen, text unread, on hearsay. Before they can expect a restoration of order in society there will have to be a restoration of order in the minds of those who are its leading citizens. Let them allay their own unrest first. So long as they go into delirium at imaginary pictures of the Russian Revolution, it will not be surprising that "ignorant foreigners" are excited when they find that the old wages will not buy the same groceries. Let our leaders put aside this opera bouffe revolution with themselves cast for Marie Antoinette. Let history make its legends if it must. But let us stop living in a legend. Life today is grim and difficult enough without complicating it further by behaving as if it were half melodrama, half nightmare.

The most dangerous form of complication is the current fashion of treating almost every economic or political incident as a phase of an imaginary revolution. For the moment the universal question is not whether this is right or wrong, desirable or undesirable, wise or foolish, but whether it fits in with this fictitious revolution that so many pretend is in progress. All our judgments are disturbed by this unreal criterion, and we shall not have restored sense until we begin again to deal with things on their merits, according to the facts, in the light of the sane tradition of American life. If everything that is suggested in America is to be viewed in the light of what Lenin thinks and does or is supposed to think and do, we shall never recover our self-possession. Take the case of a lawyer with years of experience in railroads who after long study evolves a railroad bill to untangle the railroad question. He proposes to compensate the owners at a price fixed by the courts. He proposes to win, if at all, by persuasion, perhaps in the last resort by a direct appeal to the voter. There surely is a proposal to be examined entirely on its merits. His plan may be wrong in principle or detail. It may be a mistake as the Payne-Aldrich tariff was a mistake. But it is not a massacre. Yet the scheme is treated by many who should know better as if it were the Russian Revolution at last arrived on our soil.

The time has come when those who lead opinion will have to make up their minds what they propose to regard as revolutionary. That the overwhelming majority in this country is against revolution is not open to question. But at the same time, in spite of all appearances, a decisive majority is progressive to radical. That which in 1912 went to the making of liberalism in all parties but the Republican rump and the bourbon Democracy is not extinguished and cannot long be frustrated. It swung the election of 1916 for Wilson, and it is abroad today. As a party the Bull Moose is dead, as a way of behaving it will not down. For it represents the persistent dream of all Americans, that whatever Europe's experience may be, here at least obstinacy and fanaticism shall not have their way; here at least citizenship shall overpower class.

A spirit more unrevolutionary is not conceivable. There is place in the scheme of class war and revolution for Mr. Gary and Mr. Haywood. Both gentlemen are cut to specification. Both behave exactly as Capitalist and Proletarian are pictured in the socialist books of prophecy. I say there is place in the revolutionary scheme for Mr. Gary and Mr. Haywood. But there is no place for the Theodore Roosevelt of 1912 or the Woodrow Wilson of the fourteen points. Those two leaders in those two episodes in our recent history mark the zenith of American effort to rise entirely above and beyond the plane where the class war is fought, above and beyond the assumptions, the emotions, and the terms of that struggle. This effort is the enduring part of the American ideal. It recurs again and again, this sense that our game shall not be played under the European rules, that somehow by force of will and contagious hope the whole business will be lifted above the categories of class. In the days of free land and open opportunity the ideal grew naturally on this soil. It was just exactly what pioneers would believe who felt enormous open spaces around them. For class war is a doctrine of congestion, of crowded cities or preempted land. Today in America the memory of that old physical freedom appears in the midst of a massive industrialism. It is fighting a desperate battle for the survival of the American impulse against accepting class war as the order of our life.

How does it happen, then, that our leading citizens should confuse the American liberal with the pacifist, the pro-German, and the Bolshevik? So far as this confusion exists in ignorant minds the explanation is easy. There have been numerous occasions when liberals have had the thankless task of defending this unpopular trinity, and undiscriminating people who have only the formulae and not the spirit of the American faith simply cannot comprehend the attitude of anybody who is willing to defend the rights of those with whom he disagrees. Pacifists have rights which it was necessary to defend against the mob spirit and against the fanatical zeal of officeholders. The German nation had certain contractual rights under the armistice which conscience and wisdom required us to honor. The Russian civil war was not a thing for Americans to incite or sustain; blockading people with whom we were not at war was indecent, invading their country without a declaration of war was too much like what we deplored in the Germans. Only a fool or a knave would ever confuse these convictions with pacifism, pro-Germanism, Bolshevism. But so thoroughly confused are they that the universities, the United States Congress, the government departments, every newspaper office is stocked with men who are in mortal terror of those terrible epithets. They tip-toe by day and quake by night, because they know that at this moment the man who in domestic policy stands about where

275

Theodore Roosevelt stood in 1912 and in foreign affairs where Woodrow Wilson stood when he first landed in Paris, and in his doctrine of toleration where John Milton stood two and a half centuries ago, is certain, absolutely certain to be called pacifist, pro-German, and Bolshevist. It cannot be helped.

For the very essence of any sincere belief in the liberty promised by the First Amendment is a willingness to defend the liberty of opinions with which you disagree. That means protecting some pretty poor opinions, ignorant, wild and mean opinions, occasionally even sinister ones. What is it that induces any American to take upon himself the thankless task of saying things which at first glance are sure to sound pacifist, pro-German, or Bolshevist though he himself is none of these things? There are pleasanter occupations. There are less costly occupations. There are more thrilling occupations. There are more soothing ones. Think about it a minute. A man in New York City who speaks no Russian, has no relatives or friends in Russia, is well fed, warm, comfortable, hopes that the Bolsheviks will be supplanted, is at heart an almost pedantic believer in orderly and continuous procedure, finding himself in agreement with Mr. Lloyd George and General Smuts, gets up and says that the starvation of Russia should stop, that Russian babies, and Russian mothers should have food, that the hospitals should have anaesthetics and surgical supplies. Those words cost him the black looks of some of his acquaintances. But he keeps on saying it though old friendships are strained, and he notices that some draw away from him, and that Mrs. So-and-So has begun to chatter to Mrs. Somebody Else. He keeps on, if he is any good, though pretty soon he finds himself figuring as a friend and disciple of Lenin. I can't imagine a less productive enterprise, measured by the standards of this world.

To see in him a conspiracy, a sedition, or disloyalty or any of the other noisy epithets so easily employed is to forget most of what history teaches. It is to forget that from Louis

276

XVI to Nicholas II the confusion between constitutional reform and violent revolution has been the true source of revolution. Everybody who ever paused to think knows that to be the truth. It has been preached so long that we have almost forgotten its importance. It has been practiced by every statesman who ever steered a people through a crisis. The rule that reform is the antidote to revolution comes as near as any rule can be in politics to being a universal rule. It is no new discovery. It is no one's sudden bright idea. It is not a paradox invented by the intellectuals, the intelligentsia or the parlor Bolsheviks. It is old wisdom, but in high places it has been forgotten. The established leaders are once again flying in the face of all experience by treating every substantial reform as the prelude to and not the preventive of revolution.

This has led to grotesque performances which can be grouped under one heading, as the tendency to see a conspiracy when there is none. Conspiracies occur occasionally, but they are never harder to detect than when they are conceived to be everywhere. Yet playing Sherlock Holmes has its fascination even for the adult mind, especially in wartime when those who are denied a part in the great adventure are almost irresistibly impelled to imagine adventures in which they have a leading role. The more ludicrous phases of the spy mania originated there. I am thinking of the kindly ladies who turned German nurse girls into the streets so that these girls should not be able to communicate the important military secrets which were the property of their households. Instead of serving their country by keeping the nurse girls safely interned in the nursery, it seemed more romantic to pretend that they might learn something of interest to the German General Staff. I have sometimes thought how severely these ladies would have disapproved the policy of the military authorities in France who ordered German prisoners to wear German uniforms. For if certain of our more excited and hysterical had been running the war they would surely have insisted on stripping the prisoners of the pro-German field-grey and upon clothing the Huns in horizon blue or khaki. They would have called that stamping out pro-Germanism. No wonder Bolo Pasha fooled so many of them. He did not talk like a pro-German, and he consorted with our leading citizens. They could not remember that the real spy and the real traitor would avow himself a two hundred per cent American. The man who in wartime states any opinion different from that which prevails may be a fool or a nuisance if you like, but for conspiracy and treason he is ipso facto impossible.

Yet some very active people seem heroically determined to forget this. Recently, for example, in New York City the Lusk Committee, figuratively preceded by a brass band and actually accompanied by a platoon of infantry, raided the so-called Soviet Mission in New York. The Committee found nothing; only an absolute booby would have expected to find anything. Russians are pretty good conspirators, for all of them went to school under the Czar. Now if you are conducting a conspiracy you do not carry it on from an office building after you have advertised the address in all the newspapers and invited everybody to come and call and do business. That would not be the ideal headquarters for a secret conspiracy. Such an office might be a blind (I am not for a moment implying that it is), but it is certain as daylight that no trace of conspiracy would be found at such an office. A schoolboy with no more detective skill than can be acquired from reading detective novels could have told Mr. Lusk and Mr. Stevenson that.

Finally, and this is the most critical of the preliminaries to a restoration of common sense, the leaders of the community should mitigate the habit of wrapping themselves in the American flag. It offends most patriots when a chorus girl appears in red and white tights and a star-spangled corsage and vociferates about the land of liberty. It is just as vulgar and just as offensive for men to dress up luridly when they are urging their views of public policy. Americanism is cheapened and debased when it is put forth as the compelling reason for somebody's notion about military legislation, industrial control, or foreign policy. People who flaunt Americanism on all occasions do not inspire respect, and if the aristocratic virtues are to be preserved even in the most democratic society, the huckster and the shyster must be rigorously suppressed, most particularly among those to whom the community is told to look for light and leading. Our most prominent citizens cannot afford to display too much bad taste. It is a cheap soul that is continually braying about the eternal verities. For thou shalt not take the name of the Lord thy God in vain.

The panic which afflicts us is directly traceable to the absence of a policy which would organize the nation for work, and the lack of authentic information which would organize its emotion in contact with a vast and overpowering experience. Consider what we have been through: Period I— Be neutral in fact as well as in name. Period II—Fight like thunder to make the world safe for democracy. Period III— Stop before your anger is exhausted and spend the better part of a year standing around undecided while peace is made for you in secret. Some months of supreme, but unfinished concentration enclosed by two periods of vacillation and drift. During that whole time of exhausting strain and still more exhausting idleness, most people were dealing with facts that they had to imagine because they did not see them. No nation, I suppose, ever fought a great war on so abstract a basis, except of course the Canadians, the Australians and the New Zealanders. The Hun was not at our gate, even as he was at England's. The whole conflict was far away, and the troops who went forth sailed into the dusk of the censorship. The American at home could know the European war only as he was told about it: he had no vivid personal encounter with it himself unless he invented one in the person of a German bartender or music teacher. Now what Americans could learn about Europe was subject to two conditions: First the censor came along, and with one blow of his axe abolished all possibility of telling the unprejudiced and unvarnished truth. Either the news gave information to the enemy, or it hurt morale, and for one or the other of those two reasons almost anything could be suppressed. So the censor made the news vacuum; then the propagandist filled it. The assumption underlying practically all propaganda was that the citizens of the Allied countries were on the verge of being pacifists, pro-Germans, and later Bolsheviks. The second 'assumption was that the only morale capable of standing the strain of war was built upon frightfulness. It was for this reason that a vast machine extending all over the world was constructed to keep constantly before the minds of people that particular selection of atrocities which it was believed would keep up their morale. For five years we have learned about the world what government officials had decided they wished us to know. Our leading citizens did not escape it. They are saturated with propaganda like the rest, and twenty years from now they will wonder how they ever could have believed some of the things they took for granted in 1919 A.D.

A time when all information is what the Europeans call tendentious, when the people are alternately let down, frustrated, screwed up, frustrated, and let down is one in which realistic judgment is difficult. In the meantime the world having been harrowed its length and breadth, the sense of uncertainty, of strange complexity, of lurking danger pervades a community. And thus the nation finds itself in the face of aggravated problems without any source of information that it can really trust, and without leaders to interpret events. Of course people become restless and uncertain, and highly sensitive to moral epidemics. The one thing, the only thing that could stabilize men's mind in the gigantic flux and shift of the present world, is trustworthy news, unadulterated data, fair reporting, disinterested fact. "Your eyes were un-lidded, your ears were unstopped."

In some measure our leading citizens are so extremely credulous because they are so perplexed. They hesitate to move because they cannot foresee the consequences, because everything is too uncertain. They have been fooled time without number. But while they wait, while the men who have the power to lead a reconstruction worthy of our pride and our ideals hesitate in uncertainty, the meaner elements whisper in their ear and break their nerve. This whispering has for its ostensible purpose the downing of pro-Germans and Bolsheviks. The actual result has been to scare well-to-do people so completely out of their wits that they are temporarily incapable of listening to reason.

The most dangerous form of unrest at this moment is that which prevails among the leaders of the community, among those who exercise the force of the state and set the temper of debate. The basis of revolution does not now exist in America. But the possibility of great disorder we have always with us. Mobs form rather easily, and rather easily get out of hand; and being a high strung people rather than a phlegmatic one, there is considerable commotion when the mob goes on the loose. The real peril as distinguished from the bogey is that the difficult readjustments just ahead of us will be accompanied by a nerve-wracking and distracting disorder. Revolution there will not be, but a great deal of rioting there may be. A fly alighting on the nose of a philosopher could disturb his profoundest thoughts, said Pascal. A riot, though only a few shins are bruised, will pretty nearly always dissipate the constructive mood of a community. For disorder captures attention, arouses pugnacity and fear, infuriates dogma; disorder is the environment in which the demagogue and the jingo are selected, and the reform which both preserves and enriches is lost. There is instead a turmoil of bitterness, which can have no result except to scotch reform until at last the basis of revolution has been laid. The appalling thing at this moment in America is that so many of our leading citizens are in a state of mind to do those things which cannot but provoke chronic and fanatical disorder.

It is an open secret, for example, that many powerful business men have been saying for months that there was needed a "show down" with labor. It was commonly said before the steel strike that Mr. Gary was ready and that it would be an excellent opportunity to smash the overweening pretensions of the A.F. of L. The management of the steel strike has been, so far as the employers are concerned, in the hands of men who have sought a fight to the finish, not with the I.W.W., but with the A.F. of L. For as every competent observer has realized the thing which is most at stake is the relation of the A.F. of L. to the American labor movement. The much advertised Mr. Foster symbolizes the issue.

If a constitutional regime is established in industry under which organized labor is given a genuine share in management, the break with the I.W.W. temptation will probably be final. But if the hope of such a regime is finally closed by Mr. Gary's triumph, if in other words the A.F. of L. is driven out of the partnership which it won and earned during the war, then only by a miracle of leadership can a secret drift towards the I.W.W. be averted. How could it be otherwise? It would be perfectly clear to a very large number of workingmen all over the country that the A.F. of L. had been beaten at the most critical point in the most decisive conflict. For while Mr. Gompers owns a Distinguished Service Medal presented by the United States Government, he cannot induce Mr. Gary to answer his letters.

The rank and file of labor is betwixt and between, in doubt as to what leadership to follow. The amazing thing is that a certain number of powerful and responsible people should be willing at such a moment to take the risk of destroying the prestige and effectiveness of the most conservative trade union body in the whole civilized world. In the steel strike, on the floor of the President's Industrial Conference, above all in the newspapers, no single thing has been left undone which would weaken the leadership of Mr. Gompers. In a cloud of feverish talk about Bolshevism, a group of leading citizens professing to represent the practical, conservative, far-sighted American business man, has aimed what was intended as a fatal blow at the one labor organization which throughout the world stands as the symbol of anti-Bolshevist labor.

If Mr. Gary's group did not comprise the bold men of a frightened flock, they would never have been permitted to gamble so recklessly. The recklessness does not consist in the fact that they disagree with labor unionists. Far from it. From the point of view of efficient production and sound social policy, the average leadership in American trade unions is by no means what it might be. It is bound to reactionary dogma and split by petty jealousies, it is often badly disciplined; the psychology of the Tammany politicians pervades some of the officialdom. The record of organized labor in respect to scientific management is understandable but it indicates no high order of leadership. Nor has its record in American politics been anything to boast of. On specific questions of wages and hours, of shop control, or even on that of the jurisdiction of collective bargaining there must be serious differences of opinion, for the capitalist and the manager are in contact with phases of industry that do not enter the calculations of the wage earner. There is no recklessness in disagreeing with organized labor. The recklessness of Garyism consists in denying the very existence of organized labor. Actually Mr. Gompers may have walked out of the room, and the employers may have remained in it. Technically he bolted. But what had actually happened was that the employers had voted that he represented nobody. It is as if the Republicans in the Senate should vote a resolution saying that they would not recognize the credentials of the Democrats. There would be no Senate after that vote. Likewise there was no conference. Sam Gompers might still have sat in that hall, but President

Samuel Gompers of the American Federation of Labor had been voted out of existence.

It is a pregnant moment in American history. For the first time the whole of organized labor and the leading group of capital have defined an issue which makes their differences a matter of kind, and not simply of degree. No formula however ingenious can any longer conceal the existence of two irreconcilable dogmas. The easy thing to do is to let one's sympathy decide between them, to throw in our lot with Gomperism or Garyism. And once our prejudice is dominant, it is simple to find evidence and reason to sustain it. But we dare not do that. We dare not allow the leaders of a class to present the American people with a dilemma, and we dare not allow ourselves to regard a conflict as fatally determined.

The idea that there is a Public Group, that it is the guardian of the Public Thing, that somehow it manages to represent the disinterested thought of the community—this idea persists in the American tradition. The skeptics jeer at it as a pure fiction, and the sinister often use it as a masquerade. But if it did not exist we should have to invent it. No class of people enumerated in the census are the "Public." But all individuals at some time or other are part of it. They are part of it whenever they are individuals and not mere conscious or unconscious members of a class. The Public is the name of those who in any crisis are seeking the truth and not advocating their dogma. Thus it was altogether right that Mr. Rockefeller should be a member of the Public group at the President's Conference because he was acting on considerations infinitely wider than those with which his name is commonly associated. But it was absurd to put Mr. Gary in the Public group because for him the issues of the conference were an incident in the labor policy of his corporation. The idea of a Public is simply a short way of expressing the great faith that a group of men and women will always disentangle themselves from their prejudices and will be sufficiently powerful to summon the partisans before the bar of reason; and that evidence, not mere jaw, will then decide.

In the lean and bitter time which may be ahead of us we shall find our way through if we are loyal to this ideal. Each of us will have to make some sacrifice of personal comfort and of ambition. But the supreme sacrifice demanded will be the sacrifice of dogma, the yielding of that worst form of pride, the pride of opinion. We shall have to yield our pride, and not merely insist that our opponent yield his. We shall have to put veracity above vehemence, and a willingness to seek the truth above the luxury of bawling the other fellow out. Recently it was said that the amalgam is running out of civilization. If that is even partially true, it is because we have in a moment of great perplexity stood upon the arrogance of opinion. It will be well for us to remember what Montaigne wrote, in the days when Europe was wracked by religious wars and by persecutions: "After all, it is setting a high value upon our opinions, to roast men alive on account of them."

Without a disentangled Public the unending clash of Ins and Outs, Haves and Have Nots, Reds and Whites is likely to be sheer commotion. No doubt there is much that is insincere and much that is maudlin said about the Public. The news system of the world being what it is, and education being where it is, it is possible to fool most of the Public a good part of the time. The Public is one of those ideals, if you like, which we miss oftener than we attain. But it is a precious ideal. It is the only way we have of formulating our belief that reason is the final test of action, that mere push and pull are not by themselves to set the issues and to render the decision.

As I look at it, any person is part of the Public when he is dealing with party, sect or class, not as their attorney, not as their opponent, not as their censor or their laureate, but as one seeking to learn from them, to discover in them, to draw out of them, and propose to them plans which employ in their most productive and harmonious form the energies of men. His temptation and constant danger is that he will be sucked into each controversy as it comes along, compelled to fight not for those things which he believes in most but on behalf of that party which he fears least. He tends to be swept out of a public into a partisan position chiefly because when presented with an alternative, the contagion of debate seizes him, and his mind becomes infertile. Especially if things are bitter, it is difficult to maintain enough composure for the invention of those great expedients which dissipate a struggle by repolarizing the energies involved. It is necessary but it is difficult to recall Emerson's advice that "when classes are exasperated against each other, the peace of the world is always kept by striking a new note."

This is illustrated by the Industrial Conference. The hope of that gathering lay in the Public group and in the Administration as representative of the Public. It was perfectly well known in advance that the unions on one side and the employees who accepted Mr. Gary as leader were locked in a decisive battle to decide the fate of unionism itself. Both groups were obsessed by the issue. The Public group, on the other hand, drifted into Washington unprepared and unled, without conviction and without plan, and with no resource except the attempt to supply ambiguous formulae as compromises for clean-cut differences. Capital and Labor were narrowly but completely concentrated; the Public mind on the contrary was distracted and almost vacant.

Consequently, two dogmas were permitted to occupy the whole conference and to wreck it. Now those two dogmas are very important, but taken by themselves, they are insoluble except by force. I say "taken by themselves," as a question of "I will" and "I won't" or "You must" and "You shan't," they can result only in bicker and scuffle. So *stated,* and that is the only way they were stated, they are not the industrial problem, but simply two sets of pugnacities that have grown like parasites within the industrial problem.

And so men who had come together to prepare for something that might be called peace should have insisted on keeping this issue out of the forefront of the discussion. Not in order to evade Garyism, for it cannot be evaded, but in order to dissolve its stony simplicity. There were possibly two ways of dealing with the matter, in view of the fact that Mr. Gary had laid down the assumption of an antagonism to and not a partnership with organized labor. The most statesmanlike would have been to convene the conference on the basis of the labor provisions of the Treaty of Peace, and to make acceptance of those provisions the test of membership. This would have been to assume what no publicly-minded person any longer disputes. It would have meant that the Administration had supplied a leader and not merely a chairman. And if the fact that the Treaty was not yet ratified was embarrassing to the Administration, the Treaty itself need not have been cited. The real obstacle to such a policy lay in the unfortunate fact that Mr. Gary rather than someone like Mr. Rockefeller is leading the employers of the country. I am told that Mr. Gary would probably have declined an invitation by the President based on terms which acknowledged as one of the rights of labor what the nations of Europe now at war with Bolshevism have accepted as a minimum. And if Mr. Gary had declined to come, the most unmanageable element of the employers, and temporarily the most powerful element as well, would have been out of the conference.

Under the circumstances the only other course for the Public group was to postpone Garyism to a later stage. This is just what President Eliot sought to do. Roughly speaking, industrial relations divide into a question of wages, hours, conditions, and a question of power and efficiency. The stock argument against admitting labor to a share of power is that it destroys efficiency. But the exclusion of labor from participation in power, for which essentially Garyism stands, is also notoriously inimical to efficiency. What the conference could have done without constituting itself an arbiter in any pending dispute was to undertake an analysis of the whole question of power and efficiency. This problem, although vital, is not as a matter of fact in the foreground. What is of greatest concern to the rank and file is the relation of wages to prices.

That background is not known. There are haphazard guesses and some estimates and much anecdote as to what has happened to the real wages of workingmen since the outbreak of the war. A comprehensive trustworthy study does not exist, though each of us knows from his own experience that there has been a veritable convulsion in the meaning of money. It is very difficult for anybody to calculate on the basis of a fifty cent dollar, and when men's expectations go astray the thing called unrest exists. But it so happens that the Public group was in such a hurry "to get things done" that it completely neglected to organize the kind of price and wage and standard of living inquiry which would have made possible a perspective on the unrest. Instead of starting with a disinterested appeal to the facts which underlie the whole dispute, facts which are neutral to the contentions of Mr. Gary and Mr. Gompers, the Public group let the contentions have the floor. It tried to be umpire not analyst and inventor; and what it organized was a debate not an inquiry.

The method of inquiry before decision or debate would have had some opposition from labor. Garyism is so terrible a threat to the unions that they are bound to grapple with it on every occasion. Nevertheless, a clear demonstration to workingmen that the conference was primarily concerned with that which most harasses them; that the conference was dealing with concrete matters and not with Mr. Gary's dogmas, might have permitted Mr. Gompers to avoid his sensational exit. For in the light of the facts as to prices and wages the whole industrial problem takes on a cooler and more manageable aspect.

It ceases to be a thriller about plots and secretly drilling armies and dark red foreigners. Then if men doing essential work in society ask for a reconsideration of their wage schedules on the ground that their wages have risen only 37.5 per cent in seven and a half years the thing to do is to find out whether their facts are correct and then to transact business with them on the basis of the known facts about the cost of living. To shriek soviet and publish ethnic data about the number of Austro-Hungarians among them, when most of these alien-enemies derive from our recently liberated Allies is of a piece with the plastering of Mr. Margolis's opinions all over the front pages and the relegating of Mr. Royal Meeker's data somewhere to the region of the millinery advertisements.

For a reduction of this panic my own hopes are in what might be called the latent public, in that community, shifting more or less from day to day, of those whose attitude defies classification, who do not run true to class because in their own way and with all their limitations they are looking for the truth. Intolerance may submerge them for a time and timidity paralyze them and conformity subdue them. They are there. They can be summoned. They will arise and assert the supremacy of confidence over fear, of reason and charity over suspicion and hysteria. They will prevail and restore the good humor of America when enough men, realizing the drifting embitterment of our life, break loose from their calculations and shout: Damn your Bolshevism, the time for chatter has passed. There is work to do.

November 12, 1919

ARTS AND
OTHER MATTERS

LEGENDARY JOHN REED

Reed and Lippmann were both members of the Harvard class of 1910. [*A.S., jr.*]

Though he is only in his middle twenties and but five years out of Harvard, there is a legend of John Reed. It began, as I remember, when he proved himself to be the most inspired song and cheer leader that the football crowd had had for many days. At first there was nothing to recommend him but his cheek. That was supreme. He would stand up alone before a few thousand undergraduates and demonstrate without a quiver of self-consciousness just how a cheer should be given. If he didn't like the way his instructions were followed he cursed at the crowd, he bullied it, sneered at it. But he always captured it. It was a sensational triumph, for Jack Reed wasn't altogether good form at college. He came from Oregon, showed his feelings in public, and said what he thought to the club men who didn't like to hear it.

Even as an undergraduate he betrayed what many people believe to be the central passion of his life, an inordinate desire to be arrested. He spent a brief vacation in Europe and experimented with the jails of England, France, and Spain. In one Spanish village he was locked up on general principles, because the King happened to be passing through town that day. The next incident took place during the Paterson strike. Reed was in town less than twenty-four hours before the police had him in custody. He capped his arrest

293

by staging the Paterson strike pageant in Madison Square Garden, and then left for Europe to live in a Florentine villa, where he was said to be hobnobbing with the illegitimate son of Oscar Wilde, and to be catching glimpses of Gordon Craig. He made speeches to Italian syndicalists and appointed himself to carry the greetings of the American labor movement to their foreign comrades. He bathed in a fountain designed by Michelangelo and became violently ill. He tried high romance in Provence. One night, so he says, he wrestled with a ghost in a haunted house, and was thrown out of bed.

He lived in those days by editing and writing for *The American Magazine*. But that allegiance couldn't last. Reed wasn't meant for sedate family life, and he broke away to join the staff of the *Masses*. They advertised him as their jail editor, but as a matter of fact he was the managing editor, which even on the *Masses* carries with it a prosaic routine. For a few weeks Reed tried to take the *Masses'* view of life. He assumed that all capitalists were fat, bald, and unctuous, that reformers were cowardly or scheming, that all newspapers are corrupt, that Victor Berger and the Socialist party and Samuel Gompers and the trade unions are a fraud on labor. He made an effort to believe that the working class is not composed of miners, plumbers, and workingmen generally, but is a fine, statuesque giant who stands on a high hill facing the sun. He wrote stories about the night court and plays about ladies in kimonos. He talked with intelligent tolerance about dynamite, and thought he saw an intimate connection between the cubists and the I.W.W. He even read a few pages of Bergson.

But it was only a flirtation. Reed's real chance came when the *Metropolitan Magazine* sent him to Mexico. All his second-rate theory and propaganda seemed to fall away, and the public discovered that whatever John Reed could touch or see or smell he could convey. The variety of his impressions, the resources and color of his language seemed inexhaustible. The articles which he sent back from the border were as hot as the Mexican desert, and Villa's revolution, till then reported only as a nuisance, began to unfold itself into throngs of moving people in a gorgeous panorama of earth and sky. Reed loved the Mexicans he met, loved them as they were, marched with them, raided with them, danced with them, drank with them, risked his life with them. He had none of the condescension of the foreigner, no white man's superiority. He was not too dainty, or too wise, or too lazy. Mexicans were real people to him with whom he liked to be. He shared their hatred of the *cientificos,* he felt as they did about the church, and he wrote back to us that if the United States intervened to stop the revolution he would fight on Villa's side,

He did not judge, he identified himself with the struggle, and gradually what he saw mingled with what he hoped. Wherever his sympathies marched with the facts, Reed was superb. His interview with Carranza almost a year ago was so sensationally accurate in its estimate of the feeling between Carranza and Villa that he suppressed it at the time out of loyalty to the success of the revolution. But where his feeling conflicted with the facts, his vision flickered. He seems totally to have misjudged the power of Villa.

Reed has no detachment, and is proud of it, I think. By temperament he is not a professional writer or reporter. He is a person who enjoys himself. Revolution, literature, poetry, they are only things which hold him at times, incidents merely of his living. Now and then he finds adventure by imagining it, oftener he transforms his own experience. He is one of those people who treat as serious possibilities such stock fantasies as shipping before the mast, rescuing women, hunting lions, or trying to fly around the world in an aeroplane. He is the only fellow I know who gets himself pursued by men with revolvers, who is always once more just about to ruin himself.

I can't think of a form of disaster which John Reed hasn't tried and enjoyed. He has half-spilled himself into commercialism, had his head turned by flattery, tried to act like a cynical war correspondent, posed as a figure out of Ibsen. But always thus far the laughter in him has turned the scale, his sheer exuberance has carried him to better loves. He is many men at once, and those who have tried to bank on some phase of him, to regard him as a writer, a correspondent, a poet, a revolutionist, or a lover, lose him. There is no line between the play of his fancy and his responsibility to fact; he is for the time the person he imagines himself to be.

Reed is one of the intractables, to whom the organized monotony and virtue of our civilization are unbearable. You would have to destroy him to make him fit. At times when he seemed to be rushing himself and others into trouble, when his ideas were especially befuddled, I have tried to argue with him. But all laborious elucidation he greets with pained boredom. He knows how to dismiss in a splendid flourish the creature

> "Who wants to make the human race and me
> March to a geometric Q. E. D."

I don't know what to do about him. In common with a whole regiment of his friends I have been brooding over his soul for years, and often I feel like saying to him what one of them said when Reed was explaining Utopia, "If I were establishing it, I'd hang you first, my dear Jack." But it would be a lonely Utopia.

December 26, 1914

FREUD AND THE LAYMAN

Lippmann had been the first lay writer in the United
States to refer to Freud in a book (*A Preface to Politics,* 1913). Freud was still regarded with much suspicion and hostility in 1915. [*A.S., jr.*]

In discussions of Freud's work, the perfect bromide is to
say that his theories are exaggerated. They may be, for all we
know. Since the history of scientific thought makes it clear
that later research modifies practically every hypothesis, it is
altogether safe to insist that Freud's theories will appear crude
to men of the future. Yet in the mouths of laymen, and even
of ordinary neurologists, the remark is a most uninteresting
truth. When made by people who have neither the knowledge
nor the technique to understand or to criticize Freud, the
comment is sheer platitude. They do not know wherein he
exaggerates; they cannot give evidence that he does. They
simply take a chance and assert it. It is as if I walked into
the Rockefeller Institute, spent an hour or two in Dr. Noguchi's laboratory, shook my head gravely, and remarked:
"Well, you'll see. Much of what you are doing will be thrown
aside by your successors." Wouldn't Dr. Noguchi reply with
great politeness, "No doubt you are right, but how do you
know you are right?" And wouldn't I be entitled to feel that
I had made a remark about as helpful as that of the small
boy who stands by the roadside and advises passing motorists
to get a horse?

Yet people will criticize Freud on the basis of a dinner-table conversation or perhaps on the reading of his book about *The Interpretation of Dreams.* I have heard physicians deny the theory that dreams are realized wishes, on the ground that people are subject to nightmares. They seem to think that in the lifetime which Freud has devoted to the study of dreams he might possibly have overlooked the nightmares. I have heard laymen resist the theory of infantile sexuality, because in their opinion children have no sexuality. Yet they would not dare for a moment to raise such offhand objections to the latest discovery in physics and chemistry; they would assume that a man who has become the center of world-wide scientific discussion would have taken account of at least the obvious objections to his theories.

It is clear why we who are laymen cannot remain entirely passive about Freud, why we cannot sit still and listen and simply try to understand. We ourselves are the subject matter of his science, and in a most intimate and drastic way. The structure of matter can be left to objective analysis, but these researches of Freud challenge the very essence of what we call ourselves. They involve the sources of our character, they carry analysis deeper into the soul of man than analysis has ever been carried before. The analysis hurts, but even superficially there is enough compelling truthfulness about it to make an easy escape impossible. We recognize in the analysis items that we have never quite dared phrase even to ourselves, and it is not possible to repel the attack altogether. Freud has a way of revealing corners of the soul which we believed were safe from anybody's knowledge. This uncanny wisdom is to most people both fascinating and horrible. They can neither take hold nor let go. So they rationalize their difficulty and build out of it a defensive compromise. They say that Freud is a clever man but that he exaggerates, that there is some truth in his teaching and much untruth. There is no better way than this of holding an idea at arm's length. It enables us to escape its consequences by blunting its force.

The Freudians themselves are well aware that they cannot

at present hope for a really disinterested discussion. If the arguments of archaeologists and chemists cannot be conducted without the injection of passionate prejudice, what hope is there for argument about passionate prejudice itself? Because Freud is discussing the very nature of interest it becomes very difficult to consider Freud disinterestedly. The defenses which we set up against a revelation of ourselves, he disintegrates at the outset. The challenge is so subtle and so radical that our whole organism seems to concentrate for resistance.

Our attitude is like that of a lady with whom I once went to a bull-fight. She thought the spectacle horrible, so she held her hand over her eyes. Then by looking between her fingers she watched the fight. Freud's theory has much the same attraction and repulsion. Our craving for it and our resistance to it are both below the level of reason, and our intellectual attitude is very largely determined by this conflict. And as civilized people try to conceal the fact that they are deeply disturbed, the fascination and the tendency to withdraw neutralize each other in the conscious mind, and the product is to the effect that Freud carries his ideas too far. The lady, when she spoke to her friends later about the bull-fight, said nothing about the fight. She said the Spanish costumes were very picturesque.

The difficulties of relating ourselves to a teaching like Freud's are, however, part of a larger problem. We live in a world where knowledge is becoming more and more highly specialized, and as laymen we cannot hope to have the equipment for really adequate judgment. The day is gone when we could turn for guidance to someone whose authority was unquestioned. Even science, which is the surest method of knowledge we have, is based on the denial of infallibility in any scientist. We assume that Darwin or Freud must be wrong on innumerable points. But we do not know enough to say when and where they are wrong. We are called upon to make decisions which we are not trained to make. This is almost the central problem of the modern intellectual life. How shall we distribute our faith without going it blind, how shall we have the loyalty to believe without losing the capacity to doubt? How much trust shall we put in a man like Freud, for example? How can we react in a way that will not stultify, either by petty resistance or petty acceptance?

We cannot begin to test his facts nor follow his experiments. But what we can do is to get the sense of his method and the quality of his mind. We can say that we recognize in him or fail to recognize in him the type of imagination, the sense of reality, the honesty before fact, the logical penetration, and the background of experience which are likely to yield fruitful results. We know in a general way the qualities of thought which lead to important conclusions. No doubt truths have been reached in other ways, by tossing a coin, or guessing, or saying vehemently whatever happens to be vegetating in the mind. But truths reached this way have to pass a much closer scrutiny than truths which are the normal products of what we call the scientific spirit. In the complexity of specialized knowledge our best guide is to test the working of the thinker's mind. For our first credulity it will probably serve more accurately than any other.

In such a test Freud would, I believe, emerge triumphant over practically all of his lay opponents, and most of his professional ones. There has rarely been a great theory worked out so close to actual practice, an hypothesis that has been so genuinely pragmatic in origin. Freud is first of all a physician, an applied scientist using his theory to carry him forward in dealing with his patients. The amount of industry that the psycho-analytic method requires is an added guarantee of his good faith. He has offered no short cut; in fact, one of the real objections raised by his critics is the time needed to make an analysis. He has formulated no immutable doctrine; the history of his career is the history of opinion bending and modifying before experience.

When I compare his work with the psychology that I

studied in college, or with most of the material that is used to controvert him, I cannot help feeling that for his illumination, for his steadiness and brilliancy of mind, he may rank among the greatest who have contributed to thought. I know how easy it is to be deceived, but I take it that this is a small risk in comparison with the necessity for recognizing in his own lifetime a man of outstanding importance. After all, there were people who welcomed Darwin, and saw how profoundly he must affect our thinking. In Freud I believe we have a man of much the same quality, for the theories that have grown from his clinic in Vienna have always flowered in endless ways. From anthropology through education to social organization, from literary criticism to the studies of religions and philosophies, the effect of Freud is already felt. He has set up a reverberation in human thought and conduct of which few as yet dare to predict the consequences.

April 17, 1915

SCANDAL

Judge Ben B. Lindsey of the Juvenile Court in Denver, Colorado, was a notable reformer later celebrated for his advocacy of "companionate marriage." [*A.S., jr.*]

One of the effective ways of damaging an opponent is to set some scandalous rumor in circulation about him. It is the safest form of attack because modern civilization provides no effective method of meeting it. You cannot challenge the gossip to a duel; you cannot in good frontier fashion catch him and thrash him. The law is a clumsy method, which few people care to use. In a large city where people know little of each other the gossip is comparatively safe. He starts a rumor, and the thing grows and changes as it passes through people's conversation. A few kind friends come to the victim and ask him to make a reply. But what reply? Shall he write to the papers and advertise the rumor by denying it? If he does, people simply shake their heads and say: Those who excuse themselves, accuse themselves. Shall he go to the gossip and ask him to stop? More likely than not the gossip will twist the request into fresh scandal, or will find something else to gossip about.

Moreover, the victim must ask himself whether he can afford to let any slanderer put him on the defensive, whether he can afford the cost of time and irritation which the pursuit of slander involves. It is pretty clear that a man who once takes to answering insinuation soon does little else. It is a task well symbolized by the cleaning of the Augean stables.

For the moment a person is known outside a circle of immediate friends, at that moment there begins to develop a legend. Women in public life suffer from this especially. Somebody somewhere is certain to have a nasty suspicion, which becomes associated with some half-observed fact and then begins to flower through suspicion until innocent and well-meaning people are repeating the scandal as truth. There probably isn't a single politician, reformer, publicist, labor leader, about whom somebody isn't saying something profoundly mean. The man is said to be drinking, or it is whispered that he is sexually illicit, or that he is corrupt, or that he indulges in what are so plainly described as unmentionable practices.

Anyone in this country who has been through a big political fight, or a strike, or an election, knows that the circulation of rumor which never reaches the publicity of print is one of the deadliest weapons that either side can employ. It was years before Colonel Roosevelt found an opportunity to deal with the rumor that he was a drunkard, and that opportunity came only by good fortune, when an editor in an obscure town made the insinuation plain enough to justify a libel suit. Judge Lindsey is only now beginning to secure a vindication for the wretched slander which has been spread about him, and thousands of people will never know he has been vindicated. There are enough lies afloat about President Wilson to sink him at the pit of Billy Sunday's hell, and he has no defense against them. If he issued denials, a hundred accusing fingers would be pointed where now there is one.

Every reporter is a receptacle of scandal. But the honest reporter has a moral code which says that the use of gossip for personal ends or to serve a personal grudge is as low an activity as that of a doctor who would talk about his patients at a dinner-table. It is expecting too much to ask a reporter to weigh the evidence of every rumor, but a reporter who has realized the importance of his work in a democracy where public opinion rules will certainly never stoop to the employment of what he hears for the sake of satisfying his own malice. Yet there are reporters who are like "Typhoid Mary" —they spread their infection without conscience. Often they are the tool of some politician, some special interest. Occasionally they imagine themselves to be serving a cause. And there are always plenty of people ready to believe them, for people still have a peculiar awe of reporters, regarding them as very much on the inside of life.

There are few of us who do not enjoy this sense of really knowing what's what. It extends our experience, and gives us a vicarious importance. If we cannot live great passions, we can at least read about Mme. Du Barry's boudoir; if we cannot be smart, we can at least feel that we have an insider's knowledge of the smart set. The moral earnestness and deep attention which people will devote to discussing other people's domestic affairs suggests that gossip is perhaps a genuine primitive art in which there is catharsis through pity and fear and pride and joy. One woman leaves her husband; a hundred women chatter about it, and their passionate interest might make a cynic wonder whether they are not living through all the emotions of a great adventure without the risk of moving away from their own steam radiators. Gossip is experience without responsibility. It is a means of taking part in interesting or important events without any of the risk that comes of being an actor in them. Gossip, in short, is the pleasure of the spectator at the business of life.

There is always some kind of truth in a rumor. It may describe an actual fact, it may distort it a little, it may distort it grossly. Or it may be founded on no objective truth whatever, and may simply reveal the expectation or the prejudices of the gossip himself. A good deal of the scandal about actresses, for example, betrays an unconscious desire on the part of the scandalmonger. Much of the foulness imputed to public men betrays a wish on the part of their opponents for the existence of something sufficiently damaging to destroy. The human mind soon weaves a fantasy to suit its purposes, and not even the most critical intelligence is proof against its own will to believe. A classic case for all time was the rumor in England last August that a vast Russian army was passing through on its way to France. That rumor was supported by evidence so perfect that it would have hanged a man in court. And yet what was it?—the frantic myth of a people in despair, a people whose army was being shattered, who needed help. The English people found temporary hope and comfort in their myth, and for a time some of the ablest men in England were using all their intelligence to find reasons for believing it. It is well to remember this when the statement is made that where there is much smoke there must be some fire. The gossip which sooner or later attaches itself to everyone whom people talk about reveals something, no doubt, but what it reveals about the gossiper as well as his victim requires more analytic power than is usually displayed in casual conversation.

Because of its formlessness and irresponsibility, people expect the victim to pay very little attention to gossip. They quite rightly classify as cranks those men who are always seeking vindication, calling upon their honor, assuming noble attitudes, and inviting the lightning to strike. To venture forth in defense of honor armed with a demand for damages seems, even when it is feasible, a somewhat ridiculous proceeding; the trouble with dueling or "beating up" is that truth dwells so often with those who are poor shots or who hate scuffles.

In general it may be said that public men become callous to scandal; only those with a good epidermis occupy a public office with comfort. And the result of this process of selection is that only the fit survive, the fit being those who are born or have made themselves somewhat insensitive. Men of quick feeling and thin skin suffer much, and many of them can endure public life only by shutting themselves off from contact with the world and seeing only those associates who have learned to protect them. They lose by this, of course, for they shut off, together with the painful criticism, the criticism that they need to hear. There is a dilemma here which few have solved. How, for example, is a man to work with any ease if he begins his day by receiving a caller who tells him that all the people in one place think he is a drunkard, and all the people somewhere else believe that he has had corrupt dealings with a corporation? How much disinterested and composed thought is he capable of devoting after that to his real duties? He may determine to forget the slander, but its poison will work on his nerves, sap his strength, lower his vitality. Yet he can't spend his time issuing statements, demanding investigations, hurling challenges. So if he is wise he does not react, lets the rumor play itself out and die, as rumors do, for lack of nourishment. Only if the rumor crystallizes can anything be done about it. Only when the gossip has taken public responsibility for his gossip can the victim strike back.

April 24, 1915

THE FOOTNOTE

John Dewey, professor of philosophy at Columbia and influential proponent of instrumentalism, had written *Influence of Darwin on Philosophy and Other Essays in Contemporary Thought* in 1910. [*A.S., jr.*]

When he says that the true American philosophy must be one of radical experiment, Professor Dewey opens up a curious question. He is urging us to do something never done before by any other people. He is urging us consciously to manufacture our philosophy. There would be no more complete break with the tradition of thought. The whole value of philosophies up to the present has been that they found a support for our action in something outside ourselves. We philosophized in order to draw sanction from God, or nature or evolution. The theory was that our philosophies determined us; we conformed to them. Now comes Professor Dewey to argue that we ought to make our philosophies for our own needs and purposes. At first it will surely seem a light-minded performance to say that because a people lives under certain conditions and has certain problems to meet, this people ought to have a philosophy which will help it to deal with these problems. The absolutists will assert that philosophies are not like clothes which change with the climate and the occupation, but steadfast principles by which man guides his course in a mazy world.

What justification is there for this ultimate impudence which would allow a people to make its own philosophy? The justification is in the fact that people have always made their own philosophies. They have made them unconsciously, and because they did not know how or why they had made them, the systems if they worked well seemed very noble. But as a result of modern research we know too much about the way ideas are created to have any very sentimental illusions about the divinity of their origin. As Professor Dewey says in an earlier part of the book from which the passages printed above are quoted: "Every living thought represents a gesture made toward the world, an attitude taken to some practical situation in which we are implicated." We may add that the gesture can represent a compensation for a bitter reality, an aspiration unfulfilled, a habit sanctified. In this sense philosophies are truly revealing. They are the very soul of the philosopher projected, and to the discerning critic they may tell more about him than he knows about himself. In this sense the man's philosophy is his autobiography; you may read in it the story of his conflict with life. From almost all philosophies you can learn more about the men who made them than about the world which they strove to interpret.

But if once we grant that most philosophy is not a revelation of absolute principles, but a human being's adjustment of his desires to his limitations, then we can hardly turn round and regard your own philosophy as less human in its origin. We cannot say: "These others wrote biographies, but I am writing eternal truth." We have to assume that we too are making our adjustment to life, and we refrain from taking our ideas at any superhuman valuation. Being forewarned and on his guard the modern man asks himself: Why have I come to believe so-and-so? He means to ask not only what the external evidence is, but why he should be interested in a particular idea, what there is in his spiritual life which makes him welcome a certain system of ideas. Why are certain principles congenial to him, why does he find these "facts" particularly convincing?

By the time he has been through such self-examination, a man will unquestionably have corrected part of the more obvious personal bias of his thought, and he is not likely to be in any very grandiloquent mood. But if he has real integrity he will not assume that even his corrected philosophy is more than his personal reaction to the world. To be sure, other people may have much the same reactions, the greater part of a nation or a continent may have it, and in that case his philosophy will have a following. But to each person for whom it has any meaning at all that meaning will be that it expresses his human relation to particular times and particular problems. And so no pious mumbo-jumbo need surround any system of ideas.

Here then is the justification for an experimental philosophy so radical that it is ready to experiment with philosophy itself. All philosophies are experiments, but they are unconscious ones. They all represent an attempt to make ourselves better at home in the world. What Professor Dewey urges us to do, if I understand him correctly, is to recognize the real nature of philosophizing and to make the best of it. Instead of spinning our thoughts blindly and calling them absolute truth, let us spin them deliberately and be ready to change them. Let us continue to write autobiographies, but let us be sure we know they are autobiographies. Let us recognize that the true use of philosophy is to help us to live, and having recognized that, let us pour into it all that we know and can learn of what we ourselves are and what the world is like in which we move. It is perhaps inevitable that we should write our autobiographies, but this at least is clear; they will be known for what they are, and they will be less capricious because we have made them with our eyes open.

I began by saying that Professor Dewey had broken with the whole tradition of philosophy. Perhaps it would be more accurate to say that he had broken with the pretensions of philosophy. Professor Dewey is really urging us to do what philosophers have always done; he has asked us, however, to put away the illusions of divinity with which they shrouded their work. That pretentiousness is the enemy. It turns human thoughts into monstrous absolutes, and takes the impossible position that some of man's thoughts are too sacred for man's criticism.

July 17, 1915

INCONSPICUOUS CREATION

Apart from the sheer human wonder aroused by the wireless telephone communication with Honolulu, the most remarkable fact seems to be that this application of research has been carried out by a business corporation, and that the inventors and scientists remain anonymous. As evidence of human motives there is much to think about here. What is the incentive which impels these unknown workers, what secret have these corporations discovered which enables them to tap so inexpensively the most useful minds in America? When next we read that enterprise would collapse without dazzling rewards, that human nature is so and so, we shall not be able to refrain from thinking of these nameless benefactors of mankind. Their incentive seems somehow to be as good as those of the men who are piling up fortunes in war speculation, or of those who had grandfathers with a vision of real estate development.

October 16, 1915

"PLUMB INSANE"

Tom Shevlin was a Yale football star. Heinrich von Treitschke did for Prussia and Germany what the wooden fence did for Yale. [*A.S., jr.*]

If reports are true, Mr. Thomas Shevlin has made a memorable utterance: "Against Princeton you must all go insane, plumb insane—but keep your heads." The result is known to all the world, and how all the world feels about it can be seen from an account written for the New York *Evening Post*: ". . . through utter willingness to give the final measure of physical sacrifice, those men of Yale lifted from the muck a bedraggled, bedaubed blue banner, holding it on high so that it floated and snapped proudly once more, glorified by the light of victory." Treitschke would hardly have done better than this: "If there was a Yale graduate who did not feel the impulse to stand in his place and uncover silently . . ."

That it is a splendid thing to go insane, to keep your head, and to uncover silently is not to be denied. The glory of football is that it permits such things. A struggle in which a man can be an absolute partisan is a comfort indeed. No Yale man need question that Yale ought to win. Harvard men and Princeton men can be as certain. They can be loyal without a quaver of conscience, they can desire victory without thinking of consequences. Wherever they happen to belong, there they can put their faith. And even those hyphenates who go from Yale to the Harvard Law School may be for Yale and no questions asked.

"Plumb Insane"

If only life were like football, what a splendid education young America would be receiving. It would be learning that loyalty is greater than discrimination, that the crowd you are in is the best crowd of all. A Yale freshman who wanted to see Harvard win because Harvard contributes to human culture would be an ass. He would be treated by his classmates as Englishmen are now treated who admire German professors. For the point you are trained to in intercollegiate athletics is that there are only two sides to a question, and that the side you are against has nothing to recommend it.

There have been highbrow eulogies of football. It is, we are told, a harmless outlet for pugnacity; it introduces a dionysian element into our drab lives; it purges through pity and fear; it is to America what the Saturnalia was to the ancients. Perhaps. Yet one difference must be noted. The Greeks never supposed that the passions they put into their festivals were the passions that ought to dominate human life. In the spiritual democracy which they preached they gave representations to all the elements of man. With us this is not the case. We like to regard college spirit as a model. We expect a man to feel towards his country, his city, his corporation, his political party, about as the freshman feels towards his team. We like to cultivate the habit of being partisan, and the habit attunes itself to any notions. We fail to say: "Go insane about Yale, but not about American concessions in Mexico. Go insane about DeWitt Clinton High School, but discriminate about Germany."

It is perhaps a rule of spiritual hygiene that a man who doesn't go insane about something is likely to go insane about everything. And Yale is as good an object to go insane about as almost anything we can think of at the moment. But the trouble with insanity as an ideal of education is that it doesn't exactly prepare for the sort of world we live in. That world requires the faculty of doubting, of making distinctions, of caring enormously without sinking into credulity. Just what colleges are doing to cultivate these faculties it is

313

sometimes a little hard to see. There are professors awake to the problem who would like to abolish football, because in the competition for attention it wins so easily. That is the stupid easy remedy. After all, football puts the professor on his mettle by showing him how far he is from enlisting human passion in the cause of science; and the grim joke which gives football coaches a bigger salary than teachers is a fairly good indication of what education has still to accomplish. There have been teachers whose memory was brighter than the brightest victory.

November 20, 1915

ANGELS TO THE RESCUE

Louis Boudin is remembered today as the author of
a Marxist history of the Supreme Court. [*A.S., jr.*]

After playing a hard game of chess and losing I often find
myself repeating the crucial plays in imagination. And the
wonderful thing about these imaginary games is that I am
always triumphantly successful. Combinations which seemed
impregnable melt away, the attack is neat and decisive. My
part of the game is conducted with certainty, yet invariably
when I have taken the trouble to set up the pieces in order
to try out my victory, it has turned out that I had overlooked
an important pawn that destroyed the whole scheme. The
oversight has usually proved to be gross, and no one looking
at the actual pieces on the board could have made it. But in
imagination the error resisted detection. It was as if in the
free play of the mind a deus ex machina was set upon remov-
ing the chief obstacle to victory.

The other night I attended a dinner where competent socialists were to discuss the future of the International. One
of the speakers was Mr. Louis Boudin, generally regarded as
the ablest Marxian scholar in America. Mr. Boudin has a
reputation for hardheadedness, and his writings are full of
scorn for those who deal in "ideologies" and pretty hopes.
He had before him an audience of men and women who were
a bit disheartened by the breakdown of their highest hope—
the dream of a world-wide solidarity which would prevent
war. They were looking for a renewal of faith that would rest

315

on firm foundations. What did Mr. Boudin do? He denounced the nationalism of European workingmen, he asserted that the "economic basis" of internationalism existed, he arraigned the leaders of socialism for disloyalty to the gospel, he called them politicians, and he ended by shouting that the real International must be based on real internationalism.

Judged by the applause, Mr. Boudin met the situation splendidly. Yet his evasion was obvious. The fact was that internationalism had failed in the test; that the leaders of socialism, professing it in their speeches, had failed to make it a reality; that after forty or fifty years of high talk the vision had broken down in less than a week. What everyone wished to know was why this had happened. Mr. Boudin said it was because the socialists weren't true internationalists, but that dictum merely opened up the much more crucial question of why they weren't true internationalists. They weren't, said Mr. Boudin, because they were politicians. The query what made them politicians he left unanswered. That pawn in the game he refused to use in his imaginary triumph, and having overlooked it he was able to say with much eloquence that the new internationalism must not be led by politicians. Where his analysis faltered he called upon fine sentiment to cover the difficulty, and the rustle of angels' wings could be heard in his peroration.

The President used the same method recently in laying the proposal for a continental army before Congress. The President knew, everyone who had studied the plan knew, that the real question was, can the continental army be recruited? That issue the President touched off by appealing to the patriotism of employers. When that sentiment is used for an appeal, analysis stops. The difficulty of releasing several hundred thousand men for military service is immense. It would require a great readjustment of economic life. But patriotism belongs to the angels, and where a problem is uncomfortable they can conceal it.

Public discussion is full of this amiable form of self-decep-

316

tion. Schemes are put forward every day which require an amount of virtue that exists only at the conclusion of orators' speeches. Difficulties are evaded by calling upon brotherly love, citizenship, patriotism, public spirit, and all the other glowing abstractions which mask an incompleted analysis. Realistic statesmen, men with imaginations that clinch reality, do not rely upon virtuosity in virtue. They do not cover a rocky path with a silk rug. That is why they are so often regarded as hard and cynical and lacking in imagination, whereas their imaginations are too honest for the trick of summoning the angels to win imaginary victories. But their reward is that occasionally they win a real victory.

It is a good sign that men are coming to suspect political writing pitched in too noble a key. We are unlearning our taste for those treatises which are set in spacious halls of white marble inhabited by dignified men in purple togas. These treatises cannot be read with any comfort in a Bronx flat. They make no allowances. They screw us up to a pitch of morality which would produce a fine political system, though the world as we know it would be unrecognizable. Such treatises are now being classed with fairy tales, with all those accounts of human life which shirk its chief difficulties.

Yet the love of them is inexhaustible. Essentially there is no difference between a world where men have eyes in the back of their heads, a world in which all chess games are victories and all employers are patriots and practitioners of the golden rule. They are easy worlds to imagine, and would be easier to live in than ours. We are all everlastingly busy constructing them, and their common quality is that they assume in the premise the conclusion which is desired. Much pacifism, for example, consists in imagining a world in which the incentive to fight was reduced, and then telling how peace is preserved in such a world. Many a scheme relies for its success upon a state of unselfishness which if it existed would make the scheme unnecessary.

Whenever a man wins his victories by ignoring the chief

piece of the opposition we call him a doctrinaire if he is dull, a visionary if he is exalted, a dreamer if he is charming, and a fool if he interferes. His retort is that the realists lack imagination, that they are so interested in earth they cannot look to heaven. As a result, idealists and realists begin to get on each other's nerves. But the real difference is in the capacity for appreciating the immense gap of blue inane which separates earth from heaven, and in the realist's unwillingness to assume that men have angels' wings. If we are to get into heaven, says the realist, we must climb in, and the lower rungs of the ladder must not be beyond the reach of the smallest.

January 1, 1916

"AMERICANISM"

The sight of a baby sucking and biting father's watch, and cooing as contentedly as if it were having a meal, is a reminder that mankind is after all rather easily satisfied. To chew what has no nourishment, to bite though you have no teeth, to bustle though you have no goal, to shout though you have little meaning, seem to be ways of living temporarily at least a strenuous and red-blooded existence. For how else is any one to explain the fact that statesmen will suckle their followers on an arid phrase while they take as much pleasure out of it as the baby from father's watch? It is not what we do, but the fact that we do, which appears to make us happy. The best of us are not above sitting for a long time with acute maternal emotions on a glass egg.

The latest glass egg of American politics is the word "Americanism." For many months now we have heard that "the issue is Americanism," and noble as it sounds, often as it has been repeated, it is still an open question whether the phrase has any meaning whatsoever. The only way to test a word is to inquire what those who use it most intend to do, and then contrast their intention with that of the pariahs who are not allowed to call themselves American. Beginning at the bottom there are the gentlemen who tried to put bombs on munition ships. Almost all of us are against them. So they may be eliminated. Their policy is not Americanism. For the purposes of a political campaign it is not possible to divide this country into the bomb and anti-bomb party. That issue is between the police and the criminals, not between Mr. Wilson and whoever is chosen at Chicago. In fact it may be asserted with considerable confidence that the Democratic convention will not declare for bombs either openly or secretly.

Next in the scale may be put the propagandists of foreign governments, and all those who have been visiting the lobbies of Congress to threaten and cajole officials into a policy inspired by the interests, real or imaginary, of another Power. It is certain that Wilson Democrats and Root or Roosevelt Republicans can not come to any issue here. Politicians of weak virtue are at least equally divided. It is perfectly simple to match Colquitt and O'Gorman with Burton and Nicholas Longworth, or Richard Bartholdt with Jacob Gallinger. On this issue Mr. Wilson stands nearer to Mr. Roosevelt than does Mr. Cummins. The men who are truckling to the so-called hyphenated vote are not the Democrats, and the heroes are not the Republicans. It is necessary only to look at the not very favorite sons to escape that delusion.

Planting bombs, alien propaganda, and fear of the unassimilated vote are issues of our national life, but they are not issues between the two great parties, and no amount of rhetoric can make them issues. Courageous opposition to them may be "Americanism," but if it is, no one can honestly say that there is any difference of opinion on this matter between Mr. Roosevelt and Mr. Wilson.

The next group to be thrust outside the circle of Americanism is the pacifist vote. But here it is necessary to suspend judgment for a moment. Mr. Ford, who is a Republican, Mr. Bryan, who is a Democrat, may be preposterously wrong in their theories about armament and foreign policy. But that they are American, of our soil and character, only a madman would deny. The Ford peace ship, for example, can be described as noble nonsense, but it was not un-American. If ever a gesture revealed a deep and historic strain in the soul of a people, that cargo of goodwill and trust and thoughtlessness revealed it. No other people could conceivably have

320

set it afloat. It was un-German, un-British, un-Continental, un-European, unworldly if you like, but it was made out of the confidence of a nation which has conquered the prairies and remained isolated from mankind. It was a supreme illustration of the defects of our qualities.

If it is impossible to raise the issue of Americanism here, it is surely impossible to say that Americanism is the difference between the preparedness à la Hay and preparedness à la Roosevelt. Mr. Hay is no doubt a cheap politician, not above prostituting an army bill to a militia lobby or to the desire of giving his friend Judge Carson of Virginia a good job. But cheap politics is not an issue between the Republicans and the Democrats, and many of those who are loudest for "Americanism" are cheap politicians. If any examples are needed there are those who voted against George Rublee —rejected by such patriots as Senators Gallinger, Lodge, Weeks, Wadsworth, et al., rejected without a word of protest from Roosevelt, Root, Burton, McCall or any of the other protagonists of Americanism. If Hay, the Democrat, is ready to debauch the army to politics, Lodge, the Republican, is no less ready to debauch the Federal Trade Commission.

As an issue "Americanism" will not stand much analysis. Stripped of its confusion, its rhetorical question-begging, and its rather casuistical attempt to appropriate an emotion for party purposes, what remains is the thing which Mr. Roosevelt described as the "heroic mood." It is a vague sense that in a world crisis America should be playing a more decisive and affirmative role. What the role should be has never been defined in terms of statesmanship. But there is a feeling that sharper action would have increased American prestige and given us a more powerful strategic position in the society of nations.

It is a civilized and useful feeling, one which directed by a trained intelligence would do much for the world. But it is not "Americanism." It is what Americanism might come to be. It is no more Americanism than is equality of opportunity, or the abolition of industrial tyranny, or the sane use of our natural resources, or the honest administration of public office. It is the aspiration of a minority. It is the idealism of a small group. Americanism as an historic thing is the America of fact, the America which exists in New York and Pittsburgh and Lincoln, Nebraska, where idealism is at once a redeeming hope and a brutal mockery. The Americanism of the idealists is no more the reality than is the Statue of Liberty, which by this time has learned to blush as the immigrants come by.

It is idle then for Mr. Roosevelt to speak of Americanism as of something from which we have fallen. If the word means anything it means something to which we might rise after a long struggle with the historic Americanism of isolation and scramble and planlessness and oratorical confusion.

June 3, 1916

MISS LOWELL AND THINGS

Amy Lowell's first anthology of "imagist" poets was published in 1915. [*A.S., jr.*]

Ever since Miss Amy Lowell explained the "new manner" in poetry I have been trying to imagine life lived as she describes it. For she says that there has been a changed attitude towards life which compels a poet to paint landscapes because they are beautiful and not because they suit his mood, to tell stories because they are interesting and not because they prove a thesis. I don't understand this "externality"; I don't know what it means to be interested in "things for themselves."

Let Miss Lowell try it some morning and see what happens. I pass over all the things that might catch her poetic attention between the first sound of the alarm clock and her appearance at the breakfast table. I assume that her human interest in breakfast carries her past them, and prevents her from lingering immeasurably over their color and form and polyphony. So she arrives at breakfast, and beholds a sliced orange. It fascinates her. She "never tires of finding colors in it," and sometimes the colors so occupy her that she takes them separately, unrelated to the sliced orange, as it were. She goes on gazing at "colors, and light and shade, in planes and cubes with practically no insistence on the substance which produces them." Says someone at the table, disconcerted: "Eat your orange, Miss Lowell." "Impossible," is the unhesitating reply. "I am interested in things for themselves.

It is an inevitable change, my dear, reflecting the evolution of life."

My guess is that Miss Lowell does not live at this pitch of externality. I imagine that among the thousand objects which might attract her attention—oranges, eggs, umbrellas, dust-heaps—she chooses some one about which to write a poem. And I imagine that she chooses it because it interests her for the particular mood she happens to be in. And I imagine that she feels she has written a good poem when her mood has got itself expressed about the object. I imagine she is external when it interests her to be external. To be sure, if she doesn't choose to be interested in her own feelings about the objects she selects, that is her affair. But she shouldn't ask us to believe that she has transcended them, and is now contemplating the world with the detachment of Aristotle's God. Nobody has ever yet succeeded in being external to himself, and I doubt whether Miss Lowell will succeed.

She speaks in her article about the universality of life, and then tells us that "noble thoughts" are anathema to the modern poet. Of course they are, if you put them in quotation marks. But there are noble thoughts which poets have not always ruled out of the universality of life, and those thoughts expressing the depth and variety of human desire are the elements which Miss Lowell's school somehow seems to avoid.

Much of their work often reminds me of the art collections which museums put in the basement—Persian pottery, a choice array of Egyptian beetles, six hundred and fifty specimens of Roman drinking cups, and a fascinating group of curious watches made at Nuremberg in the sixteenth century. All interesting enough if you have the time to look at them, and if properly distributed, amusing and delightful. A few specialists may be seen poring over the showcases, and an occasional party of tourists comes through bent on seeing all there is to see. But upstairs there is a crowd in front of the Madonna and Child, the famous Venus, and somebody's battle picture. Those are the art works the people remember, and hang photographs of in the parlor. It is the art with which they live.

And I wonder whether they're not more right than Miss Lowell, when they ask the artist to express human responses to the central issues of life and death. If art is a solace and a stimulus to men, are they such utter philistines in saying that the significant artist is not he who deals with things for themselves, but with things in relation to human need? I grant Miss Lowell that there are colors in the dustheaps, but what I'm afraid of is that her horror of noble thoughts has frightened her away from the effort to find color and significance in those more difficult objects about which human life revolves. I'm afraid that Miss Lowell calls a preoccupation with incidentals a brave attempt to be external and universal.

March 18, 1916

SCIENCE AS SCAPEGOAT

Roy K. Hack, a former Rhodes Scholar, was in the classics department at Harvard. [*A.S., jr.*]

The *Atlantic Monthly* has just published an article by Mr. R. K. Hack called "Drift" which sets itself the task of explaining why the world is in such confusion. The true father of the essay is Mr. Chesterton, though the breed has been crossed with that peculiar hysterical pedantry which has affected Boston culture since August, 1914. Chesterton is visible not only in the vein of jocose theology and overwhelming intimacy with God but also in that famous rhetorical trick which consists in beginning with an earthly joke and ending with a divine pun. Used by Mr. Chesterton the method, when it does not rattle and creak like a penny-a-liner, often produces a flamboyant wisdom and a gorgeous playfulness. But in Mr. Hack's hands it produces screaming nonsense like his description of Hobbes as "the great atheist, coward and logician," and the worst case of muddle-headedness recently printed in a responsible periodical.

Mr. Hack begins by asking why we are where we are. He turns to the historians, and in two pages rejects them. The historians he has happened to read did not predict the war; therefore, says Mr. Hack, "let us not blame them overmuch, but let us not trust them at all." That there is a whole library of books by students of affairs which predicted the war with extraordinary accuracy Mr. Hack seems entirely unaware. He doesn't like "historians" as a species, and he has a thesis to prove. This thesis is that we drift because we have been wrong for a century in our ideas about the function of the state and the function of science.

No doubt we have been wrong about the state and no one will quarrel with Mr. Hack for offering a homily about the evil of blind partisanship and the seriousness of indifference on the part of the ordinary citizen. But it is not carrying the diagnosis very far. Partisanship and indifference must after all have causes which cannot be controlled until they have been studied by that method which drives Mr. Hack to angry epigrams, the method known as science.

Mr. Hack's view of science is based on a simple formula. The Germans are the most scientifically trained people in the world. With science they have produced the Zeppelin which is used to kill babies. Therefore the world is idolatrous if it trusts its future to science. There is true and false science. True science deals only with things that are not "alive." False science includes all the studies which "pretend to deal with living beings"—biology, psychology, sociology, philology, politics, economics, and history. These false sciences have perverted our souls, and that is why we drift.

The formula may be compressed. The Germans are science. Science is the Zeppelin. The Zeppelin is murder. Therefore, science is hell. But is it? Can any one be mad enough to argue that the development of science in the nineteenth century suddenly made mankind cruel? There were "Huns" before the Germans, and we doubt whether Attila ever read a book on political science. No one would accuse the people who produced the massacre of St. Bartholomew or the Armenian slaughters of a passion for science. It was not "science" which created the inquisition, the pogrom, the Roman circus, or the old days at Sing Sing. It wasn't science which demanded the burning of witches, the exposure of innocents, the conquest, rapine, and greed of human history. One wonders why a man is endowed with a mind if it leads him to believe that cruelty, greed, and delusion are new phenomena due to a century's application of ordered intelligence to experience.

Because Germany has used science so widely, it does not follow that she has used it everywhere. Indeed, it is precisely to those political ideas which have irritated the world that Germany has not applied her science. If it is true that the Emperor regards himself as a ruler by divine right, he will not find any support for the theory in modern sociology; if Professor So-and-So believes that the Teutons, whoever they may be, are a "race" with a divine mission he is drawing upon his inner consciousness. If somebody else thinks that war is "holy," that is due not to the careful use of his intelligence, but to his rather eccentric notion of what is holy. If Germany had tried to conduct the technique of her commerce and her warfare with the habit of mind in which her spokesmen often glorified her, Germany to-day would be as inefficient as Venezuela and as helpless as Persia.

Were Mr. Hack to take anything more than a literary interest in scientists he would soon discover that they are quite capable of reserving larger parts of their souls from analysis. They can be scientists about physics and commonplace or superstitious about politics, and that, it seems to us, is what the articulate Germans have proved themselves to be. In those areas which Mr. Hack calls "living" they have remained romantic and obscurantist and religiously patriotic. The moral of the war is not that science has given men the Zeppelin where formerly they had to be content with the spear and the arrow, but that the scientific habit has not yet invaded those dogmas of glory and power and self-interest which are our primitive inheritance.

The political ideas which generated this war, the theories of national interest, prestige, honor, patriotism are not the products of science, but territory which science has still to conquer. The brute and the fool in mankind were not produced in the laboratory. Mr. Hack may rest assured that they are a good deal older than Newton or Darwin. Only in spots has man learned to transfigure the mud from which he rose, but that transfiguration is due to the disciplined use of his intelligence. He has hardly begun to apply his mind to politics, but the beginning is an endless promise, and it is a realization of that promise which has made this war intolerable beyond any other.

October 7, 1916

THE LOST THEME

A man was taken the other day to a soirée of artists and serious thinkers. He had never been to such a gathering before, and he was totally ignorant of the rules. Fool that he was, he thought it expected of him to show that he too liked art, and it pleased him to think he had been to a recent exhibition. He plunged in and began to describe a picture. It was of a high cliff running down to the sea, and on the little strip of beach lay the body of a young girl. The sun was rising in the background. Those who heard him were horrified, and the friend who had introduced him perspired visibly. "She had such a wonderful expression on her face—you must have noticed it?" he concluded. "Never looked at it. . . . I'm not interested in brewery advertisements," replied one of the party, and left the man feeling as guilty as if he had murdered his aunt.

But he was a dauntless person, and after much careful lecturing from his friend he began to attain artistic respectability. He has worked out a rule of conduct for himself. If the picture looks interesting, he hurries past knowing that it contains a story or a moral, and such things are no longer for him. Among the subjects he has learned to avoid are pretty girls, dancers, Eve and Venus, affectionate dogs, moonlight on snow, mermaids, and motherly old women by the fireside. He has learned to pause in front of torsos, fragments of arms, and sketches consisting of not more than a dozen lines. He has been seen to stand immovable for ten minutes before the portrait of an apple, to imitate the curve of the shadow with a tense motion of his thumb, and walk away scowling at the wretchedness of the lighting arrangements. His conversational apparatus has grown prodigiously. By taking a beam or two from Bergson, a wheel from Freud, some gearing from William James and the discards of alchemists, Hegelians and mental healers, he has provided himself with a vehicle of explanation. This enables him to avoid the vulgar habit of liking too many things, and he rarely makes a ˉbreak at a soirée. The high quality of his artistic insight is established by the fact that he is able to grow eloquent over a spot in the upper left hand corner of the most obscure picture in the gallery, while he treats the rest of the exhibition for the low-lived, ill-bred thing it is.

It is not the business of outsiders to criticize him. For he and his circle of artist friends are a close community, and only those who can speak their language are admitted. Philistines say it isn't a language at all, but merely an elaborate and noisy form of the inarticulate. It has even been said that there are circles within the circles using deeper and deeper symbols of the incommunicable, and that in the last analysis the best work done by men in this group is incomprehensible to the men themselves. There is a rumor that one of them remarked: "When I have evolved artistically, I shall like that painting of mine—some day it will reveal infinity to me. I shall grow to be worthy of it."

In the meantime the less gifted people have meted out a curious fate to him and his kind. They know nothing of the infinities revealed; after two or three efforts to understand his manifestoes they betray no particular desire to know. But often enough they like the patterns, and are busily engaged in using them for sofa cushions, neckties, wall paper, and ladies' evening dresses. At any hour of the day or night it is now possible to see men and women dressed in the scattered remnants of a mysterious metaphysics. Musical comedy costumes are deeply affected by them, magazine covers flaunt them, advertising is full of them, they are to be seen on candy-boxes and doilies and whimsical shoes.

Nor are the outsiders ungrateful. They are much obliged for the improvement in neckties, believing that if it requires a mystery and a cult and a jumble of philosophy to produce it, the price is not too high. But there is a persistent question in their minds which they hardly dare to utter aloud. Standing in front of one of the new products, they have tried their level best to purge themselves through pity and fear, or find a hint of open country beyond. But almost in vain. "Is this all?" they ask, for they had been led to believe that art was something more than the decoration of life. "These things," they say, "are often good carpets and good trimmings, but men pray on a rug, not to it; we have been given better clothes, but we are naked."

According to this theory of the outsiders, art is made to increase life, by which they mean that it cuts paths for the impulses which are not consumed in ordinary living. It enables men to be heroes and lovers and prophets and villains in a world where there are no practical costs, a world which is literally immortal because death and defeat are vicarious. In that realm they can spend the evening in Purgatory or know the Liebestod before bedtime, abduct Helen and play ball with Nausicaa, do a thousand things they were made to do, and still remain law-abiding citizens. They can compress time and space, and obliterate distance, be omnipotent and free and gorgeously sad. They can live a thousand lives, lift the roofs off houses, open sealed caskets, and see the other side of the moon. Individual man is limited by circumstances, squeezed outrageously in the world of custom, law, responsibility, thwarted by weakness and poverty and the shortness of time. But his soul is profuse, errant, and multiple, not to be contained or employed in a career. It is made of contradictions, some of which must go under in the pressure of events. It cannot satisfy itself in the restricted area of permissible

332

emotions. It longs for things that would kill it, and is everlastingly adjusted to compromise and prudence.

This overflow is the itching plague of mankind, haunting it with crimes and heroisms that it is unable to achieve, the corridor of its mind a ghost-walk of lives that it might have lived. Miser and murderer and libertine, grandee and lover and hero tumble after each other in this pageant of lost causes forever conspiring against the peace of that exterior which men show to the world. Art is the liberator of these submerged selves because it enables them to walk in daylight, to be incarnated and to find expression, without wrecking the continuity of organized life.

But art cannot do its work if it remains incommunicable. Man cannot live vicarious lives in a medium in which he does not understand. Above all, he cannot find utterance in decoration or "externality" alone. That is why he will not accept the heresy which tells him that the subject of art does not matter, that the picture of a daffodil is as significant as the picture of a soul. He believes persistently that design and pattern are not the end of art, that the artist must respond to those moral conflicts which constitute the living theme of great works. He need not quarrel with those who are unable to be more than craftsmen engaged in making the costumes, utensils and furniture of life. His quarrel is with their pretension that they have usurped the avenues of human expression.

In some such way as that the outsider might reply to those who claim to speak for modern art. In the effort to establish his argument he could do more than point to those creations which have meant most to the inner life of mankind, or ask the obvious question whether there is no qualitative difference between a Greek tragedy and a Greek vase. He would be inclined to turn on the *illuminati* and ask them whether they have found what they need, and whether in the test of experience they have attained answers to craving and struggle, either rest or new life when they wanted it most? And whether there is not already a creeping disillusionment with trifles and abstractions and incidentals heaped up to leave them unfulfilled? And whether the immense pretentiousness and trumpetings of the millennium and the scrapheap of explanations and titanism are not the signs of men whistling to keep up their courage, shouting to conceal their doubts?

The layman may even hint at a possible explanation. The avoidance of significant themes, the emphasis on treatment and decoration are perhaps due to the fact that we are living now in a society of a scale never known before, in an environment enlarged and complicated beyond anything mankind has ever experienced. We have not learned to adjust human passion to this new situation, to value human motive in the terrifying intricacy of modern life. Moral science, as Socrates understood it, is in perplexity and confusion, and if ever any order is attained it will be by long study and invention. Only then might the material of human conflict be sufficiently understood to furnish art with its greater themes. For painters, poets, novelists are happiest when they live in a moral tradition. The lack of it to-day has robbed them of themes on which to work.

So they have turned away from the theme and concentrated on the externals of their craft, on technique, or form, or pattern, or color, or on the less important objects of the natural world. Having turned away, they try to justify their result by endless theorizing aimed to show that what they are getting is all that an artist should seek. They despise the theme because to-day the theme is infinitely difficult to grasp. They have transformed an evasion, a necessary and perhaps an inevitable evasion, into a virtue. They are trying to make their central failure a criterion of success.

April 8, 1916

THE WHITE PASSION

It is not necessary to identify Isadora Duncan to admirers of Vanessa Redgrave. John P. Mitchel was a reform mayor of New York City, 1914–1918. [*A.S., jr.*]

Some one inquired recently why utopias have gone out of fashion. For the last gallant attempt was by Mr. Wells, and from his recent work it appears that he cannot endure the thought of those well meaning people who take his utopia too seriously, and fail to see "the subtle protesting perplexing play of instinctive passion and desire against too abstract a dream of statesmanship." Since this renunciation by Mr. Wells, no first-rate mind at least in the English-speaking world has dared to write another utopia.

Any one who has been sentenced as I was once to study ten or fifteen descriptions of a perfect society knows why the fashion has passed. They read like the epilogue of little Eva in heaven spread out into a five-act play. They are the happy endings of a drama which the author was unable to write. They give the result which is obvious and shirk the process which is difficult. Therefore no critical person is any longer interested in a finished picture of what might be, and the modern visionary cannot rest, like the advertisements of hair restorers and obesity cures, when he has said, look here upon this picture, and on this. One of the loveliest utopias I ever knew was of sunburnt philosophers playing with shells on a coral island written by a friend of mine living in Washington Square who wished he could spend the winter in Bermuda.

It filled him with passionate revolt to think that Manhattan was not a coral island peopled with the lithe, brown naked bodies of laughing philosophers. Well, it filled him with revolt, and left Manhattan otherwise unchanged. And I remember that he stared at me as at an unfeeling and unimaginative person because I urged him to write another essay showing how Manhattan was gradually transfigured into a red island on a blue ocean together with the history of how its inhabitants gradually became lithe and brown and philosophical, and lived wantonly under a luxuriant growth of decorative palm trees. He said my cynicism showed how little I understood the free play of fancy, that I talked as if I read *The New Republic,* and that if I'd spend an hour a day digesting the *Little Review* and thinking of Isadora Duncan, I might be fit to talk to.

I tried that one day in a room on MacDougal Alley when the man I had come to meet inconsiderately spent four hours over lunch instead of the customary three. All the room offered for entertainment was *Breezy Stories, Snappy Stories, The Parisienne, Top Notch,* one Japanese print, some Fatima cigarettes, no matches, the *Little Review,* and the thought of Isadora. In fifteen minutes I had exhausted everything, and turned resolutely to Isadora. I remembered a solemn afternoon at her studio when vision and reality almost touched hands, when New York was within an ace of God knows what. For some one had induced Mayor Mitchel to come and sit on a gray divan under an orange light while the girls danced. The idea was that he as the head of the government was to be struck mad by a vision of beauty and that we were all to dance on Fifth Avenue. There was the inevitable ass who wanted to know in a stage whisper whether sandals would be permitted, but what really spoiled it all was Isadora's casual remark to the Mayor that of course the family would have to be abolished if there was to be beauty and freedom in New York. Courageous as I know Mr. Mitchel to be, that was more than the Mayor of New York had any

336

right to hear, and it ended Isadora Duncan's activity in practical politics.

There was at least this to be said for her effort, that no one in the world's history had ever before made so direct an attempt to apply vision to life. No one else had ever shown such divine impatience with method in an inspired enthusiasm for the result. And yet it showed that Isadora Duncan was an old-fashioned person. Essentially she was doing what every archaic moralist does who tells men to be good, be true, be beautiful, and forgets to say how. She was merely repeating what lawyers do at banquets when they talk of justice, or theologians when they set the City of God upon a hill, and tell men in the valley to have a good look at it. She was sister, I fear, to some of the writers in the *Masses* who are fond of saying: that pile of stones would look better if it were on top of that mountain, and having indicated this desirable conclusion, go home to dinner.

That after all is a comparatively easy and primitive kind of vision. The modern imagination has a harder task to perform. Its work is to abolish the old dualism of fact and fancy in which existence lay inert and unresponsive to the kiss of hope. Vision to-day will compel no one if the hope is extravagant or the fact distorted; and they see the world most effectively who see reality luminous in a cold dry light dissolving into a warm aura of probabilities. It is a limitation against which only the dilettante rebels, he who would rather dream ten dreams than realize one, he who so often mistakes a discussion in a cafe for an artistic movement, or a committee meeting for a social revolution. It is a form of lazy thoughtlessness to suppose that something can be made of nothing, that the act of creation consists of breathing upon the void. To create is to transfigure the given in the light of desire, and for the artist anywhere, but especially for the artist in human relationship, the margin of freedom is something offered to him, not made by him. He is a disciplined creator who can estimate truly how much men can be expected to change within a definite time, how much those who desire a change can prevail against those who ignore or resist it, how much the technique of change can be quickened by what some men know and others may hope to know. On the certainty of these guesses depends what Mr. Wells calls the state-making dream.

That is why the modern utopia cannot have the finish and neatness of the old. It is not a picture composed to suit the artist, it is not planned and executed at his leisure. It is a living picture with the pace and rhythm of existence, necessarily a fragment and a guess. It cannot be comprehensive or final, and it requires a vitality of soul and a toughness of perception to which no one is equal at all times and few at any., But it means a life of vision, not merely a life and a vision. It is the test of a true culture, this ability to make the opaque world translucent, to see fact and dissolve it into hope, to know pinched things and see them grow wide, to feel throttled things shake themselves free, and know in all relevant life the longing which effort could realize.

Only by living in that fringe where reality and desire play against each other do we escape the staleness which perfection suggests. The kind of vision men are practising to-day may account for the style they use, for that tone of nimble and varied aggression which some call brilliant and others smart. "Into the crowned windbag thrust," says Meredith, "that we may come to know the music of the meaning of Accord." A little hard on the windbag, but without the thrust accord is only too readily as maudlin as an Easter postcard. For we beat our vision into existence by an everlasting attack on the inert, the frozen, the mechanical and the unctuous. We spank it as the doctor a newborn infant till it breathes and cries out and takes its place in the world.

In that living zone where fact is yielding to desire men are chary of too much articulate nobility, and not a little impatient of pretentious emotion. They feel the defenselessness of virtue in a world at war, and will not drag it like a slut through all their discussion. The old Persian potters cracked their best rounded vessels because they feared the jealousy of God, the Gothic builders left embedded in their art fragments of the malice and brutality of life, the modern visionary is ascetic and economical in faith. Even Chesterton, the least reticent of believers, has saved face by his militant tone, flaring vivacity, roaring grotesques, and volcanic fun. He has said his say with aggression persistent as a steam hammer and gorgeous as a peacock's tail.

There too is a reason for the decline of utopias. More than ever before man seems to realize that he cannot live unless he lives against something, that hope is dull unless its edges are sharpened on fact. Certainly if every stone wall were a sofa cushion, if the mountains stood aside as we walked, it is altogether probable that mortal men would fall down and beat the earth and cry for joy at the solid indifference of it. Perhaps this is the ultimate disharmony, that we are so irretrievably beings who want and struggle that the only utopia we can endure is the process of making it. For in the heavens of our freest fancy, only our fancy is at rest. There the world has forgotten that it is a coquette. The coaxing and wheedling, the trials and errors, the setbacks and thrusts, all the elation and depression, the humor and the gallantry, the eddies of insignificance, all this that gives life its quality and its dimension are gone. We have ceased to be ourselves, have become thin flames ascending gilded staircases, and even the face of the beloved is dim. If ever we actually strayed into it we should flee from a universe where fish jump into the net, where nothing resists, and we step jerkily on air.

Sometimes when too grandiose a vision is presented, I wonder whether nature having found a voice isn't saying as she watches the fret of our desire: "I have lured you to interminable hope, for all your hope is banal to me. It carries you on. It gives you purpose, and when you are particularly vain you like to think it is my purpose. I'm not sure I have a

339

purpose, or that you would grasp it if I had. But I have fixed you so that no one of you can find the last repose while life is upon him. Remember that many of you have sought Aladdin's lamp. There is no record that any one ever kept it."

October 21, 1916

INDEX

absolutism: and democracy, 51
absolutists: and philosophers, 307, 308
"acids of modernity," *x*
Adamson Act, 216, 217, 218, 220
Ade, George, 120, 122
administrative collectivism, 149
Advance Rate Case, and Louis D. Brandeis, 113
aggression, 7; as defined by U.S., 34; German, 65, 67
Alliance, vital supplies of, 78
Allies, 70, 75; and America's position, 23, 43, 44, 50, 63–67, 74; and Bolsheviks, 280; and World War I, 42, 60–62
America. *See* United States of America, the
American Federation of Labor, 224, 228, 282, 284
American Magazine, The, 294
American President Lines, W. G. McAdoo and, 180
Americanism, 119, 125, 142, 279; and the Chicago convention of 1920, 189; and the League of Nations, 190; and politics, 319–322; as slogan, 115, 212
Angell, Norman, 46, 49
Anglo-French loan, 23
arbitration, 212–218, 221–222, 258, 288
Arkansas, 262
armament, 26, 39, 55, 320
Armenians, massacre of, 60
armistice, the, 271, 275
arms: embargoes on, 10; manufacturers of, 5
army, 12, 16, 157, 168, 316

art, 330–334
Asia, 38, 86, 88
Asia Minor, 60, 61
Asquith, H. H., 155, 156
Atlantic Monthly, The, 326
Atlantic Powers, *xi,* 69, 73
Attorney General. *See* Knox, Philander C.
Australia: and labor, 258; and war, 279
Australian Commission of National Association of Manufacturers, 258
Austria-Hungary, 7, 16, 24, 62
autobiography, as philosophy, 308, 309

Bacon, Robert, 130
backward countries, *xii,* 26–30
Bahamas, the, 184
balance of power: international, 15, 63, 66; between labor and management, 215
Balfour, Arthur James, 64
Balkan Peninsula, 7, 61–62, 73, 82
Ballinger case, 112
Baltimore platform, 93
Barbados, 184
bargaining, collective, 220, 228, 231
Bartholdt, Richard, 320
Belgium, 13–15, 34, 40, 60–61, 72–73, 81, 115
Berenson, Bernard, 23
Berger, Victor, 294
Bergson, Henri, 294, **331**
Bermudas, 184

341

democracy (*continued*):
of, 151; Woodrow Wilson and,
140
Democratic Party, 94, 137, 146;
and Americanism, 115; and
Baltimore platform, 93; bourbon, 274; Convention of 1916,
121, 320; Convention of 1924,
180; doctrine of, 196; and
Hoover, 191; liberal, 60; and
W. G. McAdoo, 180; platform,
64; and progressivism, 139,
145; and propagandists, 320,
321; Republican attitude toward, 116, 129; sectionalism of,
146
Denmark, 31, 45
Dennison, Congressman, 204
department stores, 234, 243–244.
See also retail stores
DePew, Chauncey, 129
de Sade, Marquis, 48
Detroit, Michigan, 21, 166
Dewey, John, 307–310
Diaz, Porfirio, 151
Dickinson, Goldsworthy Lowes,
46, 49
Die Zukunft, 46
disarmament, 12
discipline, industrial, 259
discrimination, 268, 313
disputes, industrial, 217, 218. *See
also* strikes
dogmas, and science, 328
domestic issues, and Chicago
Convention of 1920, 190
Drift and Mastery, vii
Dublin executions, 42, 44
Duncan, Isadora, 335–337

economic associations, and a
league of nations, 79
economic democracy in industry,
251
economic law, and minimum
wage, 239–240
economic life, and military, 316
economic nationalism, 78–79

education, 17, 149, 285, 313–314;
compulsory, and child labor,
204; nationalization of, 117,
148
efficiency: administrative, 147;
industrial, 243, 245, 246, 247,
259, 260; and labor, 238, 287,
288; and minimum wage, 242
"eight-hour-day," 212–218
elderly, pension for, 249
election: labor union, 266; of
1916, 141
Eliot, Charles William, 287
Emerson, Ralph Waldo, 286
Emery, James A., 205, 206
employers: and the American
Federation of Labor, 282; and
cheap labor, 250; and child
labor, 203, 250; and Samuel
Gompers, 283; and the Industrial Conference, 226–227; and
minimum wage, 201, 235–251;
and National Association of
Manufacturers, 261; and working hours, 254. *See also* business; corporations; management
Entente diplomacy, 47
enterprise, freedom of, 264
espionage, Russian, 277–278
equal opportunity, 321
Europe, 33, 61, 62, 65, 78, 81,
85, 88, 115, 280; American attitude toward, 21; and Americanism, 116; and Bolshevism,
287; and the U.S.A., 44, 86,
89, 143, 275
Executive branch: relation of
Legislative to, 196; conduct,
and the Supreme Court, 101;
policy, and Congress, 195

Factories, 104; inspection of, 203;
laws concerning, 240; and
wages in New York, 233, 244
Factory Investigation Commission (New York), 234
Falkland Islands, 118
Famine, threat of, 77, 79

Government (*continued*):
can Party and, 173; and strikes,
215; structure of, 102
Great Britain, 13, 24, 28, 31, 40,
41, 43, 52, 55, 70, 72–73, 143,
149, 246; and America, 23, 44,
50, 51, 53, 59, 118; Americans in, 44; liberalism in, 44–
45; and nationalized railroads,
118, 216; naval power of, 38,
51, 69, 73, 118; and Paris Conference, 88; and Russia, 16
Greece, 7, 32
Grey, Viscount (Sir Edward), 43,
130
"Gum-Shoe Bill," 151, 152

Hack, Roy K., 326–329
Hackett, Francis, *vii*
Hague, the, 14, 15
Haiti, investments in, 28
Hamilton, Alexander, 196
Hammond, M. B., of Ohio, 247
Handicapped workers, 249
Harden, Maximilian, editor of
Die Zukunft, 46, 49
Harding, Warren G., 169, 187,
189, 191, 194, 195
Harvard University, *ix,* 48, 160,
254, 313
Hassgesang gegen England, Ger-
man play, 46
Havana and Leonard Wood, 161
Hays, Will, 180
Haywood, Big Bill, 270, 274
Health, and low wages, 261
Hearst, William Randolph, 97
Hegelians and art, 331
Helsingfors, 272
Hitchcock, Frank, 120
Hobbes, Thomas, 326
Holland, 31, 70, 72, 73
Holmes, Oliver Wendell, 102, 132,
136
Honolulu, and the wireless, 311
Herbert Hoover, 164, 174, 178,
184–192

Hours, working, 214–217, 220,
223, 250, 253, 254, 257, 283;
and arbitration, 221, 222; and
labor, 287; as social policy,
218; and strikes, 229
House of Representatives, first
woman in, 139
Housing: and labor, 241; and
tenement law, 245
Howe, Frederic C., 26–29
Huerta, Victoriano, 7, 9
Hughes, Charles E., 102, 120–
140; candidacy of, 122–123,
129–138; as conservative, 165;
and direct primary, 136; and
the League of Nations, 65
Hymn of Hate by Ernst Lissauer,
46

Ickes, Harold, 144, 145
Idealism and Americanism, 322
Illinois, courts of, 104; and
Frank Lowden, 163, 177, 178;
State Board of Equalization,
175, 176
Illiterates, employment for, 249
Illness, insurance against, 230
Immigrant labor, conditions of,
165, 167, 248–249
Immigration, 249, 317, 318, 337
Independents, 139, 192
Industrial Commission of the
State of Colorado, 247, 268
Industrial Conference of 1919,
226–227, 286
Industrial conflict, and the United
States, 216
Industrial Relations, U.S. Com-
mission on, 246, 262
Industrial Representation Plan,
266–269
Industrial Welfare Commission
of Washington (state), report
of, 259
Industrial Workers of the World
(IWW), 270, 282, 294; and
minimum wage for women,
201

353